The PROXY WAR in UKRAINE

The PROXY WAR *in* UKRAINE

A Geopolitical Strategy of the Global Elites

MARK FULMER

LIBERTY HILL PUBLISHING

Liberty Hill Publishing
555 Winderley Pl, Suite 225
Maitland, FL 32751
407.339.4217
www.libertyhillpublishing.com

© 2024 by Mark Fulmer

All rights reserved solely by the author. The author guarantees all contents are original and do not infringe upon the legal rights of any other person or work. No part of this book may be reproduced in any form without the permission of the author.

Due to the changing nature of the Internet, if there are any web addresses, links, or URLs included in this manuscript, these may have been altered and may no longer be accessible. The views and opinions shared in this book belong solely to the author and do not necessarily reflect those of the publisher. The publisher therefore disclaims responsibility for the views or opinions expressed within the work.

Unless otherwise indicated, Scripture quotations taken from the New American Standard Bible (NASB). Copyright © 1960, 1962, 1963, 1968, 1971, 1972, 1973, 1975, 1977, 1995 by The Lockman Foundation. Used by permission. All rights reserved.

Paperback ISBN-13: 979-8-21835-375-9
Ebook ISBN-13: 978-1-66289-471-8

Table of Contents

ACKNOWLEDGEMENTS ix

INTRODUCTION xi

CHAPTER ONE The Gates of Europe: A Brief History of Ukraine and its Role in International Affairs 1

CHAPTER TWO Revolutions for Radicals: Setting Zelensky's World Stage 21

CHAPTER THREE The Bear Provoked: Understanding Russia's History and Its Military. 77

CHAPTER FOUR Understanding Putin and Russia's Vision for Eurasian Foreign Policy. 115

CHAPTER FIVE Proxy Wars, Covert Operations, and Political Corruption in the Deep State 161

CHAPTER SIX Conclusion: Getting America Back to the Vision of Our Founders After Decades of Foreign Policy Disasters 195

Acknowledgements

I would like to express my appreciation for the many friends and colleagues who have encouraged me in the past nine months with the research project that became the basis of this book. Great grassroots patriot organizations like Citizens Defending Freedom, Flash Point, and Patriot Academy all whom I support have been tremendous assets in inspiring the vision for this book. Also, I am most thankful for the spiritual discipleship from my church Mercy Culture in Fort Worth and their vision for servanthood reformation through their For Liberty and Justice organization. As reformers they have taught me the essence of what it means to develop *Presence Driven Activism* through daily personal faith encounters with God.

I have also been blessed through many personal relationships and family members too numerous to reference here. Therefore, I wish to dedicate this book to several individuals who have challenged me and inspired me. The first of these is Mary Houston who turned one hundred years old during the writing of this manuscript. "Miss Mary," as I call her, had childhood families in Ukraine and Poland and witnessed firsthand the atrocities of Nazi Germany. Her Christian faith is an amazing testimony that has inspired me. The second such person is my niece Tatsiana who was born in Belarus during the Chernobyl disaster. Tatsiana or Tanya as we call her, has demonstrated the most remarkable resilience for overcoming her physical birth defects. She was born without fully developed legs and hands because of her mother's exposure to the ravaging effects of deadly radiation. Tanya has defiantly refused to be limited by what others would call a handicap and is an amazing athlete who has competed in local marathons in St. Louis, Miami and two 200-mile relay races. And finally, I dedicate this book to my wonderful wife Linda, who has been a daily source of encouragement as I worked to complete the manuscript and get it ready for publication. Linda is my greatest team partner and an amazing conservative patriot who has cheered me on to the finish line. Together Linda and I share the "Great Adventure" in "Pledging our lives, our fortunes and our sacred honor" to serve, protect, and to defend this great constitutional republic in which we live.

Introduction

Shortly before dawn on February 24, 2022, Russian President Vladimir Putin announced on Russian media that there would be a special military operation in Ukraine. Putin remarked that the purpose of the invasion was a defensive mission to protect the inhabitants of Donbas and included objectives for demilitarization of the region. Within hours international media showed images of Russian infantry and armored divisions advancing into the eastern part of the nation toward Kyiv and shared reports of multiple missiles strikes. Although there had been various levels of military conflict in the Donbas region in the past decade this was seen as a major escalation in post war Europe. As images of the armed conflict were rapidly emerging on all mainstream and social media platforms, the American public was compelled by a powerful sense of overwhelming humanitarian ethos. We saw masses of Ukrainians huddled in makeshift bomb shelters and refugees fleeing the devastating chaos.

In the United States where there are over one million people who are of Ukrainian descent and over two million of Russian descent. We began to see every day American citizens sympathizing with the nation of Ukraine. Almost overnight local business owners began to display the blue and yellow flag of Ukraine. Soon large US corporations were also pledging humanitarian support to Ukraine: including Amazon, major airline carriers, VISA and Mastercard, G.E., big pharma (e.g., Pfizer, Johnson & Johnson). For most American citizens who were shocked by scenes of modern warfare in Europe, the most logical response would be one of compassion. With the catastrophic impact of any war always brings grim consequences of death and destruction. We began seeing daily reports of innocent women, children and other civilians who were the victims of this invasion. As with most wars, the conclusion is easily drawn as to who is the victim and who is the villain. It appeared obvious that the Russian Federation under the leadership of Vladimir Putin was the hostile aggressor, whereas Ukraine was an innocent sovereign nation under invasion from a hostile enemy. Therefore, on March 1, 2022, US President Joe Biden in his first State of the Union Address directed his speech toward the Russian Federation, who he called "invaders" as he praised the "fearless courage" of Ukraine. In the halls of the US Congress, with senators and representatives of both parties wearing the colors of the Ukrainian flag, it appeared to be a truly bipartisan moment as Biden remarked, "Throughout our history we've learned this lesson: When dictators do not pay a price for their aggression, they cause more chaos. They keep moving and the cost and threats to America and the world keep rising."[1] Biden would later go on to comment about renewed relationships with NATO and the EU as well as other nations from the international community with whom the US would be providing support for Ukraine in both humanitarian as well as military aid. Then, on December 21, 2022, Ukrainian President Volodymyr Zelensky addressed a joint meeting of US Congress, asking for financial and military support for the war against Russia: "Your money is not charity, but rather an investment in global security and democracy."[2]

Faced with countless foes throughout the centuries it is no wonder that the Ukrainian national anthem begins with the somber words,

---

[1] US Department of Defense, *US Stands with Ukraine, Biden Says in the State of the Union*, March 1, 2022. Sources accessed on July 3, 2023, from https://www.defense.gov.

[2] The New York Times, *Full Transcript of Zelensky's Speech Before Congress*, December 21, 2022. Accessed July 3, 2023, from https://www.nytimes.com.

"Ukraine has not yet perished." Although such a refrain hardly inspires optimism, it reflects the heart and soul of a people who have journeyed through much misfortune in their nation's history. Ukrainian citizens have suffered greatly at the hands of governments, regimes, and totalitarian dictators while facing the atrocities of war. Therefore, I would like to point out that the heart, spirit, and culture of the Ukrainians is quite admirable, they are a resilient culture with an inspiring heritage. I do not deny the reality of the unfortunate suffering in Ukraine. My wife and I recently interviewed a young woman by the name of Allison who is the strategy director for a Christian organization called *Unbound Now* that works with women who are victims of sex trafficking in Ukraine and throughout the world. Allison recounted story after story of how young women in Ukraine (some of them children) are taken captive by traffickers promising them refuge after becoming displaced from their families and homes.[3] This is just one of the many human atrocities caused by the war. The harsh reality is that the citizens of any nation are vulnerable to being geopolitical pawns at the hands of a much larger and sinister force. Even within my own nation of the United States, I believe that there is a Deep State which operates in our government and threatens our great constitutional republic. I will address in much further detail how the people of Ukraine are victims of the globalist elite.

Although we must have compassion for the people of Ukraine, we must also understand with objectivity the larger geopolitical co.nstruct in which they suffer, it is at the hands of an ambitious one-world government, a global cabal that uses proxy wars to accomplish their totalitarian agendas. Here we must be careful not to resort to oversimplified reductionist[4] logic by vilifying Russia or Putin as the source of Ukraine's

---

[3] Unbound Now's European Division works to free women from international sex trafficking. You can support their work in Ukraine through their site: https://unboundnow.org/europe/.

[4] Reductionism is a philosophical idea regarding the associations of between phenomena which can be described in terms of other simpler or more fundamental phenomena.

problem. In this book I intend to reveal the situation regarding the war in Ukraine by looking at a larger, more complex system as the sum of its parts, more specifically how geopolitical forces are using Ukraine to advance their globalist ideologies and to usurp national sovereignty to strip free nations of their individual rights. It is about much more than the unfortunate casualties of war; it is about how the emerging global new world order orchestrates everything from pandemics to armed conflicts to accomplish its agendas. Yes, I realize that all of this seems remarkable and sounds like a grand conspiracy theme. However, Deep State operatives are skilled at crafting catastrophic global events to carry out their dark and sinister plots while using the mainstream and social media to not to believe in what they brand as right-wing conspiracy theories. Although my viewpoints are largely from a conservative geopolitical and foreign policy context, I have taken great care to reference subject matter experts from a wide variety of fields: history, military, intelligence, foreign policy, and academia as well. These subject matter experts represent both sides of the debate over the war in Ukraine.

Intelligence history has proven that covert and clandestine operations are carried out on a regular basis around the world behind the scenes and well hidden from the view of an unsuspecting public. Even our own federal agencies such as the CIA are involved with nefarious plots to overthrow governments and to assassinate leaders. We find ourselves in our own nation living in dangerous times with the FBI and DOJ being weaponized against conservatives who would outright challenge the liberal and progressive' authoritarian regime. It is incredible to see our own federal agencies enforcing a totalitarian police state or to come under the boot of censorship as freedom of speech goes out the window. Yet, the average public citizen maintains a rigid skepticism that such events could possibly take place. They are convinced that conspiracy theorists should be written off with disdain and distrust. Nearly two years ago when I published my book *The Wuhan Incident: Bioweapons & the Emerging Global Reset* on the lab in China and gain of function research as related to the origins of the COVID-19 virus, I was immediately labeled as a conspiracy theorist. The mainstream media promoted their version of COVID origins claiming that it did not come out of a lab but developed through naturally occurring biology. Anyone who dared to question this narrative was written off as being *anti-science*. Yet, we are now hearing more disclosures about the dark and nefarious research projects with bat coronaviruses which were conducted in secrecy between our own US agencies and the Communist Chinese. Now in this book, I have a feeling of Déjà vu all over again, not with a lab in China, but with the proxy war in Ukraine. There is a grand conspiracy that lurks in the geopolitical construct of this incident. The dark and secretive elements behind this war are much greater than what the average citizen realizes. Sometimes these elements are right out in the open, but the media creates distractions with their narratives, hoping to prevent the public from seeing the truth behind the bigger picture.

Mainstream media and social media serve the global elites in much the same way as the Orwellian version of Big Brother's state-controlled media through the Ministry of Truth (a process referred to as "Newspeak"). This fictional state-controlled media bears semblance to our present-day media with their mainstream narratives and censorship complex to get the public to believe exactly the opposite of truth. Orwell wrote of the state-controlled Ministry of Truth's propaganda which supported the slogans of his fictional totalitarian party: "WAR IS PEACE. FREEDOM IS SLAVERY. IGNORANCE IS STRENGTH." Although these statements were contradictory, the masses were convinced by Big Brother that the media narrative was the truth. This contradiction of truth is still the strategy of the liberal media today. It confirms what the Hebrew prophet Isaiah proclaimed in Israel in the 8th century B.C.: "Woe to those who draw iniquity with cords of falsehood...Woe to those who call evil good and good evil." (Isaiah 5:18, 20). Deception is behind most media narratives while they condemn what is true as conspiracy theories. I will discuss the conspiratorial nature of certain international incidents in more detail in Chapter Five and show that most of these conspiracy theories are revelations of truth!

My conviction is that we must stop funding the proxy war in Ukraine with billions of dollars that contribute to an out-of-control national debt. The Ukrainian government is deeply entrenched with corruption at the highest levels, but the Deep State in Washington is a co-conspirator as well. Yes, Russia is also a corrupt authoritarian regime, but it is in our best interest to not to use a proxy war by funding a corrupt socialist government to fight Russia while DC bureaucrats line their pockets with shady business deals from Kyiv. First, we must understand the overall geopolitical goals of the progressive international order that are behind the proxy war in Ukraine and realize that these are nefarious forces which seek to undermine our national sovereignty. Then we must develop fiscally conservative foreign policies that put America first and not fund the ideologies of global elites. And we must invest in America by securing our borders, strengthening our national security, and fortifying our military at home as our priorities. In this book, to expose the geopolitical strategy framers of the new world order, I will not only quote mainstream media narratives but will also reveal how they often contradict one another. I will also utilize historical events to explain the complexity of Ukraine's role in the emerging global reset that has taken generations to develop. I will quote direct sources from US and international agencies which are part of this grand conspiracy to use Ukraine as a global pawn. I will also "follow the money trail" to expose how Ukraine has become a conduit for billions of dollars for one world globalists. And in the final chapter I will look at how essential it is to develop an America first strategy and to reorder foreign policy matters through the values and convictions of our nation's Founders. My hope is that readers will look at the big picture in world events not only with Ukraine but also with anything else that threatens our liberty and freedom as we live in this great Constitutional Republic. Let us as our nation's Founders proclaim: "We pledge our lives, our fortunes, and our sacred honor" to be Patriots who will always defend the truth at no matter the cost. God bless these United States of America!

Chapter One

The Gates of Europe – A Brief History of Ukraine and It's Current Role in International Affairs

The gates of cities and nations throughout ancient empires served as entrances and corridors of trade routes as well as military outposts to defend local inhabitants. Serhii Plokhy, Harvard Professor of Ukrainian history brought an apt description of the nation of Ukraine by referring to it as the gates of Europe: "Located at the western edge of the Eurasian steppe, Ukraine has been a gateway to Europe for many centuries."[5] This description of a gateway is not merely figurative. Early historical narratives tell us that in 1019 A.D. Yaroslav the Great constructed a massive entrance in his fortified citadel in the ancient city of Kyiv known as the Golden Gate. Throughout the course of its history, the nation of Ukraine has been a gateway on the European continent as it is the second largest country after Russia. It is bordered by Belarus to the north, Poland, Slovakia and Hungary to the west and Romania and Moldova to the southwest. Its coastline runs along the Black Sea and the Sea of Azov to the south and southeast. The extensive land masses of Russia border Ukraine to the east and northeast.

---

[5] Serhii Plokhy, *The Gates of Europe: A History of Ukraine.* (New York, Basic Books, 2021), xxiii & 35.

Historically, the nation's unique geographic positioning has caused much adversity. Because of its vulnerable position on the continent Ukraine has had to defend itself from the full force of invaders and hostile forces throughout the centuries from the Middle Ages during the Slavic expansion it had to face ruthless Mongol raiders. Later, with the Ottoman Empire in the thirteenth century it had to contend with the Cossacks and still later, its adversaries were the Russian Imperialists. In the twentieth century Ukraine was under the iron boot first from Stalin's Communist regime in Russia and later from the Nazi Third Reich in Germany. Ukraine's role as a gateway in Europe should not merely be viewed in terms of its past military adversity in history, but in terms of its essential geopolitical presence in European and global current affairs. Looking toward the future, in the interests of an emerging global economy the global elites see vast potential in Ukraine. The ideological perspective of globalism is best understood within the construct of socialism. Socialism is an ideal espoused by global elites such as Klaus Schwab and George Soros and organizations such as the World Economic Forum (WEF). Many recall the popular 2016 WEF essay written by Denmark's Socialist Democrat Ida Auken that was incorporated into a viral video. Auken in support of the United Nations 2030 Sustainability Goals stated, "You will own nothing and be happy." This is cornerstone doctrine of global socialism.

Ukraine – a Socialist State

Like many of its European neighbor nations in the nineteenth century, Ukraine has existed as a socialist state. The earliest development appears in 1848 after a revolution that was part of a resistance movement opposing early Russian Imperialism. That imperialism was overthrown during the Bolshevik Revolution sixty-nine years later, giving place to a communist state. Lenin who dreamed of a world revolution that would spread to China, India, Germany, France, and the United States, included neighboring Ukraine within his grand matrix. According to

Plokhy, Lenin's assumption was based upon his belief that Ukrainians and Russians were one and the same people. This view persists even in present times within the Russian Federation. Prior to Lenin's revolution, the most influential political thinker in developing Ukraine's socialist ideologies was Mykhalio Drahomanov. While in Geneva Drahomanov wrote about the idea of a European federation that included Ukraine in *Books of the Genesis of the Ukrainian People*.[6] The political science professor is said to be one of the earliest to have embraced a socialist philosophy in Ukraine prior to Karl Marx and Frederick Engels who published the *Communist Manifesto* in 1848.

Later, in the 1890's, local Ukrainian students refused to join all Russian parties and sought to merge socialist and nationalist ideas through their own political activist groups calling upon local peasants to revolt against the Russian imperialists. The political dissidents soon created a liberated social democratic party that had nearly 7,000 members by 1905. Ukrainian peasantry later became politically dominated by the Ukrainian Socialist Revolutionaries Party prior to the Bolshevik Revolution in 1917. On December 25, 1917, the Ukrainian People's Republic of Soviets was formed by the nation's parliament. In 1921, representatives of Soviet Russia, Ukraine, and Poland signed a treaty establishing a Polish-Soviet border. A driving force behind the development of the USSR to bring it to the forefront of industrialized society in the 1920's was Vladimir Lenin. Lenin knew that the communist state war machine would need to harness electric power to operate factories. Ukraine not only played an important role in agricultural commodities to feed Russia's military but also had the ideal location to strategically position one of the largest hydroelectric dams in the world for power production. The ambitious Dnieper Dam was constructed within five years with the assistance of American engineering. The chief American consultant was Colonel Hugh Lincoln Cooper, an engineer who was involved with massive projects in the US such as the Toronto Power

---

[6] Plokhy, The Gates of Europe, 169-170 & 233.

Station at Niagara Falls and the Wilson Dam of the Tennessee Valley Authority. Lenin readily deposited $50,000 into Cooper's account to initiate the project. The construction of the hydroelectric dam would utilize as many as 36,000 Ukrainian workers. The Russians built brick cottage residences to house Cooper and his American engineering team, complete with tennis courts and golf courses. In addition to the engineering assistance, the US also manufactured turbines and generators for the Soviets. It is interesting to learn that America provided a communist state with such assistance, but Russia was considered an ally in the war. After the dam was completed in 1932, Cooper and his engineering consultants were awarded the Order of the Red Banner of Labor for their contribution to communism. Oddly enough this strange partnership between Americans and communists would further increase the Soviet empire's domain.

The Geopolitical Interests of the United Nations & NATO

Because of the dominant influence of Soviet Russia, Ukraine would not become an independent state (at least not officially within the Europe) until after the collapse of the USSR. Thereafter, there would be tensions for the next several decades with Ukrainian autonomy and the post-Soviet Russian Federation. Depending upon your perspective on the issue of Ukrainian autonomy, there are two sides to the coin. One is from the perspective that the Russian Federation historically considers Ukraine as an inclusive part of their domain and a natural buffer from the forces of the West and NATO. The opposite perspective is to see Ukraine as an independent state that should assert its place within democratic Europe. I would like to interject that the issue of Ukraine's autonomy is not all "black and white" and is much more complex than what we see in the mainstream narrative. The fact is that there is extensive and deep-rooted corruption in both Ukraine and Russia. It is easy to vilify Russia (and Putin as an authoritarian warmonger) and to sympathize with Ukrainian autonomy. The popular view is one that empathizes with Ukraine in light of the assault from the Russian military forces, the humanitarian assumption of compassion for its citizens who have been devastated by the war. And we must be concerned with the humanitarian needs in Ukraine as their people have been casualties of war during the Russian invasion. However, we must not merely evaluate the war in Ukraine with our "gut-level compassion." We need to ask what is driving this war and who are some of the responsible global key players. It is necessary to look at the larger context of a proxy war against Russia and see that funding it with American tax dollars with no accountability from Ukraine and no clear strategic outcome is insane. It does not make sense to pour billions of dollars into one corrupt nation to fight against another corrupt regime the Russian Federation who also is dangerous. I will address this larger context in relation to the dynamics of globalism when I focus upon Russia in later chapters. For now, to understand an essential dynamic of Ukraine's place in global affairs, look at the specific attributes it has in terms of its geographic elements and relationship with NATO. To naively believe that NATO is a European ideal of world peace, and that the EU has the best interests at heart for fostering the democratization of nations to build a liberal international order are fallacious assumptions. We must examine the driving ambitions that the U.N., NATO, and the EU have for Europe and specifically Ukraine.

Because of Ukraine's extensive borders within an area of 233,000 square miles, from a topographical perspective has historically been well suited to the geostrategic deployment of military forces. NATO expansion in the past two decades has contributed significantly to the strategic land mass surrounding Ukraine. If Ukraine were to be factored into the NATO alliance along with Poland, the Czech Republic, Hungary, Slovakia, and Romania there would be a substantial increase of 563 miles of common border with member nations. Former Ambassador Yuri Shcherbak who served during the Clinton administration describes the NATO alliance as follows: "Understandably, this will mean a sharp change in the geostrategic situation, not only of

Ukraine, but of Europe at large."[7] To understand fully the relationship dynamics of NATO's thirty-one nation state members from Europe and the US it is important to consider its early formative history in global affairs. Upon Germany's surrender in the Second World War, the big three international power leaders Roosevelt (US), Churchill (UK), and Stalin (USSR) met at Yalta in 1945 to decide upon demilitarization of the former Nazi controlled state.[8] Stalin had negotiated control of eastern Germany by promising free elections in the nations liberated by the Soviets from Hitler's forces and by joining the United Nations. However, once the Eastern Bloc had solidified under the USSR, it became apparent that Stalin was not going to honor his word for fair and open elections. Roosevelt's successor President Harry Truman quickly assumed a defensive posture by consideration of a European alliance. Up until this time the United States had largely been what some historians called *isolationists* or even *secluded nationalists* as the practice was one of non-involvement or non-interference with international wars and conflicts not belonging to US territories. In other words, America did not see itself as needing to fulfill the role of an international police force and focused upon its own borders and national security. However, it was Senator Arthur Vandenburg, a republican from Michigan in Truman's administration who became the chief architect of the Truman Doctrine. This doctrine was a major shift in America's momentum toward international engagement.[9] I will address the work of Vandenburg, Truman, and other twentieth century progressives more extensively in the final chapter regarding American foreign policy, but for now I will briefly address their role in the context of Europe after the Second World War. Vandenburg of course utilized the Pearl Harbor

---

[7] Shcherbak, *The Strategic Role of Ukraine: Diplomatic Addresses & Lectures (1994-1994)*, (Cambridge, MA: Harvard University Press, 1998), 103.

[8] *Yalta Conference*, History.com Editors, November 1, 2022. Site accessed May 25, 2023, from https://www.history.com.

[9] The Vandenberg Coalition, *Who is Arthur Vandenberg?* Site accessed on May 25, 2023, from https://vandenbergcoalition.org.

attack as the chief rationale behind his doctrine that for the US to have a greater defensive posture, it needed to also be proactive in international affairs. In June 1948, our US Congress passed US Senate Resolution 239 known as the Vandenberg Resolution. This resolution committed our nation to support the U.N. by serving as an international peacekeeper. Following is a direct quote from this resolution:

> Therefore be it Resolved, That the Senate reaffirm the policy of the United States to achieve international peace and security through the United Nations so that armed forces shall not be used except in the common interest, and that the President be advised of the sense of the Senate that this Government, by constitutional process, should particularly pursue the following objectives of the United Nations Charter...Maximum efforts to obtain agreements to provide the United Nations with armed forces as provided by the Charter, and to obtain agreement among member nations upon universal regulation and reduction of armaments under adequate and dependable guaranty against violation.[10]

The organization named after Vandenberg – the Vandenberg Coalition describes their mission values as follows: "Vandenberg ultimately came to argue that internationalism – what he called enlightened self-interest was not only consistent with US values, but also critical for US interests and national security." I urge a great deal of caution to my fellow conservatives not to buy into the "enlightened" international thinking of Vandenberg. If an armed conflict does not clearly pose a security threat to America, then it should be hands-off. The result of America playing the role of an international police force is only contributing to a new world order and increasing its chances of being another pawn for global

---

[10] Vandenburg Resolution, US Senate Resolution 239; 80th Congress, 2nd Session, 11th June 1948. Source accessed on May 25, 2023 from www.nato.int.

elites. My position is one of distrust when it comes to the U.N. and its affiliate organizations such as the World Health Organization (WHO) and, especially international agencies such as the WEF. What is the reason for my lack of trust, it is simply this: we need to invest in our own borders and national security, especially with the catastrophic results of our porous borders down south with millions of undocumented illegals invading our nation. We must not relinquish our national sovereignty to international organizations. One only needs to read the mission statement of the U.N.'s 2030 Sustainable Development Goals or the basic creeds of the WEF to realize that by becoming part of the international new world order, we endanger our rights, liberty, and freedom. Yes, I realize that many will call me a harbinger of right-wing nationalist conspiracy theories, but I am living in this post COVID world in the aftermath of what I believe to be a grand global cabal experiment. More on this in the final chapter!

Shortly after the Vandenberg Resolution established the precedent for American support of the United Nations Charter, on April 4, 1949, the North Atlantic Treaty Organization (NATO) treaty was signed in Washington, D.C. with twelve founding members. NATO'S authority is granted and recognized within the U.N. charter, Chapter VII; Article 51 which states: "Nothing in the present Charter shall impair the inherent right of individual or collective self-defense if an armed attack occurs against a Member of the United Nations."[11] The globalist focus organization in the US known as the Council on Foreign Relations (CFR) whose members describes its mission as a foreign policy think tank wholeheartedly endorses American support for the U.N. and NATO. CFR is quite outspoken on its condemnation of Putin and the Russian Federation. CFR even goes as far as planning for a post Putin Russia by encouraging the development of "emergency response plans" with NATO to prevent what it calls the threat of

---

[11] United Nations Codification Division Publications, *Repertory of Practice of United Nations; Chapter VII; Article 51*. Source accessed May 26, 2023, from https://legal.un.org.

radical right-wing nationalism. The agency has applauded the Biden administration for their response to events escalating between Russia and Ukraine: "Close coordination, such as US President Joe Biden's phone call with leaders in London, Paris, and Berlin, and outreach by top US diplomats and military leaders to their European counterparts, ensured a united transatlantic message in a moment of crisis in Russia."[12] In addition to affirming the Biden administration's role in the global cabal, CFR is in lockstep with NATO and the U.N. especially regarding the agency's description of their interest in Ukraine according to the U.N. Codification document: "Ukraine has long played an important, yet sometimes overlooked, role in the global security order. Today, the country is on the front lines of a renewed great-power rivalry that many analysts say will dominate international relations in the decades ahead." For the context of our focus upon the war in Ukraine it is important to highlight the given purpose of the NATO Treaty quoted in the historical archive of the US State Department: "The North Atlantic Treaty Organization was created in 1949 by the United States, Canada, and several Western European nations to provide collective security against the Soviet Union."[13] Notice that the primary focus is for NATO to provide a defense against the USSR. Although one might easily relegate this to a cold-war era doctrine, it still bears testimony to the definitive mission of NATO. Given NATO's posture in Europe, it is easy to see why this continues to be a source of contention with the Russian Federation. NATO's current statement still maintains this: "Collective defense is at the heart of the Treaty and is enshrined in Article 5. It commits members to protect each other and sets a spirit of solidarity within the alliance."[14] Furthermore, NATO states one of its chief military objectives:

---

[12] Council on Foreign Relations, *For Europe, Time to Plan for a Post-Putin Russia*. June 28, 2023. Site accessed on July 3, 2023, from https://www.cfr.org.

[13] US State Department Office of the Historian, *North Atlantic Treaty Organization (NATO), 1949*. Source accessed May 26, 2023, from https://history.state.gov.

[14] North Atlantic Treaty Organization, Founding Treaty, Rev. 02 Sep. 2022. Source accessed May 26, 2023, from https://www.nato.int.

"NATO is committed to the peaceful resolution of disputes. If diplomatic efforts fail, it has the military power to undertake crisis-management operations. These are carried out under the collective defense clause of NATO's founding treaty Article 5 of the Washington Treaty or under a United Nations mandate, alone or in cooperation with other countries and international organizations."[15] Breaking this down further, NATO is declaring that by invoking Article 5 under a U.N. mandate it can utilize military force to resolve international conflicts through what is called "crisis-management operations." NATO crisis management operations are defined as the engagement of an integrated military command structure; in other words, a war room planning scenario. Following the historical narrative after World War Two, the United States under Roosevelt and Truman entered a European alliance recognizing the U.N. charter authority and solidifying it further by drafting and signing the NATO Treaty. This treaty opened the door for America to provide military support to NATO members under the alliance of the United Nations. Now I will look at the military engagement of NATO in relationship to Ukraine.

The Crimean Peninsula is another land feature that forms a strategic geographical area for NATO and Ukraine. This area provides international trade and economic ties to the Black Sea region's access for international shipping and naval fleets. The large port cities of Odesa, Kherson, Mykolaiv, Kerch, Sevastopol and Izmail are key access points for marine passenger and freight routes. Because Ukraine's naval fleet is considerably small with fewer than 100 warships, it relies upon NATO for support because the military history of the Black Sea and Mediterranean areas was strategic for forces during the Second World War. Since 1997, Ukraine has been doing joint naval exercises in the Black Sea region with the following NATO nations: the US, Italy, Turkey, Greece, and Romania. Ukraine is also a member of the Parliamentary Assembly of the Black Sea Economic Commonwealth which links

---

[15] NATO, *What is NATO? Political & Military Alliance*. Source accessed May 26, 2023, from https://www.nato.int.

Trans-caucasus Corridor for oil transport. NATO forces are comprised more than 20,000 military personnel in missions around the world from Kosovo and the Mediterranean and the Baltic States. Although Ukraine to date has not been granted membership into NATO, a press release dated May 25, 2023, titled *NATO and Ukraine Boost Partnership through Greater Cooperation* describes a meeting of NATO and Ukraine in Brussels to "expand the NATO-Ukraine partnership:"

> Along with their bravery, we praise the creativity, agility, and innovation that the Armed Forces of Ukraine embody. NATO stands behind Ukraine, including in their innovation efforts...This is the biggest war since World War II and at the same time the most technological war in human history. Innovations play a special role in confronting the enemy, which is many times superior in terms of weapons and personnel. The launch of the NATO-Ukraine Innovation Dialogue is an important step that will bring cooperation between our country and the Alliance to a new level. We are also ready to share our experience with our allies.[16]

European Union

It is worthwhile to consider the importance of the relationship that NATO has with another significant globalist power organization influencing events in Ukraine the European Union (EU). The EU is geopolitically concurrent with NATO and the U.N. and shares similar global ambitions. Described as a *supranational* in a class by itself, the EU is outright in its condemnation of nationalism which it sees as a threat to internationalism. It has twenty-seven member nations from Europe, nineteen of which are also NATO members. By sheer volume

---

[16] NATO and Ukraine Boost Partnership. 26 May 2023. Source accessed May 26, 2023, from https://www.nato.int.

the EU boasts of 1.6 million square miles of territory and comprises the third largest global economy which easily bestows the status of a recognized global super power. Although the EU's history goes back as early as post-history World War Two in 1948 under what was known as the Treaty of Brussels, the most recent development was at the NATO summit held on July 11-12, 2018. At this international summit NATO and the EU signed a new joint declaration. In a statement made by the acting president of the European Council, Donald Tusk remarked on Donald Trump's reluctance to support the EU:

> Speaking on the eve of the NATO summit here in Brussels, I would like to address President Trump directly, who for a long time now has been criticizing Europe almost daily for, in his view, insufficient contributions to the common defense capabilities, and for living off the US–Dear president Trump: America does not have and will not have a better ally than Europe. Today, Europeans spend on defense many times more than Russia, and as much as China. And I think you can have no doubt, Mr. President, that this is an investment in common American and European defense.[17]

Tusk obviously attempted to snub Trump's common sense anti-globalist foreign policy stance. This is a game that leaders in the international community often play by making statements which belittle anyone's efforts not to relinquish their national sovereignty for the sake of a one-world order. Trump was clearly a nationalist looking out for the best interests of our country by not selling out to the global cabal as the Biden administration would later do full throttle. The EU stands by their support of Ukraine while vilifying Russia: "The EU stands united

---

[17] European Council on the European Union: NATO Summit 2018. Site accessed July 3, 2023, from https://www.consilium.europa.en/meetings/international-summit/2018/07/11-12/.

in its solidarity with Ukraine and will continue to support Ukraine and its people together with its international partners, including through additional political, financial, and humanitarian support. The EU has reacted swiftly and decisively to Russia's aggression by adopting further restrictive measures in response, that will have massive and severe consequences for Russia."[18]

At the root of Ukraine's desire to become a member of NATO is their concern over Russia. Shcherbak states that "Any attempts to restore the (Russian) empire or to forcefully reintegrate the post-Soviet countries under Russian control will accelerate the movement of Ukraine toward NATO." Ukraine's trajectory course into a strategic collaboration with NATO was also accelerated during the Clinton administration when Leonid Kuchma became the nation's second post-USSR era president in 1994. Clinton had been influenced by Polish President Lech Walesa in 1993, who urged him: "After decades of Soviet domination, we are all afraid of Russia. If Russia again adopts an aggressive foreign policy, this aggression will be directed against Ukraine and Poland. We need America to prevent this."[19] For Clinton the way to prevent further Russian aggression would be for Ukraine to become part of the NATO alliance. However, Ukraine's new government was politically unstable and faced serious challenges in its course of development. President Kuchma's legacy was marked by political corruption, scandal, and government censorship which set the stage for recurring governmental depravity in the nation. Ukrainian historian Plokhy calls Kuchma "a crook and even a murderer."[20] The corruption in Ukraine precedes Kuchma going back to the days of Leonid Brezhnev who spent much of his career in the nation as the leader of the political clan known as the *Dnipropetrovsk Mafia* named after a leading industrial city. Later Kuchma appointed Yuri Shcherbak as ambassador to

---

[18] European Union, *In Focus – EU Solidarity with Ukraine*. Site accessed on July 3, 2023, from https://european-union. europa.eu/index_en.

[19] Plokhy, *The Russo-Ukrainian War*, 75.

[20] Plokhy, *The Gates of Europe*, 332.

the US under Clinton. Shcherbak speaks highly of his leadership role model Robert Lansing who worked closely with Woodrow Wilson to promote globalist policies against nationalism which were expounded at the 1919-1920 Paris Peace conference. Shcherbak is also known for his organization of the Green Party in Ukraine as a response to the Chernobyl disaster. This party later would evolve into a radical global environmental group. Shcherbak described Kuchma and Clinton's collaboration as being aimed at the integration of Ukraine into European global affairs as well as renewed relations between Ukraine and the US government: "This course has been aimed at the integration of Ukraine into Euro-Atlantic structures...I presented my credentials to President Bill Clinton on the eve of the state visit of President Kuchma to the United States, which instituted a new level of friendship and cooperation between our two nations."[21] Both Democrats and Republicans have shown favoritism to the socialist state of Ukraine because of the nation's strategic position as a gateway in European affairs. The Clinton Administration began steps to create policies supporting what would be known as the *democratic transformation* of Ukraine's government in the 1990's a trend that has continued in both parties until this present day. Because the terms are frequently utilized throughout this book, I will digress briefly here to inject my personal views on the use of the term *democratic* or *democracy*. There is confusion on the distinction between a democracy and a republic even among some conservatives. My view is best summed up by conservative American historian Dave Barton: "We have grown accustomed to hearing that we are a democracy; such was never the intent. The form of government entrusted to us by our Founders was a *republic*, not a democracy. Our Founders had an opportunity to establish a democracy in America and chose not to. In fact, the Founders made it clear that we were not, and were never

---

[21] Yuri Shcherbak, The Strategic Role of Ukraine: Diplomatic Addresses & Lectures (Cambridge: Harvard University Press, 1998), 12-13.

to become a democracy."[22] Barton references quotes from American founders such as John Witherspoon (signer of the Declaration): "Pure democracy cannot subsist long nor be carried far into the departments of state, it is very subject to caprice and the madness of popular rage." Another founder's quote about the shortcomings of democracy is from John Adams: "Remember, democracy never lasts long. It soon wastes, exhausts, and murders itself. There was never a democracy that did not commit suicide." Progressives, socialist Democrats, and Deep State bureaucrats love to use the word *democracy* especially when it collectively refers to the *democratization* of foreign nations such as Ukraine. What they are implying is the assertion of a socialist rule of order upon a nation that takes place through tyranny and big government. A democracy was such as was birthed through the bloody mob-directed French Revolution. A republic not a democracy was forged by the founders who fought in the American Revolution and its principles are outlined in our Constitution. The trend in supporting the development of European Democratic Socialism is a renewal of the past ambitions of Wilson, Roosevelt, and Truman who also opened the door for the US to have a greater geopolitical presence on the European stage.

Washington Deep State Bureaucrats and Ukraine

Ukraine's government corruption was no obstacle to the Democratic party's ambitions of the Clinton administration to utilize the Ukrainian government to support their global collaboration strategies. Deputy Secretary of State Strobe Talbot was a close friend of Bill Clinton and because of his former role with Russian foreign policy he also worked as adviser to Secretary of State Warren Christopher regarding "New Independent States" such as Ukraine that emerged shortly after the collapse of the Soviet Union. Talbot and Christopher were deeply involved in US collaboration with global foreign policy. In chapter six we will

---

[22] David Barton, *Republic v. Democracy*. Election-Year Stewardship. Source accessed November 27, 2023, from https://www.khouse.org/articles/2004/546/print.

cover in more detail how global foreign policy evolved. Talbot later served as a president of the Brookings Institution, a socialist global policy think tank whose mission fully supports all that the global elites love: climate action and justice, U.N. 2030 sustainability goals, diversity, equity and inclusion, EU-US trade relations, etc.[23] It was here that Talbot distinguished himself by raising more than $650 million in support of global policy research and analysis focusing upon Europe and Russia. Christopher also went on after his career in government to become director for the Yale Center for the Study of Globalization, a policy think tank within academia. Both Talbot and Christopher played a significant role in the formulation of strategic policy with Ukraine under the Clinton administration. On May 16, 1997, Ukraine's President Kuchma and US Vice President Al Gore signed the Joint Statement of the Ukraine-United States Binational Commission. This joint statement between the US and Ukraine affirmed the following:

> The Sides underscored the importance of deepening cooperation to ensure the security interests of Ukraine and the United States, and to promote the integration of Ukraine as a central European state into European and Euro-Atlantic Institutions. They affirmed that Ukraine should play a key role in ensuring peace and stability in Central and Eastern Europe and the continent as a whole.[24]

The words of the statement that talk about Ukraine playing a "key role in ensuring peace and stability in Central and Eastern Europe" will become the ideological cornerstone for Ukraine's strategic geopolitical role especially regarding the current conflict with Russia. Talbot reinforced this view by stating "the fate of Ukraine is key to stability

---

[23] Brookings Institution, source accessed June 28, 2023, from https://www.brookings.edu.

[24] Shcherbak, *The Strategic Role of Ukraine*, xii.

in Central Europe – that if Ukraine could develop as an independent, sovereign nation, secure in its current borders, with normal, peaceful relations with its neighbors, then the entire region would have a better chance for peace and prosperity." Adding the peace element to Ukraine's role in the world sounds quite humanitarian; after all, world peace is one of the greatest utopian aspirations. However, we will see that world peace is the favorite language of the global elites who say that they are for peace on the one hand but on the other hand are quick to utilize war to accomplish their objectives. The peace machine of global leaders is bought and financed with billions of dollars that go toward funding international conflicts. Peace is only an illusion and a smokescreen for shaping public opinion even when world events can potentially escalate into nuclear holocaust. Socialists and communists alike have utilized the promise of peace as nothing more than a baited hook to deceive the masses. Mao Zedong who was a devoted student of Stalin, climbed China's ancient Gate of Heavenly Peace as a symbolic gesture to reassure the masses that his revolution would usher in a new era of peace for the nation. However, Mao's act of peace was later exposed as deceptive rhetoric during his bloody revolution as his regime executed millions. This peace at *at whatever the cost* approach sounds like the Apostle Paul's apocalyptic warning: "While people are saying, there is peace and security, then sudden destruction will come upon them."[25] I will discuss further about how the global elites speak of peace while playing with the risk of a nuclear Armageddon. The Clinton administration loved to promote global peace by financing international conflicts. Clinton's Secretary of Defense William Perry committed over $20 million dollars to Ukraine's strategic military defense in the name of peace, this only initiated the disastrous policies that we see today with billions of dollars going toward the financing of the proxy war machine. This peace ideology was forged by such individuals as Yuri Shcherbak

---

[25] 1 Thessalonians 5:3 (NEV) – this text talks about a time of future divine judgement known as the "Day of the Lord" which will be a harbinger within the eschatological context of world leaders who deceive the nations with false promises of peace.

who outlined his work in the Clinton administration for the Ukrainian Research Institute at Harvard as follows:

> The proclamation of an independent Ukrainian state on the ruins of the Soviet Empire has changed the geopolitical reality of Europe and has drawn the close attention of political leaders, military specialists, political scientists, and all those engaged in strategic analysis and planning. Interest in Ukraine on the world stage is seen as early as the beginning of this century, especially in connection with the First World War.[26]

Yuri served as one of the early architects of Ukraine's geopolitical dogma. His work and that of the Harvard University Ukrainian Research Institute have greatly influenced not only Ivy League academia but have also shaped public opinion about Ukraine in America. Madeleine Albright another significant player in the Clinton Administration helped to shape foreign policy and public opinion regarding Ukraine. Albright who served on the National Security Council added that Ukraine's geopolitical role not only contributed to bringing about world peace, but also global economic prosperity: "A prosperous Ukraine will be a major world market and a strong contributor to the global economy. A peaceful Ukraine will be a vigorous partner in European and international affairs."[27] On the peace and prosperity note, globalists love to pour US taxpayer money into socialist nations to fund globalist agendas. With the help of the Clinton administration, Ukraine soon was established as a global corridor for international banking transactions. Over sixty financial agreements between crooked Ukrainian President Kuchma and the US opened the door for USAID funding, credits from the Import-Export Bank, the US Department of Agriculture, and the

---

[26] Shcherbak, *The Strategic Role of Ukraine*, 3.

[27] Ibid.

US Department of Defense. On September 30, 1996, President Clinton enacted the Foreign Operations Appropriation Act earmarking $225 million in US Assistance to Ukraine under the Freedom Support Act. The International Monetary Fund (IMF) and the World Bank also began to attract international investors; by 1996, over one billion dollars from international investors was pouring into Ukraine.[28] Later I will look at how billions of dollars pass through Ukraine not because of a desire to assist the nation or to help its citizens, but to promote the agendas of the global elites to use Ukraine as a pawn on their chess board.

In 1994 at the 49th U.N. General Assembly, Ukrainian Minister for Foreign Affairs Hennadiy Udovenko, formulated the principles for the nation's new policies with a summary statement: "The main task for Ukraine as a historically old but politically new state is the gradual integration into European and world processes as a reliable link to the new global system of international relations." Udovenko's statement was prophetic, a new global system was emerging – a system by which countries would eventually relinquish their national sovereignty to transition into a one-world governance. More specifically the infrastructure was already being laid for the nation of Ukraine to have a key role in this new world order. Just a couple of years after the Ukrainian minister for foreign affairs spoke of the nation's importance for a "new global system," Ambassador Shcherbak in an address to the Center for Strategic and International Studies focused upon European and global security in Ukraine's future: "In a practical sense, there can emerge a kind of security corridor which could become a means for a very active and positive political, economic, trade cultural, and scientific route on the map of the European continent."[29] This security corridor will be the focal point of the global elites with the war in Ukraine. It is, in effect, Ukraine's place as an international gateway that I mentioned earlier in

---

[28] Shcherbak, 69-71.

[29] Ibid.

this chapter. Shcherbak further adds to this concept that Ukraine is not only a gateway but a bridge:

> Geographically, Ukraine is a state within the Central and Eastern European region, and by God's will, it is destined to be a bridge, a joining link between political East and West. It would be a national tragedy if Ukraine finds itself between two conflicting or warring military and political blocs. It would be a universal tragedy if Ukraine becomes a pawn of expansionist powers.[30]

What an amazing coincidence that almost thirty years after the late ambassador made this statement, in essence this very tragedy did occur as his nation found itself "between warring military and political blocs." But even more tragic is that Ukraine is now a pawn not of "expansionist powers," but of the global cabal. I will now look at the revolutions that set the stage for these events and made way for its current leadership.

---

[30] Shcherbak, 31.

CHAPTER TWO

Revolutions for Radicals: Setting Zelensky's World Stage

History is a relay of revolutions; the torch of idealism is carried by the revolutionary group until this group becomes an establishment, and then quietly the torch is put down to wait until a new revolutionary group picks it up for the next leg of the run. Thus, the revolutionary cycle goes on. – Saul D. Alinsky, *Rules for Radicals*

Revolution is the path to desired change – Volodymyr Zelenski, November 21, 2020

Corridors to Power in Georgia – The Rose Revolution

After President Bush, Sr. the Clinton administration was the next to develop policies that would contribute to a preference for NATO engagement. This would be a gradual process wherein the US government would still pledge financial support for Russian disarmament while enabling nations such as Ukraine and Georgia to become more assertive in matters of succession. A positive move required Ukraine to relinquish their nuclear arms to be dismantled in Russia. This was part of the Lisbon Protocol in 1992, which committed Ukraine to joining the Nuclear Nonproliferation Treaty. The Treaty essentially followed the START-I Soviet American treaty on arms reduction. In turn the US would provide one billion dollars of compensation that would go towards converting the nuclear warheads into uranium fuel to run their nuclear plants. Not everyone agreed with this move; political scientist John Mearsheimer and Ukrainian history expert Serhii Plokhy both believe that Ukraine should be allowed to keep their nuclear arms as a deterrent to the Russo-Ukrainian War in 2022.[31] By 1995 the US was providing Ukraine with $225 million annually in addition to assistance already provided by the G7 nations.[32] Yeltsin already made concessions for Clinton which included an agreement to respect the Russian populations of the Baltic States. It was not long before NATO and the EU realized they could easily use the nations of Georgia and Ukraine, which were already at core of Russian insecurity as leverage for applying pressure on the Russian Federation. This realization was most unfortunate because it put the citizens of Georgia and Ukraine in vulnerable positions to be used as mere pawns in the larger geopolitical game of the global elites through three revolutions which were orchestrated for nefarious purposes. The first revolution which occurred in Georgia in 2003, lasted only twenty-one days and was known as the *Rose Revolution*. I will explain the significant players and circumstances in this revolution which brought about a swift transfer of power.

The nation of Georgia which occupies 27,000 square miles is sandwiched between the Black Sea and the Caspian Sea bordering Russia's Caucasus region. Georgia is a mere 900 miles from Ukraine, and it is one of the first nations involved the series of revolutions that helped to set the stage for future events we now see escalating in Ukraine. Eduard Shevardnadze a close colleague of Gorbachev served as a foreign minister in the 1990's to implement the withdrawal of Soviet troops from

---

[31] Plokhy, *The Russo-Ukrainian War*, 71.
[32] Shcherbak, 68-69.

Afghanistan and the negotiation of arms treaties with the US.[33] When there were problems within the leadership of Georgia after the demise of the USSR, Shevardnadze became a chair in Georgia's state council in 1992 and fought against organized crime and separatist violence. Two years later, the Clinton administration endorsed support for a U.N. peacekeeping force to be deployed to Georgia to bypass any intervention of the Russian military.[34] Clinton was looking for ways to use multinational forces rather than to rely upon Russia for stability. However, Shevardnadze was already working toward peaceful solutions for the nation of Georgia. This set the precedent for US and NATO engagement early on, not only in Georgia but also later with Ukraine. Globalist billionaire George Soros was also ready to influence Georgia through his Open Society Foundation in 1994. Soros who has invested over $85 million into "democratic reforms" in Georgia, stated that Open Society's goal was to "support local, independent, civil society groups that share our commitment to the values of democratic participation and government accountability."[35] Soros's Open Society Foundations has provided more funding than any other progressive left-wing organization to totalitarian regimes around the world and has advanced the cause of a new world order even in the US with the appointment of liberal judges and leftist politicians.

Shevardnadze later became president of Georgia in August 1995. On the way to a signing ceremony for the new Georgian constitution the president survived an assassination attempt by separatist rebels when a car bomb exploded near his motorcade. Shevardnadze already had enemies because he supported the Russian Federation and adopted

---

[33] Britannica, Eduard Shevardnadze; Soviet Foreign Minister & President of Georgia, accessed online on July 19, 2023, from https://www.britannica.com/biography/Eduard-Shevardnadze

[34] The Washington Post, March 8, 1994, U.N. Force for Ex-Soviet Georgia Wins Clinton Support. Accessed on July 19, 2023, from https://www.washingtonpost.com.

[35] Open Society Foundations, The Open Society Foundations in Georgia, February 13, 2020. Accessed on July 19, 2023, from https://www.opensocietyfoundations.org.

a conciliatory policy towards Moscow by blocking the flow of separatist rebels and equipment trying to reach Chechnya. The Georgian president faced challenges from resistance factions that were opposed to the Russian Federation. Separatists in Abkhazia in Western Georgia and ethnic conflicts in Southern Ossetia in the northern region were posing difficult challenges for his presidency. After reelection in November 2003, there were allegations made against Shevardnadze for government corruption. A wave of protesters arrived in the Georgian capital Tbilisi on November 3, 2003. The Rose Revolution was proclaimed as a bloodless, non-violent Revolution against the Russian Federation leadership in Georgia, and the protesters called for Shevardnadze's immediate removal. The name "Rose Revolution" was attributed to an incident in which a young girl holding a rose was lifted up above the protest rally in Tbilisi.[36] The young girl holding the rose soon became the poster child for the international media, who praised the revolution as a demonstrations of peaceful resistance to the Russian Federation-backed president.. Although pro-NATO and EU opponents of Shevardnadze were claiming that the Rose Revolution was a peaceful protest which resulted in the resignation of Georgia's president, it was a planned coup by forces behind the scenes such as Soros and the CIA. Putin had long suspected the CIA of being part of the Georgian revolution. His critics have scoffed at his claims of CIA involvement, but it is a well-known fact that the CIA had been involved with globalist plots around the world to overthrow governments and to depose foreign leaders. As early as June 1993, CIA agent Freddie Woodruff was in Tbilisi on assignment to train local security forces.[37] The CIA claimed that they had concerns about drug smuggling and separatist insurgency and needed to establish a presence in Georgia, thereby justifying

---

[36] Radio Free Europe, *She Coined the Catchphrase: Looking Back on the Rose Revolution.* Accessed on July 19, 2023, from https://www.rferl.org.

[37] Newsweek, Cristina Maza, November 13, 2018. *The Murder of a CIA Agent in an Unruly Post-Soviet Country.* Accessed on July 20, 2023, from https://www.newsweek.com.

Woodruff's mission. However, the plot began to thicken when Agent Woodruff was shot in the head and killed on August 8, 1993. Initially, claims were made that Russia was behind Woodruff's murder because there were also KGB agents in Tbilisi. It turned out that he was murdered at the hands of one of their own, a senior CIA officer by the name of Aldrich Hazen Ames. Ames was a Russian double agent who executed Woodruff. The CIA covered up the incident with Woodruff's death and the double agent Ames because they knew that it would expose some of their intelligence operations in Georgia a decade before the Rose Revolution. Shevardnadze who was working as a foreign minister in Georgia before his presidency stated that when he met the CIA director at the airport to deliver Woodruff's body, details about the murder were never mentioned giving the impression that the US merely wanted the whole incident to go away. Although Ames was arrested and brought back for espionage and murder, he would not face the death penalty because the CIA needed to debrief him. When the CIA Director James Woolsey testified before the Senate Intelligence Committee in D.C. on January 10, 1995, he could not give assurance that the CIA could avoid another spy scandal like what happened in Georgia. Insurgents within Georgia played a key role in influencing the transition of power and have been used strategically by the CIA. Such clandestine operations carried out by the CIA are well substantiated by former Secretary of Defense Christopher Miller. Miller who served under Trump, was a combat veteran and career military officer with direct experience of CIA operations and the role of foreign insurgents. Miller writes of his experiences with the CIA regarding insurgents: "By contrast, Irregular Warfare is more typical of the twenty-first century with violent struggles among state and nonstate actors not just to control geography but to gain legitimacy and influence...we support insurgents to overthrow a hostile government."[38]

---

[38] Christopher C. Miller, *Soldier Secretary: Warnings from the Battlefield & the Pentagon about America's Most Dangerous Enemies*, (New York, Hachette Book Group, 2023), 138 & 142.

However, Georgian President Shevardnadze was not a hostile government dictator and yet was forcibly removed from office in his country. There were plenty of insurgents that he had to contend with who no doubt were working with the CIA. A rightfully elected leader was removed because he supported the Russian Federation and would not accommodate NATO or the EU in their demands toward building a globalist society. This will be the trend with the so-called European revolutions especially when they concern nations that have been a part of the Russian domain. The Rose Revolution activists claimed that their new president Mikheil Saakashvili received 97 percent of the popular vote and was immediately affirmed by the EU member states and the US[39] President George W. Bush and his administration were supportive of the results of the Rose Revolution and the transfer of power to Saakashvili. Bush praised Georgia for "being a beacon of liberty."[40] Just a year prior to the revolution, Bush had a busy diplomatic schedule — he met with European leaders at the NATO Summit and inaugurated the NATO-Russia Council. In a meeting on November 22, 2002, Putin expressed his concerns to Bush about NATO expansion. Although Putin was the first world leader to offer support to Bush immediately after the 911 attacks, his concerns over NATO expansion especially regarding Ukraine and Georgia fell upon deaf ears. After the Rose Revolution Putin expressed further dissatisfaction with seven nations, three of them Baltic States that were added to the NATO alliance. Mark Galeotti a prominent scholar of Russian security affairs described Putin's feelings toward Bush as follows: "By 2006, he was feeling that Russia had been exploited, conned and marginalized, and at a keynote speech in Munich, in February 2007, he suggested that the United States was trying to create a 'unipolar' world, one in which 'there is one master, one sovereign' through the 'almost uncontained

---

[39] Dov Lynch, European Union Institute for Security Studies (EUISS): *The Rose Revolution & After*, 2006.

[40] Oxford Reference; Overview Mikhal Saakashvili, accessed July 21, 2023, from https://www.oxfordreference.com.

hyper use of force, military force, in international relations, force that is plunging world into an abyss of permanent conflict."[41]

Many of Putin's critics dismissed his remarks as whining about his perception of US-NATO unfairness. However, Putin's statement is accurate: the global elites have created a unipolar world that uses military force in international relations to plunge the world into permanent conflict. And the Rose Revolution that placed Saakashvili into power sought exactly that to set the stage for permanent conflict. Saakashvili graduated with a law degree from Kyiv University's Institute of International Relations in Ukraine. Later, he was employed by Patterson Belknap, a law firm in New York, while attending the Ivy League Columbia University's World Leader's Forum. In addition to the university president Lee Bollinger being a champion of affirmative action cases, Columbia's Forum is extensively liberal in its support of heads of state from globalist institutions around the world. Its list of esteemed speakers includes individuals such as Richard Haas (with the progressive Council on Foreign Relations) and George Soros. Saakashvili's transition to power after the Rose Revolution was praised by Soros and the United Nations Development Program Administrator Malloch Brown at an address at the WEF in Davos on January 22, 2004.[42] Soros further described the work to establish his Open Society new funding to support governance reform in Georgia. Saakashvili was instrumental in the execution of the Rose Revolution as he served on the Georgian Parliament under President Shevardnadze. Saakashvili founded the opposition party known as the United National Movement — a liberal pro-western pro-NATO party that vigorously opposed the president. On November 22, 2003, Saakashvili and his party officials launched the protests in Tbilisi and in other regions of Georgia while taking over the parliament building. Fearing for his safety, Shevardnadze fled the capital

---

[41] Galeotti, *Putin's Wars*, (London: Osprey Publishing, 2022), 85-86.
[42] Open Society Foundations: OSI & UNDP Announce New Fund to Support Governance Reform in Georgia, January 22, 2004. Accessed on July 21, 2023, from https://www.opensocietyfoundations.org.

and announced his immediate resignation. One of the witness accounts of the coup reported: "I assert this as a witness – this was the forced removal of the current lawful President from office."[43] Russian officials voiced that the Rose Revolution was an anti-constitutional coup that was well prepared in advance by foreign forces and mentioned specifically the involvement of US Ambassador Richard Miles and the George Soros Foundation.[44] Putin's advisor on EU affairs, Sergei Yastrzhembsky issued a statement saying: "The Rose Revolution was no revolution at all, but foreign interventions, violating Georgia's constitutional order and international norms." Also, State Minister Paata Kakareishvili, stated in an article in 2005: "Everyone knows that no real revolution took place in Georgia; the face of the political elite merely changed through revolutionary methods." The European Union Institute for Security Studies (EUISS) in their report on the Rose Revolution commented that "some Georgian civil society activists had received training and support in Europe and the US" which added to the momentum of tens of thousands of protesters who went into the streets.[45]

The Rose Revolution which took a decade of collaborative planning through various players such as Soros, the CIA, and both the Clinton and Bush administrations, was pulled off in a mere three weeks. After the installment of the newly appointed parliament under Saakashvili, it was on its way to accomplishing its purposes for building infrastructure for the new global order. One of the key interests of global elites in putting Georgia in the geopolitical game was for access to energy resources. Svante E. Cornell the research director for the Central Asia-Caucasus Institute, authored a report for the Strategic Studies Institute of the US Army War College titled *Georgia After the Rose Revolution: Geopolitical Predicament & Implications for US Policy* that specifically addresses Georgia's importance in energy:

---

[43] Ibid.

[44] Lynch, EUISS, *The Rose Revolution & After*, 2006.

[45] Ibid.

> The security and success of Georgia is very important to Western interests in general and to those of the United States in particular. Beyond the hope that Georgia represents for successful state-building and democratic development in both the former Soviet Union and the wider Middle East, this country is a key strategic pivot for the transportation of Eurasia's energy resources, as well as for western access to Central Asia and Afghanistan.[46]

Cornell further pointed out that Georgia is the most critical country in the South Caucasus because of its strategic place in linking the Caspian Sea and the Azerbaijan with the West. The EU's Transportation Corridor Europe Caucasus Asia program launched in the 1990's focused upon Georgia as an important transportation corridor for building rail lines linking Kazakhstan to China. In addition to oil, the second objective for the new Georgian regime was for NATO and the EU's strategic military goals. Putin's assessment of the Rose Revolution's purpose for building a *unipolar world* through military force proved to be correct. Georgia increased its defense budget to 9.2 percent of the country's Gross Domestic Product (GDP) which was five times higher than the NATO minimum.[47] NATO's interest in Georgia was vital to its military logistics for the transport of troops and equipment to Central Asia. To the satisfaction of George W. Bush, Saakashvili aided with post-war operations for Iraqi Freedom's U.N. peacekeeping force by deploying 2,300 infantry soldiers from Georgia. This new military coalition assistance incurred the favor of Washington bureaucrats who in turn provided Georgia with training and equipment. The Bush administration supported what it called a red line policy with Georgia that had the purpose of halting Russian encroachment with a Train-and-Equip

---

[46] Svante E. Cornell, Strategic Studies Institute, US Army War College (JSTOR), 2007; *Georgia After the Rose Revolution: Geopolitical Predicament & Implications for US Policy.*

[47] Galeotti, *Putin's Wars*, 123-24.

program costing over $64 million in 2002. Budget increases resulted in the purchase of helicopters and self-propelled artillery as well as T-72 tanks. NATO also provided their Individual Partnership Action Plan for Georgia's Ministry of Defense to assist with strategic military planning. Saakashvili promptly acted to reinforce ties with Ukraine and the anti-Russian Moldovan government via increased solidarity with the EU and NATO through their aggressive foreign policies. Meanwhile relations with Russia seriously deteriorated because of the US-NATO alliance with Georgia's new regime. The Georgian legislature increased the size of its military from 28,000 to 37,000 soldiers and even claimed to have shot down a Russian aircraft over Abkhazia. In the next chapter I will show how all of this came to the tipping point that led to Russia's response in 2008. For now, I will move to the second revolution that set the stage for Zelensky the Orange Revolution.

The Orange Revolution – Influencing Ukraine's Presidential Elections

Just a year after the Rose Revolution in Georgia toppled a pro-Russian Federation president, Ukraine was next to experience political upheaval. The events leading up to the Orange Revolution in Ukraine are quite complex and had been developing for over a decade. The political instability in the aftermath of the collapse of the USSR was a key contributing factor in both revolutions. Given the shaky situation in Russia with its volatile transition from the Soviet state to the fledgling Federation, Georgia and Ukraine were fair game for political corruption, crime, and were targets for global interest groups within NATO, the EU, and the US. Although Ukraine was eager to move forward with its independence from Russia and to establish its own sovereignty it had to contend with a failing economy, high unemployment, and its own political corruption.[48] Runaway inflation was at a staggering 2500 per-

---

[48] Plokhy, *The Gates of Europe*, 329-30.

cent in 1992. Geopolitical groups in Europe and around the world had competitive and varying interests for Ukraine. As mentioned previously, Russia was quite reluctant to see its buffer zone between potential hostile forces in the West give its allegiance to NATO and the EU. And on the other side the US, NATO and the EU saw Ukraine as an ideal geopolitical advantage in terms of their global agendas. Ukraine's new leaders had a desire to move toward the EU and NATO, which proved to be a source of consternation for Russia. One must understand Ukraine from ethnic and cultural, not merely political viewpoints. These viewpoints are best described by political consultant Paul Manafort who did consulting for the Ukraine Party of Regions: "Ukraine is really two different countries."[49] Manafort continued by explaining that western Ukraine from Kyiv to the borders of Poland and Romania has a strong European heritage, whereas eastern Ukraine is predominantly Russian from an ethnic and cultural standpoint. Attempts to unify the country apart from honoring the diversity of the two cultures will result in greater division. Unfortunately, leaders would emerge in Ukraine who tended to polarize the east and west in the interest of their agendas (pro-EU vs. pro-Russia) rather than try to embrace its diversity by achieving a middle ground for the two. And most often US, NATO, and EU interests in a unified global agenda tended to create greater division rather than unity, especially when it alienated Russia. The key to Ukraine's success as a nation is to avoid being exclusively one over the other and to welcome opportunities for increased diplomacy with Russia.

The first democratically elected president of Ukraine was Leonid Kravchuk a former chairman of the Ukrainian Supreme Soviet party. Kravchuk was in office from 1991 to 1994 and sought the first opportunities to move the nation toward an independent state when Soviet power began to weaken in Russia. Kravchuk did not win the following election and was succeeded by his prime minister Leonid Kuchma who served as Ukraine's president from 1994 to 2005. Whereas his

---

[49] Paul Manafort, *Political Prisoner: Persecuted, Prosecuted, but Not Silenced*, (New York, Skyhorse Publishing, 2022), 114.

predecessor Kravchuk desired to distance the nation from Russia, Kuchma had a strong rapport with former Soviets, and his administration supported privatization, free trade, and closer ties with Russia.[50] Kuchma's reforms did provide initial relief for the economy although his administration was tainted with ties to rich oligarchs which were corrupt. Nevertheless, Kuchma won a second term in office on the campaign promise for defeating the Communist Party with continued economic recovery. However, Kuchma soon had to contend with a Ukrainian version of the Watergate crisis when his opposition leader Oleksandr Moroz, head of the Socialist Party of Ukraine, released secretly recorded audio tapes that exposed him taking bribes from local officials involved with privatization schemes. The plot became even darker when another Kuchma opponent, a dissident journalist mentioned on the tapes by the name of Heorhii Gongadze was found beheaded in a forest near Kyiv. Although Kuchma's ties to the murder were never proven, the scandals would prove to be the undoing of his political career and he would pass on seeking a third term in office by backing Victor Yanukovych, a popular candidate with the working class. Yanukovych was born into a poor family and worked in heavy industrial mechanics until earning his degree in mechanical engineering. He later became a successful business executive in manufacturing. He entered the political arena in Ukraine's Party of Regions after attending law school and was favored by Vladimir Putin because of his desire to maintain ties with Russia. Yanukovych understood this dynamic relationship with Russia from a historical perspective — eastern Ukraine, as a part of the former Soviet Union was a major industrial center. Its oligarchs were all Russian educated and spoke Russian fluently. Therefore, Yanukovych's Party of Regions recognized the importance of these influential eastern oligarchs in their kinship with Russia. He realized that extricating eastern Ukraine and forcing it into a European direction would not only be detrimental to the nation's economy, but

---

[50] Britannica, Leonid Kuchma; President of Ukraine. Accessed on July 26, 2023, from https://www.britannica.com/biography/Leonid- Kuchma.

would seriously jeopardize relations with Russia. Conservative geopolitical consultant Paul Manafort also saw this dynamic as essential to the unity of Ukraine. Manafort, who was a campaign consultant for several US presidents (including Trump), later summed up the importance of Yanukovych's leadership in Ukraine: "I found that in eastern Ukraine there was an undercurrent that Yanukovych was the only national political figure who was viewed as able to protect Russian culture, language, and heritage."[51]

Yanukovych's opposition candidate was the Ukrainian prime minister Victor Yushchenko, former chairman of the Bank of Ukraine. Yushchenko favored stronger alliances between Ukraine and the West. His campaign focused upon delegitimizing Russian culture in Ukraine with false claims that the Russian citizens in the nation were undermining unity. His Orange party was bolstered by strong support from the Socialist Party of Ukraine which would later form a coalition government with several other parties.[52] The election season would prove to be quite heated between the two candidates, and when Yushchenko was poisoned there were allegations that the Ukrainian State Security Service was behind the attack although no proof was determined. In the first round of the 2004 October election each candidate won approximately two-fifths of the vote, leading to a runoff the following month. Although Yanukovych the pro-Russian candidate, was declared the runoff winner, the Socialist Party claimed that there was election fraud and Yushchenko's supporters staged mass protests. The Socialist Party protestors wore orange which represented Yushchenko's campaign color and came to symbolize the Orange Revolution. The Ukrainian Supreme Court ruled the election invalid due to fraud and called for a new runoff in December 2004. The court declared Yushchenko as the winner and inaugurated him as president in January 2005. Yushchenko's presidency was soon steeped into political turmoil when he dismissed all his

---

[51] Manafort, *Political Prisoner*, 120.

[52] Ivan Katchanovski *The Orange Evolution? The Orange Revolution and Political Changes in Ukraine.* University of Ottawa, October 2008.

ministers in September 2005 including his prime minister Tymoshenko, a fellow leader of the Orange Revolution. Manafort, who later provided consulting for Yanukovych's Party of Regions, criticized the Orange Revolution as a proxy revolution:

> The Orange Revolution was the spark that ignited a movement led by politicians from western Ukraine challenging the Russian influence exerted by the outgoing President Leonid Kuchma. Kuchma was independent but aligned his policies within the Russian sphere of influence...I was not involved with the controversial 2004 Ukrainian presidential election but came to understand that it was really a proxy election of Europe and the US against Russia. The European candidate Victor Yushchenko was elected president over Yanukovych in an election that had significant charges of fraud by all sides. The MSM *mainstream media* [author's italics inserted here for explanation of acronym] claim was that Yanukovych tried to steal the election.[53]

In addition to the Orange Revolution's outcome of an EU and US proxy election, there were also personal ambitions for power driving Yushchenko. He had an interest in the consolidation of his privately owned steel company, Kryvorizhstal and planned to illegally transfer industrial wealth to his supporters. Yushchenko would do this by seizing the properties of the industrialists who lived in eastern Ukraine. His illegal attacks on the Russian citizens of Ukraine, which were clearly unconstitutional would add fuel to the fire of Putin's growing resentment of the nation's anti-Russia and pro-EU sentiments. Serhii Plokhy in his book on the Russo-Ukrainian war addressed how the Orange Revolution helped to set the stage for the Russian invasion: "The

---

[53] Manafort, *Political Prisoner*, 118-19.

Orange Revolution put Ukraine and Russia and, subsequently, Russia and the West on a collision course that would eventually lead to war."⁵⁴ It did not help to improve relations with Russia that right before the revolution seven eastern European nations (including the Baltic states) had officially joined NATO. It's just as historian Serhii Plokhy concisely stated: "As far as Russia was concerned, the victory of the 2004 Orange Revolution in Ukraine was a major blow to the Kremlin's interests at home and abroad. 'It was our 9/11,' declared the Russian political adviser Gleb Pavlovsky, who was close to the Kremlin." The Orange Revolution resulted in a major geopolitical shift in Kyiv away from the eastern influence of Russia into more formalized relations with NATO and the West.

Not only did the Orange Revolution under Yushchenko seek to undermine the heritage and culture of ethnic Russian citizens and their constitutional rights in Ukraine, but it attempted a significant shift in ideological terms. Ivan Katchanovski, political science professor at the University of Ottawa published leading academic research on Ukraine. In his work titled *The Politics of Soviet and Nazi Genocides in Orange Ukraine* he states how Yushchenko sought to rewrite Ukrainian history regarding the Nazi occupation of Ukraine in the Second World War to affect political policies: "During his period of office President Victor Yushchenko pursued policies aimed at domestic and international political and legal recognition of these interpretations of Ukrainian history, while he avoided raising a similar issue recognizing Nazi policies during World War II as a genocide of Ukrainians."⁵⁵ Because Yushchenko was pro-EU and anti-Russia, he set forth a revisionist history of the Nazi genocides in order to influence parliamentary legislation. This should sound similar to the revisionist attempts to rewrite American history by rejecting our 1776 founding heritage and replace it with the 1619 Project in which all the founders are portrayed as white

---

⁵⁴ Plokhy, *The Russo-Ukrainian War*, 36.

⁵⁵ Ivan Katchanovski, *The Politics of Soviet & Nazi Genocides in Orange Ukraine*, Europe-Asia Studies, Vol. 62, No. 6, August 2010, 937-997.

colonial supremacists.[56] The 1619 Project was purely political and gave carte blanche to socialist progressives in support of critical race theory propaganda for those who want to play the socialist race card of division in our nation. Attempts to either blatantly ignore the Constitution or to completely revise it and then to rewrite the nation's history in support of a Marxist political agenda a nefarious attempt to undermine any nation's sovereign rights and freedoms and, in Ukraine, Yushchenko was guilty of both. It is a historical fact that the Nazi occupation of Ukraine resulted in the genocide of its citizens. This is attested to by the academically renown Ukrainian historian Serhii Plokhy:

> Ukraine would learn what that meant in practice and access the degree of difference between the two regimes during its three-year occupation by Nazi Germany from 1941 to 1944. With its pre-1914 reputation as the breadbasket of Europe and one of the highest concentrations of Jews on the continent, Ukraine would become both a prime object of German expansionism and one of the Nazi's main victims. Between 1939 and 1945 it would lose almost 7 million citizens (close to 1 million of them Jewish), or more than 16 percent of its prewar population.[57]

However, the revisionist narrative of the Orange Revolution removed the word *genocide* from the atrocities committed against innocent civilians by the Nazis and applied it exclusively to the famines in Ukraine under Stalin. While millions did perish in the famines under Stalin, especially with his aggressive policies on collectivism with agricultural

---

[56] I refer readers to President Trump's 1776 Advisory Commission written in January 2021 which challenges the 1619 revisionist narrative of socialist progressives. Although archives of this report have been removed by the Biden administration, you can obtain a copy through Tolle Lege Press in Powder Springs, GA.

[57] Plokhy, *The Gates of Europe*, 260.

land, we know historically that Ukrainians were not the only victims. Katchanovski's research further clarifies this:

> Major arguments against viewing Stalin's policy as genocide of Ukrainians are first, that it did not affect the whole Ukrainian population in a comprehensive way, because, for example, the famine affected peasants, primarily in Ukraine; and secondly, that there is lack of evidence showing clear intent to destroy the Ukrainians as a group. Historical studies based on declassified Soviet archival data show that the famine resulted in the death of not only a significant proportion of Ukrainian peasants, but also of significant proportions of Kazakh and Russian peasants since the famine also affected Kazakhstan in 1931, and several major regions in Southern Russia in 1932-1933.[58]

The pro-European revisionists of Ukrainian history diverted attention away from the atrocities of the Nazi occupation to vilify Russia. Their narrative argued that the Soviet leadership intentionally planned mass famine in Ukraine with the intent of suppressing the nation's identity and undermining nationalism among the peasant populations. However, this blatantly ignores the historical reality that not only Ukrainian citizens perished under Stalin but also millions of Russians as well. Once Ukrainian history was revised, Yushchenko developed aggressive policies aimed at adopting the revisionist narrative. This included issuing orders to state organizations such as the Security Service of Ukraine (SBU), and the Ukrainian mass media, as well as educational institutions, to commemorate the famine genocide at the hands of Russians. He even went as far as proposing laws that would make public denial of the revised historical narrative a crime. We know

---

[58] Katchanovski, *The Politics of Soviet & Nazi Genocides*, 977.

that Russia is not exempt from historical atrocities especially during the seventy-five-year reign of Soviet authoritarianism. However, rewriting the narrative to give favoritism to the Nazis so that Russia can be vilified by claiming that it targeted Ukraine for genocide by famine is not a proper accounting of history. It is about promulgating a political narrative that is contrary to history.

Yushchenko did not only stop with his efforts to revise the Constitution and to implement laws for adopting revisionist history in Ukraine, but he also went as far as making heroes out of infamous Nazis. When the "Hero of Ukraine" award was given to Nazi Stepan Bandera, it greatly offended many within the European Parliament as well as leaders in Russia and Poland. Bandera was a radical leader of the militant Organization of Ukrainian Nationalists (OUN). The OUN participated in the holocaust in Ukraine and Poland and collaborated with the Nazi mass murders of the Second World War. In 1943 the Bandera faction took leadership of the 100,000- member Ukrainian Insurgent Army which was a guerrilla force that fought the Polish Army and the Red Army.[59] The Soviets condemned the OUN, and the Bandera faction groups by exposing their participation in the Holocaust and the ethnic cleansing of the Poles during the German occupation of Ukraine. I will address in further detail in chapter four how Nazi sentiments continue to impact Ukraine today nearly twenty years after the Orange Revolution. Giving posthumous awards to Nazi war criminals is as absurd as it gets, but Yushchenko was deliberately adding fuel to the fire in efforts to demonize Russia. To accomplish this revisionist narrative, he had to sway Ukrainian sentiments away from the historical reality of the Nazi atrocities and shift the blame to Russia. The most powerful propaganda tools make an appeal to human compassion and the Orange Revolution regime exploited the tragic famine by recasting history to influence public opinion. The historical reality is that many innocent people died because of famines under Stalin's brutal

---

[59] Serhii Plokhy, *The Russo-Ukrainian War: The Return of History*. (New York: W.W. Norton & Company, 2023), 20 – 21.

communist totalitarian state not only Ukrainians, but also Russians, Poles, and other innocent civilians. Ukraine was not singled out within a grand scheme of genocide specifically targeting them because there were many others who also perished including Russians. The purpose of the famine genocide narrative is to portray Ukraine as the sole target for mass starvation at the hands of Russia. This is simply not the case in the historical record. And to hold this crime against Russia and not the former Soviet Union is politically biased. It would be like holding modern day Germany responsible for the crimes of the Third Reich or the Japanese people responsible for Imperialist Japan's attack on Pearl Harbor. The revisionist narrative of a Soviet famine genocide has had tremendous resurgence, especially since Zelensky has come to power. Zelensky who is a former actor, realizes that cinema is a powerful propaganda tool and Ukraine has widely distributed half a dozen films between 2017 and 2020 that blame the Russians for weaponizing the famine against the Ukrainians. Films like *Mr. Jones* (showcased at the 69th Berlin International Film Festival in 2019) influenced public opinion around the world in favor of the revisionist narrative. And to this day, public sentiment toward the war in Ukraine is driven more by feeling rather than by fact which is unfortunate for the innocent people of the nation who are merely pawns of a proxy war.

    Although the Orange Revolution regime under Yushchenko would continue for five years a populist movement would soon challenge the tyranny. Citizens were tiring of Yushchenko's corrupt administration. The 2006 elections provided an opportunity for reform by shifting the power axis from a presidential-parliamentary into a parliamentary-presidential republic.[60] This is best understood in terms of US politics when the American citizens grow weary of a top-heavy executive branch (presidential powers) over against the legislative branch (congressional powers) and bring the balance of power back to the people of the constitutional republic. Although, Yushchenko was trying to revive

---

[60] Katchanovski, *The Orange Revolution?*, 352.

the weakening Orange coalition through his "Our Ukraine" bloc, both socialists and communists were now moving their support towards Yanukovych's conservative Party of Regions. These reforms were further accelerated when, in the spring of 2007, Yushchenko attempted several anti-constitutional presidential decrees after dissolving the parliament in an effort to consolidate power in the Orange parties and to create a new constitution which favored preference for presidential powers. George W. Bush was supportive of the Orange Revolution and Yushchenko's presidency. Bush was concerned that Ukraine's populist movement might sway Ukraine away from NATO and closer to Russia. In April 2008 Bush visited Ukraine while attending the NATO summit in Bucharest and voiced his support of the Atlantic Treaty membership. He further cited what he called a pro-Western Orange Revolution as justification for Ukraine to join NATO. The 2008 NATO meeting resulted in what is known as the Bucharest Summit which stated the importance of both Georgia and Ukraine becoming strategically aligned with NATO within the next decade.[61] Putin quickly responded to Bush's defense of Ukraine's NATO membership by stating that "it would present an unacceptable threat to Russia's security and potentially lead to a breakup of Ukraine along regional lines."[62] Putin's concerns fell upon deaf ears not only from Bush but also from the leading US presidential candidates who were focusing upon future foreign policy issues. John McCain, Barack Obama, and Hillary Clinton all cosponsored a US Senate resolution expressing their support for Ukraine and Georgia's membership in NATO which was unanimously passed in April 2008. At the Munich Security Forum, Putin challenged the US as the world's political leader and accused Washington of acting unilaterally and destroying the foundations of the international order by its attack on Iraq. Senator John McCain shot back with this reply to Putin: "Moscow must understand that it cannot enjoy a

---

[61] Galeotti, *Putin's Wars*, 169.

[62] Ibid.

genuine partnership with the West so long as its actions at home and abroad conflict so fundamentally with the core values of Euro-Atlantic democracies."[63] This has become the primary trend with Washington bureaucrats supporting the interests of global elites toward Ukraine and Georgia becoming part of the EU and NATO alliance and opening doors to pour billions of dollars toward this effort in years to come. Their concern was not so much for the goal of a free Ukrainian society but more for the inclusion of Ukraine into a liberal international order and the development of a new world order. When Putin visited the Romanian capital in person at the Russia-NATO summit, he warned President Bush: "The emergence of a powerful military bloc at our borders will be seen as a direct threat to Russian security." Bush showing his new world order allegiance to NATO and the EU on his return trip stopped in Kyiv where, regarding their application for NATO membership, he told them: "Your nation has made a bold decision, and the United States strongly supports your request."[64]

Under Yushchenko's liberal administration the nation's economy was in poor performance and had to deal with an energy crisis, with soaring natural gas prices caused by deteriorating diplomacy with Russia.[65] Problems with the economy coupled with a decline in national approval of the president's policies caused huge losses for the Orange Party (Our Ukraine) which finished third in the 2007 parliamentary elections. However, the conservative Party of Regions was gaining traction and provided Yanukovych with an opportunity to run again in the polls. In January 2010 Yushchenko only captured five percent in the first round of presidential polling and was eliminated later in a runoff election between Yanukovych and Tymoshenko on February 7, 2010. It was a close race - Yanukovych winning with 48.95 percent of the vote. International observers declared the polling to be fair, although

---

[63] Plokhy, *The Russo-Ukrainian War*, 87.

[64] Ibid.

[65] Britannica, Victor Yushchenko; President of Ukraine. Source accessed August 2, 2023, from https://www.britannica.com/biography/Viktor- Yushchenko.

Tymoshenko denied the validity of the results. For the next four years under Yanukovych and the Party of Regions the economy experienced considerable improvement. The energy crisis was on the mend as an energy deal was brokered allowing lease extensions for the port at Sevastopol, the base of the Russian Black Sea Fleet, to be extended until 2042. This significantly reduced pricing for natural gas imports to Ukraine. Yanukovych's party also rescinded the laws of the former administration which promoted the revisionist history that claimed the Ukrainian 1932 famine was an act of genocide carried out by Russia. By 2012 the conservative Party of Regions won the largest share of seats in parliament. Things were looking good for Yanukovych's conservative reforms at least up until the next revolution in Ukraine.

The Deadly Maidan Revolution

Until 2013 there were tensions mounting in Kyiv between those who supported an EU association agreement on one side and those who wanted to remain with the Moscow-led customs union. The signing of an association agreement with the EU was not an application for membership and most felt that it would be a good middle-ground compromise that would bring open trade agreements between Ukraine and Europe. The downside in co-opting the EU association agreement would be the possibility of creating strife with the pro-Russian side of Parliament. Yanukovych wanted to strike a balance between the two sides to maintain national unity. He knew that a practical solution between the pro-EU and pro-Russian interest groups would not be easily achieved. Yanukovych was between a rock and a hard place and reluctantly agreed to sign the EU association agreement scheduled for November 28, 2013. However, a week prior to the signing, Yanukovych decided to postpone the agreement. Some say that he was influenced by pro-Russian supporters in his government and perhaps even by Putin himself who offered up to a $15 billion dollar loan on a natural gas deal to Ukraine. His decision to back out of the agreement resulted in a firestorm of protests in Kyiv from pro-EU groups who were furious with Yanukovych backing out of the agreement. The revolution that ensued is named after the area where the protestors converged on the town square known as *Maidan* (after the Ukrainian word for town square) on the evening of November 21, 2013.[66] According to Plokhy the initial majority of the protestors are described as being "young Kyivan urbanites" who were angered that the EU agreement was not signed. Like the riots in America led by Black Lives Matter (BLM) and Antifa during 2020, when historical monuments were toppled and destroyed, protestors demolished more than 500 Russian monuments.[67] Yanukovych who was concerned about violence when 20,000 protesters clashed with police on February 18, 2014, soon responded with anti-protest measures that were immediately repealed by Parliament. The number of protesters continued to grow into the tens of thousands of active marchers on the square with demands for impeachment. Things turned deadly on February 20; shots were fired upon the crowds in the downtown square, killing nearly fifty protesters. Although never proven, it was claimed by Ukrainian parliament that the assassin was a part of Yanukovych's government administration. When the Parliament and some of his own Party of Regions members voted to impeach Yanukovych, he denounced the action as a coup and fled the capital. The interim government that soon came to power issued a warrant for his arrest on charges of mass murder claiming, there were nearly 100 victims in the aftermath of the violence. After fleeing Ukraine, Yanukovych delivered a speech in the in Russia that accused members behind the government coup as fascists. Ukraine's new prime minister Arseniy Yatsenyuk swiftly condemned Yanukovych of embezzlement and moved to freeze his bank accounts. Prosecutors in Geneva also followed suit by launching money laundering investigations into the deposed leader who was now placed on Interpol's most wanted list.

---

[66] Plokhy, *The Gates of Europe*, 317; 338-39.

[67] Serhii Plokhy, *The Russo-Ukrainian War: The Return of History*, (New York: W.W. Norton & Company, 2023), 132.

In May 2017 Yanukovych was tried in absentia for high treason and murder. He was sentenced to thirteen years in prison but remained in exile in Russia. The victims who were killed were heralded as martyrs and were memorialized as the *Heavenly Hundred* for the cause of the Maidan Revolution. The media widely exaggerated the numbers, which were many fewer than 100 victims. It was confirmed by eye witness narratives a total of forty-nine protesters died. Later in 2015 an international documentary titled *Winter on Fire: Ukraine's Fight for Freedom* gave a glowing tribute to the Maidan Revolution and called it a major triumph of democracy. One thing was now certain, this revolution became the catalyst for an anti-Russian and pro-EU-NATO-Ukraine beginning with the post-Yanukovych interim government for the next five years setting the stage for Zelensky.

As with any major government coup, nothing is ever completely black and white. It will become clear that, as with the Orange Revolution there are actors within Deep State government as well as international players who contributed to this violent overthrow. Benjamin Abelow, a subject matter expert in European history and US cold war foreign policy, explained how the Maidan Revolution was supported by the US and other actors: "These protests, which were supported by the United States, were subverted by violent provocateurs. The violence culminated in a coup in which armed, far-right Ukrainian ultra-nationalists took over government buildings and forced the democratically elected pro-Russian president to flee the country."[68] John Mearsheimer, professor of political science at the University Chicago further adds: "The new government in Kiev was pro-Western and anti-Russian to the core, and it contained four high-ranking members who could legitimately be labeled as neofascists." Abelow further details the US support behind the Maidan Revolution by citing that just a month before the coup, in a phone call that was leaked between assistant secretary of state Victoria Nuland and the US ambassador to Ukraine, Geoffrey

---

[68] Benjamin Abelow, *How the West Brought War to Ukraine* (Great Barrington, MA: Siland Press, 2022), 14-15.

Pyatt. The two discussed who would replace Yanukovych. Victoria Nuland has been one of the most influential players in the European geopolitical spectrum who in addition to her current role as acting US deputy secretary of state under the Biden administration served in a long list of key roles: assistant secretary of state for European and Eurasian affairs, the US State Department, NATO representative, CEO for New American Security — a global think tank established under the Biden administration, the National Endowment for Democracy – a liberal globalist group that seeks to advance democratic socialism, the Brookings Institute, and the Albright Stonebridge Group (a firm providing global economic and business consulting in the international arena, founded by Madeleine Albright). Nuland's career was launched under the Clinton administration in the 1990's during the early formative years of Ukraine-US foreign policy. Later, she moved to serve as the principal deputy foreign policy adviser to Vice President Dick Cheney in the George W. Bush administration and then afterwards served as US ambassador to NATO. In the Obama administration Nuland became a special envoy for the Treaty on Conventional Armed Forces in Europe (this treaty established the military balance of power in Europe, and Nuland supported NATO intervention in strategic countries). Under the Obama administration, Nuland served as assistant secretary of state for European and Eurasian affairs. Although Obama denied direct involvement with Ukraine, it was during the Maidan Revolution that Nuland's role came to light. Nuland and EU representative Catherine Ashton were meeting in Kyiv to express their mutual support for the protestors.[69] Putin later refered to Nuland's visit as proof of the US role in instigating the Maidan Revolution. While most have dismissed Putin's statement about Nuland's involvement in the Maidan Revolution as a product of paranoia, the transcript of Nuland's phone call with US Ambassador to Ukraine Geoffrey R. Pyatt indicates that the US had very

---

[69] Plokhy, *The Russo-Ukrainian War*, 96.

clear ideas about what the outcome of the revolution should be – the overthrow of the pro-Russian majority.[70]

Aside from Nuland's visit to Kyiv, the other critical issue for consideration regards the deadly sniper attacks which have been hotly debated on the international scene. Controversy has been at the center of the sniper massacres ever since they occurred on February 20, 2014. The interim Ukrainian government quickly linked the attacks to the pro-Yanukovych government without offering specific proof. The massacre was also used aggressively to trump up murder charges against the former president. Ivan Katchanovski a political science professor at the University of Ottawa has published extensive research on the Maidan massacre. His research team gathered data from 1500 videos, media sources, and social media recordings, as well as over 150 gigabytes of news photos, and nearly 30 gigabytes of radio communications intercepted from police, military, and security on the day of massacre. Katchanovski and his team also conducted field research with eyewitness account interviews to include weapons ballistics and forensic data from victim's entry and exit bullet wounds. Katchanovski's research paper titled *The Sniper's Massacre on the Maidan in Ukraine*, proposes the following thesis:

This academic investigation concludes that the massacre was a false flag operation[71], which was rationally planned and carried out with a goal of the overthrow of the government and seizure of power. It found various evidence of the involvement of an alliance of the far-right organizations, specifically the Right Sector and Svoboda, and oligarchic parties, such as Fatherland. Concealed shooters and spotters were located in at least 20 Maidan-controlled buildings or areas.[72]

---

[70] Jonathan Marcus, *Ukraine Crisis: Transcript of Leaked Nuland-Pyatt Call*. BBC News, February 7, 2014. Site Accessed August 25, 2023, from https://www.bbc.com.

[71] A **false flag** operation is an act committed with the intent of disguising the actual source of responsibility and pinning blame on another party.

[72] Ivan Katchanovski, *The Sniper's Massacre on the Maidan in Ukraine*, University of Ottawa School of Political Studies, Paper prepared for presentation to the Annual Meeting of American Political Association in San Francisco, September 3-6, 2015.

Mainstream media sources have all maintained that the Maidan Revolution was peaceful. However, two violent radical parties noted here, the Svoboda party and the Fatherland party, participated in the Maidan Revolution. The Svoboda party is an ultranationalist party that has a known history of neo-Nazism and active recruitment of skin heads along with the usage of conventional Nazi symbols. This group has been noted for its violence and its anti-Russian fascist ideologies. The Fatherland Party was one of the parties supporting former prime minister Yulia Tymoshenko an Orange Revolution leader who later ran against Yanukovych. Tymoshenko was charged by the Ukrainian authorities with abuse of power, embezzlement, and tax evasion and was sentenced to seven years in prison. Although she was released from prison under a deal brokered by Parliament, Tymoshenko immediately traveled to a protest camp in Kyiv showing support for the protestors who regarded her as a symbol of resistance to Yanukovych's administration. The following is a summary of Katchanovski's research on the Maidan massacre which supports his thesis:

- Although it was maintained that the snipers were from the SBU, it was discovered that the weapons used were carbine hunting rifles which are not standard issue for SBU officers.

- No evidence could be produced through any channel of communication that Yanukovych ordered his security forces to fire upon the protesters. None of the commanders or police who were interrogated had been given such an authorization which would have been immediately challenged.

- It was reported that an unidentified person started firing at police around 9:00am on February 20, 2014.

- Although it was alleged that Vladislav Surkov a former aide to Putin, was personally coordinating the sniper attack, it was confirmed that Surkov was not present during the massacre and did not arrive in Kyiv by plane later the evening of February 20th after the incident took place.

- Stories were widely circulated about the snipers being from Russia and Belarus and staying at the Hotel Ukraina, but no reliable evidence was ever provided to substantiate these claims.

- Some 200 investigative cases of specific victims of the massacre either disappeared or were destroyed under the post-Yanukovych interim government and there was failure to further investigate the killing and the wounding of police officers.

- Lawyers representing the two Berkhut policemen stated in court on August 3, 2015, that the prosecution case was falsified. Andrii Parubii a known neo-Nazi patriot, played a significant role in the Euromaidan leadership during the protests. After he was promoted as the first deputy of Parliament he was never questioned.

- The Prosecutor General of Ukraine who is from the far-right Svoboda party stated in June 2014 that he gave the videos of the massacre to the FBI to enhance the quality, but any follow up from the FBI or Parliament to date has not been made public.

- In addition to the silence surrounding these videos given to the FBI many other videos were either unreported, misrepresented, or suppressed by mainstream media. The research discovered unreported time-stamped versions of widely publicized videos from live TV broadcasts and internet with contradictory claims.

- A photo provided by an Italian journalist reveals a protester with an assault rifle (not police or security issue) fired upon police behind protestor shields. The rounds are consistent with the 5.45mm AK-75 and the 7.62mm AKM that were discovered. Videos surfaced with protestors carrying rifles wrapped in cloth and in jackets.

- A BBC news reporter had photos of a protester with an assault rifle inside the music conservatory shortly after 8:00am just before the time of the massacre. The reporter also indicated that he saw ten other protesters armed with rifles shooting at police from the conservatory. This was confirmed by a tweet at 8:21am that there was a sniper in the building.

- Police reports were made that noticed protestors wearing the Right Sector insignia of the Social National Assembly, a neo-Nazi group in the conservatory the day before the shooting. In a BBC interview one of the shooters said that he was recruited for such a mission at the end of January 2014. This individual also stated that guns primarily hunting rifles were hidden at the post office directly across from the conservatory. There were further reports of a masked protester taking a rifle equipped with a scope from his vehicle trunk.

- A member of another neo-Nazi group the Vikings had posted on social media that he and his associate had killed four policemen. Other snipers were confirmed firing from the Hotel Ukraina and videos were released showing protestors arriving at the hotel with a handgun, an axe and what appeared to be a long rifle bag breaking into the hotel room on the 14th floor after 10:00 am on the day of the massacre.

- Some protestors reported that they were lured into the killing zones by individuals they identified as fellow protesters near the police barricades just before being fired upon.

Katchanovski concluded his research on the Maidan massacre with comments that the corruption behind the revolution was extensive, involving the far-right Svoboda, neo-Nazis, and the communist parties, along with leaders in organized crime. He also mentioned that his evidence confirms that the massacre was an operation which required advance planning and coordination. The massacre was carried out in the presence of dozens of foreign and Ukrainian journalists during the visit of three foreign affairs ministers from EU countries with the intent to blame the violence solely upon Yanukovych. The report also adds that the victims of the massacre were intentionally sacrificed by those wanting to overthrow the government.

The Deep State cover up of the tragic Maidan Revolution of 2014 is extensive and had a significant geopolitical goal for the global elites as Katchanovski clearly articulates:

> However, the misrepresentation of the Maidan massacre by the US and to a lesser extent other Western governments, apparent lack of their interest in the Maidan massacre investigation and prosecution, their backing of the Maidan opposition during the "Euromaidan" and its violent overthrow of the Ukrainian government, Ukraine turning into a US client state after this overthrow, and similar precedents in other countries, such as Iran in 1953, raise a question whether these governments had intelligence or other undisclosed information that this massacre was a false flag operation or whether there were any their direct or indirect involvement in the organization of this violent overthrow...For instance, the US President and Vice-President publicly blamed the government forces for the massacre of the protestors immediately after it happened, but the US government did not disclose any evidence that they had about this mass killing. Barack Obama said that "we had

brokered a deal to transition power in Ukraine" after the massacre and before Yanukovych fled, but the US President or other American government officials did not release any specific information about the nature of this involvement. An intercepted telephone call between a US State Department official and the US ambassador in Ukraine prior to February 20, 2014, shows them discussing which specific Maidan opposition leaders, specifically Yatsenuik, can be in the Ukrainian government after Yanukovych offered the positions in his government to the opposition leaders.[73]

The research summary above lays much blame upon the US for misrepresentations regarding the Maidan massacre calling out the primary purpose of the revolution – a "violent overthrow of the Ukrainian government" that turned Ukraine into a "US client state." We will pick up the pieces from this violent overthrow of government in Ukraine and look at the trail of breadcrumbs leading us to Zelensky.

Setting the Stage for Volodymyr Zelensky

Once the transitional post-Maidan revolutionary government in Ukraine was propped up there would be one interim president and one elected president just before Zelensky came to power. During the Maidan revolution, Russia was becoming increasingly concerned about Crimea. Crimea, an autonomous republic of Ukraine is a geographic peninsula nation lying between the Black Sea and the Sea of Azov. Russia feared that if Ukraine along with Crimea would become part of NATO, their Black Sea fleet would be jeopardized.[74] Putin acted quickly in February and March 2014 as if anticipating an opponent's

---

[73] Katchanovski, *The Sniper's Massacre on the Maidan in Ukraine*, 60.
[74] Galeotti, *Putin's Wars*, 168-69.

move in a geopolitical game of chess and proceeded to annex Crimea. I will address the Russian military's intervention into Crimea in more detail in chapter three. The Crimea incident will further substantiate that Putin was driven to protect his interest in the security of Russia. Aggressive Russian interests for self-preservation lead to events that later transpired with the invasion of Ukraine. The international community was swift to condemn Russia's move upon Crimea. Ukraine's interim president Oleksandr Turchynov a member of the Yanukovych opposition party the Fatherland now had to respond to a situation with pro-Russian insurgents in eastern Ukraine. He requested that U.N. Secretary-General Ban Ki-moon send peacekeeping forces to help stabilize the eastern region.[75] From this point forward after the annexation of Crimea, tensions between Russian and Ukraine would escalate causing future Ukrainian presidents to further solidify their allegiance to NATO and the West.

On May 25, 2014, after the brief interim transition of Turchynov, Petro Poroshenko was elected. Poroshenko served as Ukraine's national security secretary under Yushchenko after the Orange Revolution.[76] The fighting with Russian separatists intensified over the next year even after French President Francois Hollande and German Chancellor Angela Merkel attempted to broker an agreement in Minsk, Belarus in February 2015. Meanwhile the approval rating of Poroshenko was declining especially after it was discovered that he did not follow through with a campaign promise to sell his business. Instead, he transferred his assets into an offshore holding company in the British Virgin Islands, which did not sit well with Ukrainian voters who had been critical of a poor national economy. Another situation that created contention resulted when Poroshenko decided to intervene in matters regarding the local

---

[75] Time Magazine, Charlotte Alter; April 14, 2014, *Ukraine Wants UN Troops in Eastern Cities*. Site accessed on August 8, 2023, from https://time.com/61624/ukraine-united-nations-troops-east/.

[76] Britannica, Michael Ray, *Petro Poroshenko*, source accessed August 9, 2023, from https://www.britannica.com/biography/Petro-Poroshenko.

church. There had been a longstanding rivalry between the Ukrainian Orthodox Church of the Moscow Patriarchate (UOCMP) established in 1990 under the jurisdiction of the Russian Orthodox Church (ROC) and the Ukrainian Orthodox Church Kyiv Patriarchate (UOCKP) that was set up by clergy seeking independence in 1992.[77] Although the ROC remains the largest church in Ukraine with approximately 12,000 parishes, because of suspicions over ties to Moscow there had been tensions with the UOCMP which heightened after the Maidan Revolution. To resolve the rivalry between churches, Poroshenko established a new church, the Orthodox Church of Ukraine (OCU) under the jurisdiction of the Ecumenical Patriarchate of Constantinople which granted it ecclesial independence. Poroshenko's creation of a new church reeks of authoritarian governments that create religious organizations endorsed by the state something that is absolutely appalling to those of us in America who cherish religious freedom in a constitutional republic. Yet, this became a democratic precedent that would be further exacerbated under Zelensky, who also yielded state power over freedom of religion in Ukraine. Amazingly the creation of a new Orthodox church resonated with most Ukrainians who were not religious but wanted more intervention from the state, and this brought Poroshenko increased favor among voters. Later the administration became increasingly focused upon the problems with rebel insurgents and Crimea. In November 2018 after Russian vessels fired upon Ukrainian ships and seized both the ships and their crews, Poroshenko made a desperate attempt to declare martial law in ten regions to gain an edge on the military conflict. However, Ukrainians were tiring of the war in the eastern regions and the faltering economy and were now anxious for change. This time, change would not be left to the preponderance of traditional politicians. The next presidential candidate for Ukraine soon rose to the occasion from the most unlikely background of all – television. The

---

[77] Konstantin Skorkin, *Holy War: The Fight for Ukraine's Churches & Monasteries,* Carnegie Endowment for International Peace, November 4, 2023. Source accessed on August 9, 2023, from https://carnegieendowment.org.

power of public media literally influenced the choice of the next president of the nation.

A Fictional Political Party Made for Television Becomes Reality in Ukraine

Zelensky has placed the governance of his country squarely in international hands. It is not Kyiv that calls the shots in Ukraine, but Washington.
– Vladimir Putin

Initially few would hardly take Volodymyr Zelensky, who provided the voice for Paddington Bear cartoons, as a serious political candidate. Unlike Ukraine's past five presidents mostly business oligarchs who later became career politicians, Zelensky was a complete political novice. However, as an actor he knew how to utilize his experience in a television studio to craft a powerful presentation that would not only influence the opinion of Ukraine, but also the world. Zelensky began his acting career at the age of nineteen and through the years rose to fandom as he received standing ovations in concert halls and theatres in Moscow, Kyiv, Odesa, and Minsk. Zelensky's performances on TV and stage were not exactly PG rated and often included profanity laced with raunchy political sarcasm. One stage episode included a skit where he plays the piano with his genitals while the audience responds with an uproar of laughter for nearly five minutes. On the one hand, well-known Ukrainian publicist Vitaliy Portnykov criticized Zelensky's jokes as "a modern domestic sense of humor, low quality, tasteless, philistine, and shallow. If people laugh at vulgarity, they must understand that vulgarity does not and cannot have value-added categories and moral boundaries."[78] On the other hand, many of his viewers had nothing but praise for Zelensky's acting and comedy routines. Journalist Arkady Ostrovsky succinctly described the young actor: "His words contained

---

[78] Serhii Rudenko, *Zelensky: A Biography*; translated by Michael M. Naydan & Alla Perminova. (Cambridge: Polity Press, 2022), 70.

something that people in the West particularly of a younger generation had been searching for: a sense of meaning in a post-ideological society."[79] The younger generation in Ukraine and around the world resonated with Zelensky's image and his speeches. And like the younger generations who marched in the Orange Revolution and the Maidan Revolution years before, this generation also saw him as a revolutionary agent for change. Former Russian-born US intelligence expert Rebeka Koffler in the forward that she wrote for Andrew L. Urban and Christ McLeod's biography on Zelensky wrote about his popularity in the West:

> Zelensky may have won the West's heart but has that come at the expense of its head?...We have all come to see President Zelensky as a hero, but some of his decisions are not as straightforward as we in the West think. Zelensky, much like Ukraine itself, is filled with contradictions. The Ukrainians are a freedom-loving people but among the most corrupt in Europe. And while Zelensky declares his love for his nation, he failed to protect it from a destructive assault that may lead to scores of civilian deaths, the erasure of its borders, and the annihilation of its culture.[80]

I will highlight some of the underlying corruption within Zelensky's administration. Although he claimed that he did not participate in the Maidan Revolution in 2014, he said that he was active in calling for Yanukovych's resignation. The new revolution that would bring Zelensky into power would be waged almost exclusively through digital and internet communication as well as all other popular platforms

---

[79] Volodymyr Zelensky, *A Message from Ukraine: Speeches, 2019 – 2022*, (New York: Crown-Random House, 2022), xviii.

[80] Andrew L. Urban and Chris McLeod, *Zelensky: The Unlikely Hero Who Defied Putin and United the World*, (Washington, D.C.: Regenery Publishing, 2022), xi.

of social media.[81] Zelensky's videos and news clips were either live streamed or uploaded on all media platforms resulting in over three million Twitter (now X) followers and over twelve million on Instagram. When Zelensky announced that he was running for president, he lacked any official election campaign program. The solution he proposed for developing a campaign would be built entirely upon a Facebook platform where followers could click on his page titled "The Ukraine of My Dreams" which featured President Vasyl Holoborodko (the popular TV character he played) and simply leave their comments that would be used for writing the party platform.[82] He became a prominent Ukrainian celebrity through the Kvartal 95 Studio, a public television entertainment production company that he was involved with as one of the founders in 2003.[83] *Servant of the People* became a popular TV series created and produced by Zelensky as a comic political satire that ran for three seasons from 2015 to 2019. Ironically the title "Servant of the People" also became a registered political party in Ukraine in 2017 that identifies itself as being liberal, centrist, and pro-European. This became Zelensky's primary party that put him into office. The party was founded by Zelensky's close childhood friend Ivan Bakanov who later was appointed to the head of security and counterintelligence when Zelensky came to power. Many others who were involved with the TV series also received appointments to government positions. The series is based upon a fictional character a young high-school history teacher played by Zelensky, who unknowingly is recorded in a video by one of his students and uploaded on social media. The profanity-laced political rant goes viral and targets corruption in the government of Ukraine. The history teacher who is a klutzy nerd, rides bike and resembles the character of *Pee Wee Herman* more than the image

---

[81] Lisa Rogak & Daisy Gibbons, *Volodymyr Zelensky in His Own Words*, (New York: Pegasus Books, 2022), x.

[82] Steven Derix & Marina Shelkunova, *Zelensky: A Biography of Ukraine's War Leader*, (Great Britain: Canbury Press, 2023), 98-99.

[83] Serhii Rudenko, *Zelensky*, xii.

of a president. Eventually in the series he is elected president, and the stories revolve around his comic efforts to clean up Parliament. The TV series became a sensational hit in Ukraine, and Netflix purchased the screening rights. It was later released as a film in 2016. When billboards appeared in Ukraine advertising the third season in 2018, Zelinsky denied that there was a political motive behind the series, although it proved to be a powerful segway into the presidential elections by the time he would announce his decision to run. The TV series proved to be one of the most powerful campaign strategies ever in the history of Ukraine. As Derix and Shelkunova stated: "Zelensky much preferred to campaign on stage. Even in the midst of the election battle, none of his regular performances were cancelled, and Kvartal 95 continued to tour the country."[84]

On the evening of April 21, 2019, Zelensky was elected in what was claimed to be a landslide victory after receiving 73% of the vote over Poroshenko. The victory party played the theme song "I Love My Country" from the TV series *Servant of the People* which would become the political party from which he was elected their first president. Just like the fictional character, Vasyl Holoborodko, who cleaned up parliament, Zelensky in real life within a few months after his inauguration promised that as well. Streamlined procedures would decrease the need for a parliamentary republic so more power could be granted to the executive powers of office. Zelensky looked toward the July 21, 2019, elections for the Verkhovna Rada, a unicameral legislature to obtain a majority of the 450 deputy seats. An overwhelming 43.16 percent of the votes were for the Servant of the People Party, giving them 254 seats in the Rada the first time an independent party in Ukraine ever held a majority.[85] Within twelve hours, Zelensky completely transformed the leadership with new faces in Ukraine: unemployed wedding photographers, showmen, restauranteurs, and many with limited education

---

[84] Derix & Shelkunova, *Zelensky*, 101.

[85] Serhii Rudenko, *Zelensky: A Biography*, 21.

who were among the youngest generation in politics with ages between thirty and forty. Steven Derix and Marina Shelkunova in their biography on Zelensky added a most interesting moniker given by the media: "Zelsnksy's ministerial team was youthful, good looking, ambitious and spectacularly inexperienced. Within a very short time, the media started referring to them as the *Sorosyata* (the 'Soros-youngsters'), after George Soros, the American-Hungarian investor who had donated billions of dollars to promote liberal democracy in eastern Europe and the former Soviet Union."[86] The new thirty-five-year-old prime minister Oleksiy Honcharuk promoted this new image as he started his term dressed in a polo shirt, jeans, and sneakers and rode into the cabinet meeting on an electric scooter. The youthfulness of the administration was not the only new makeover in government. Beginning on August 29, 2019, all power was de facto transferred into Zelensky's hands as the Rada became one of the divisions of the office of the president. Zelensky wanted to make decisions that were exempt from parliamentary control. The administration through Prime Minister Honcharuk was given the nickname the "mad printer" referring to the record number of executive orders that Zelensky signed into law within the first few months of office.

Administration Scandals, Authoritarianism and Corruption

The lightning pace of the massive government overhaul in Zelenski's administration soon ground to a halt. The first bump in the road would be the resignation of the prime minister because he overstepped his bounds with the finance minister and the national bank director (this was later leaked in a video.)[87] Later, European leaders cringed when Zelensky fired the prosecutor general and appointed a new prosecutor to file legal cases against former President Poroshenko (the opposition candidate during the elections). The Lithuanian foreign affairs minister

---

[86] Derix & Shelkunova, *Zelensky*, 114.

[87] Ibid.

condemned Zelensky for the move: "I found it imprudent, Ukraine will start to resemble countries where the solution to the opposition is to throw them in jail." Zelensky was still determined to bring court cases and legal battles against those he considered to be adversaries and soon the heads of the tax and customs authorities were dismissed. The deputy of the Atlantic Council's Eurasia Center, Melinda Haring, issued a warning: "If I were in the Zelensky Government, I would think twice before bringing court cases against the people who had done many good things."[88] The continued dismissals and lawsuits began to slowly erode Zelensky's administration. In 2020 when the SARS-CoV-2 pandemic hit Ukraine, Zelensky responded with draconian lock downs as part of his national pandemic mitigation strategy as was the case with most European nations. As the nation's economy shrank by nearly 10 percent, this resulted in a pushback from the mayors of some of Ukraine's largest cities as well as various politicians who resisted the lock downs of businesses. They insisted that it was enough for the nation's burden to be in a deep economic recession without having to endure the tyranny of lockdowns. However, Zelensky was in lockstep with most nations who followed the dictates of the WHO and required vaccine passports along with all the mask and social distancing mandates.

Ukraine's 2014 association agreement with the EU that was established after the Maidan Revolution was on rocky ground because of Zelensky's aggressive reform tactics. Originally, the EU agreement that allowed for establishing economic ties with Europe also allowed Ukrainians to travel to what was known as the *Schengen* a visa free zone that included twenty-seven countries. To continue the terms of the association agreement the EU administration in Brussels needed evidence that Ukraine did not show an inclination toward government tyranny or corruption. Anti-corruption measures were part of a non-negotiable condition for Ukraine's loan application process with the IMF and the World Bank. Amid a faltering national economy,

---

[88] Ibid.

these loans represented a lifeline for Ukraine. Josep Borrel of the EU was becoming skeptical of the anti-corruption measures, especially of Ukraine's National Anti-Corruption Bureau (NABU) that was under government control after prosecutor Nazar Kholodnytsky was forced to resign.[89] The security council was weaponized against any Ukrainian citizen who was perceived as a threat to national security without any intervention by the judicial branch. Under the new administration the National Security and Defense Council (NSDC) increased their staff from 160 to 237 members. The NSDC imposed sanctions on everything from Russian-Ukrainian athletic apparel stores to mining and oil companies that were suspected of alignment with Russia. The NSDC also imposed flight bans on all private jets landing in Moscow. By the end of 2021 the security council had sanctioned a total of 1162 citizens. To make matters worse Zelensky submitted a bill to the Rada that nullified decisions made by the Court and in turn dismissed their judges. The measure was unconstitutional because it was stipulated that judges cannot be dismissed but serve for a lifetime appointment until they resign. The act was condemned by the European Council and the Venice Commission who declared it a gross violation of the constitution and the separation of powers. Zelensky relented of his decision and agreed to seek the advice of the Venice Commission. Human rights organizations were outraged by the president's totalitarian government regime. Concerned Ukrainian rights organizations issued a joint appeal stating: "The president's measures are not sanctions in an international legal sense – they are a directive form of governance."[90] Olena Kondratiuk of the Fatherland Party who was the acting chair of the Rada also voiced concern over weaponization of the Security Council: "You cannot simply replace the work of the country's institutions...The NSDC has effectively become the Public Prosecutor's Office, the National Anti-Corruption Agency, the tax authority, the judiciary,

---

[89] Derix & Shelkunova, *Zelensky*, 129-30.

[90] Ibid.

and the list goes on." The Security Council rubber-stamped resolutions already prepared by the presidential staff most often just before agenda meetings. Whereas there was a great deal of criticism from legislators regarding the Security Council's authoritarian role in government, Zelensky was quite pleased with the council: "It was very important to have founded the National Security and Defense Council, it has proven extremely effective as an institution...If you are a traitor, we will put you in your place."[91] The NSDC also made decrees in support of environmental policies that Zelensky's order to plant a billion trees within a year must be enforced and for the ministry of health policies that there should be an increase in the number of COVID-19 vaccinations to be increased 350,000 per day. Zelensky not only supports the EU's trends toward liberal international policies but also the global 2030 sustainability goals of the U.N. such as those which wholeheartedly endorse environmental agendas: "If we fail to reduce the pace of climate change, after 2030 the social and economic losses will be so significant that no one will be able to shut themselves off from this threat within their national borders. No one will be able to beat the climate with political populism."[92]

When Zelensky visited Joe Biden in August 2021, Washington enthusiastically supported a detailed plan outlining eighty major infrastructure projects for Ukraine over the next decade in the cost range of $277 billion. Foreign investments into Ukraine at that time were estimated at $6.5 billion. The first lady of Ukraine was praised for working with subject matter experts to develop diversity, equity, and inclusion (DEI) materials for schools and other public institutions. DEI was not the only ideological principle launched by the Zelensky administration, there was a war on capitalism as well. Whereas the prosperity of Ukraine in the previous generations came through the free market economy of influential industrial oligarchs, in June 2021 the president

---

[91] Derix & Shelkunova, *Zelensky*, 139-43.

[92] Rogak & Gibbons, *Volodymyr*, 13.

submitted a new bill to the Rada under the Security Council that all wealthy business owners must be listed on an oligarchs public register. The criteria for the register were that any personal or business income that was a million times over the poverty line of $83 per month must be publicly listed. The intent was to prevent any wealthy business corporations from financing political parties or agendas, especially those who were opponents of Zelensky. Zelensky tweeted on July 2, 2021, "The oligarchs are a thing of the past."[93] Although the president proudly claimed to be a virtuous defender of socialist principles and fought against rich oligarchs, some hypocrisy would come to light and bring his integrity into question. A collection of eleven million financial documents were leaked regarding Zelensky's business affairs called the *Pandora Papers* through a group known as the International Consortium of Investigative Journalists. These documents included an expose' on Zelensky's offshore accounts from his companies in Cyprus along with members of his entertainment company Kvartal 95 who also had businesses in the Virgin Islands. This business that operated under the name of the Maltex Corporation had received over $40 million through the powerful oligarch Ihor Kolomyski. Zelensky claimed to be fighting against the corruption of rich oligarchs in his administration, yet transaction records confirmed that he had transferred his shares just before the elections. More disclosures on these offshore businesses came to light. Zelensky was shocked to learn that the investigative reports were going to be included in a documentary film titled *Offshore 95 Secrets of Zelinsky's Business* scheduled to premiere in a theater in Kyiv. Members of the Security Services promptly responded to shut down the film, which resulted in a huge scandal. The documentary eventually was screened because of public outrage over its cancellation. Ukrainian citizens demanded to know why their president was operating offshore companies which betrayed loyalty and faith in keeping money at home for sake of economic recovery. Did the president harbor distrust in his

---

[93] Ibid.

own nation's economy to the extent that he would conduct business offshore? Not only was corruption extensive in the Zelensky administration, but also the administration turned out not to be the wonderful democracy that most of the West had proclaimed. The government was trending toward authoritarianism and putting a stranglehold on the individual freedoms and liberties of the people.

Whereas most of the West looked to Zelensky to bring vast reforms for democratic freedom in Ukraine, free speech was not fully protected under his parliamentarian regime. Under his executive powers of office, Zelensky invoked anti-terrorism laws that had been used to target separatist rebels. Now these laws would be used against Ukraine's own judiciary. Taras Kozak who represented the pro-Russian platform that had a mere 44 seats in the Rada ran content on local broadcasts that was critical of Zelensky. The president's administration condemned this as foreign propaganda aligned with Russia and under the anti-terrorism law, they froze Kozak's assets for five years. Although it was blatant censorship, the American embassy in Kyiv supported the move along with the EU which stated that Ukraine had the right to enforce measures to protect itself from disinformation. Zelensky posted on Facebook: "Open propaganda requires a swift and decisive social response."[94] Ukraine's NSDC suspended eleven pro-Russian political parties.[95] The media censorship policies culminated in January 2023 when Zelensky signed further legislation that gave broader authority through the government run National Television and Radio Broadcasting Council.[96] Members of the broadcast council are appointed by the president's administration and by members of the parliament. The regulatory agency has power to

---

[94] Ibid.

[95] Radio Free Europe, *Zelensky Signs Law Banning Pro-Russian Parties*, May 14, 2022, source accessed July 17, 2023 from https://www.rferl.org/a/ukraine-law-bans-pro-russia -parties-zelenskiy- signs/31849737.html.

[96] Brad Press, The Hill, January 01, 2023. *Zelensky Signs Law to Regulate Media*. Source accessed on July 17, 2023 from https://thehill.com.

shut down news sites that are not registered as well as to revoke media licenses and to impose fines for releasing restricted information.

Usually after freedom of speech goes out the window such individual liberties as freedom of religion are the next to topple under an authoritarian government. Although Zelensky claims widely publicized Jewish heritage, he is more agnostic than a practitioner of the Jewish faith. Not even in personal family settings, does Zelensky discuss religion, which he considers as completely divisive: "There are things that we never discuss at the table in my family. Religion is number one. We never discuss things that divide family and society."[97] On another occasion he stated, "I don't go to church, not to the synagogue, not to the mosque." For someone who claims complete neutrality in religious matters, Zelensky does not avoid confronting religious institutions in his administration. Recall I previously mentioned how Poroshenko stepped in to intervene in what he perceived as a long-held rivalry between the Ukrainian Orthodox Church of the Moscow Patriarchate (UOCMP) and the Ukrainian Orthodox Church Kyiv Patriarchate (UOCKP). Because the UOCKP proclaimed independence from Moscow in 1991 after the fall of the USSR, there were tensions over the UOCMP who was believed to maintain loyalty to Russia. Poroshenko's solution was to create a new state church the Orthodox Church of Ukraine (OCU) that he insisted was going to be completely non-partisan to any political rivalry. Of course, a state church in Ukraine would be the authoritarian dream because it would maintain complete neutrality not only regarding politics but also regarding any hint of allegiance to ecclesiastical affiliations in Moscow After all, government tyranny loves churches that are completely compliant to state authority, consider the churches under the Third Reich in Nazi Germany. Apart from a minority of pastors like Detrich Bonhoeffer who resisted Nazi totalitarianism, most churches in the Second World War in Germany were completely compliant with the government. This was the post-Maidan Revolution vision President

---

[97] Rogak & Gibbons, *Volodymyr*, 110.

Poroshenko had for the nation of Ukraine. Even before he was elected, Zelensky was known to join stand-up comics on his program at Kvartal 95 and do mocking news parodies of the Russian Orthodox Church and its clergy as Russian agents. Zelensky as president would go even further than Poroshenko he has completely banned any church with suspected ties to Moscow. In December 2022, the administration passed laws which targeted churches that had any questionable allegiance to Russia. Zelensky stated, "We will ensure spiritual independence. We will never allow anyone to build an empire inside the Ukrainian soul."[98] With the passing of this law the nation's largest and oldest branch of Christian Orthodoxy was outlawed. One of the ideological tenets on which Zelensky's administration targeted the Russian Orthodox Church was because its leader Patriarch Kirill, in Moscow, expressed his opinion that Russian's war in Ukraine was justified as a metaphysical struggle to prevent liberal ideological encroachment from the West. I will talk more about specific ideological distinctions in both religion and philosophy in Russian in chapter four. For now, the issue I address here is that Zelensky was banning a particular church based on its expressed political viewpoint. Even a historical monastery in Kyiv, the Pechersk Lavra (regarded as a world heritage site by UNESCO) came under complete government scrutiny. The security service of Ukraine ordered a search of the monastery after the priest made favorable references to Russia in a sermon.[99] More than 350 church buildings were also searched by government security including another monastery and all churches of the Rivine regions just 150 miles west of Kyiv. Orthodox Christian clergy were detained for questioning under polygraph examination to determine whether they were involved in subversive activities. The

---

[98] Hanna Seariac, *Zelensky Seeks Ban on Moscow Connected Religious Groups*, Deseret News, December 2, 2022. Source accessed on July 17, 2023, from https://www.deseret.com.

[99] AP News, December 2, 2022, *Ukraine Bans Religious Organizations*, source accessed on July 17, 2023 from https://apnews.com.

security services declared that they would continue their systematic work to counter politically subversive activity in churches. What was considered as any pro-Russian propaganda literature was confiscated from seminaries and parish schools. The bans after the Russian invasion escalated violence on Russian Orthodox Christians in Ukraine. On January 2, 2023, at an Orthodox church in Vinnytsia a man burst through the doors, turned over a crucifix, broke several religious icons, threw banners on the floor, and then slashed the priest's throat with a razor.[100] In the city of Chornomorsk parishioners disarmed a man in camouflage who was about to stab a priest with a knife. In the village of Chechelnyk, a man shouting profanities brutally beat a priest in the streets. Such violent incidents against churches and clergy are inexcusable, yet the Zelensky administration condoned it for the sake of political expediency. While Ukraine's new presidential regime was busy with their authoritarian socialism, a fast-approaching storm was on the horizon in the east.

The Russian Invasion of Ukraine

Zelensky's first encounter with Russia occurred when Putin offered Russian passports to Ukrainian citizens in the separatist-controlled regions in the east. Zelensky ridiculed Putin and posted on Facebook that he would counter his offer by extending citizenship to any Russians who wanted to defect from "the authoritarian corrupt regime."[101] Putin also was known for taking an occasional jab at Zelensky but never used his name in public. In a meeting in St. Petersburg in April 2019 when an interviewer asked Putin if he was going to congratulate Zelensky, Putin was

---

[100] Yevhen Herman, *Zelensky Vs. the Ukrainian Orthodox Church*, The American Conservative, January 25, 2023. Source accessed on July 17, 2023 from https://www.theamericanconservative.com.

[101] Michael Ray; Britannica, *Volodymyr Zelensky President of Ukraine*. August 8, 2023. Source accessed on August 10, 2023, from https://www.britannica.com/biography/Volodymyr-Zelensky.

matter of fact in his reply: "He is still pushing a certain rhetoric. He labels us enemies and aggressors. Perhaps he should think about what he really wants to achieve, what he wants to do."[102] And later when the interviewer pressed Putin in asking by asking if he was prepared to meet Zelensky, he smirkingly replied, "Listen, I do not know this man. I hope that we can meet one day. As far as I can tell, he's amazing at what he does, he's a marvelous actor. But seriously, it's one thing to play a person, but quite another thing to be that person."[103] Unfortunately, Zelensky underestimated his adversary because it would take much more than social media taunts to challenge the Russian Federation military that was already at his backdoor. As Russian intelligence expert Rebekah Koffler put it:

> For the past 20 years, Putin has planned to reverse the outcome of the Cold War. In his mind losing Ukraine to Western influence is not an option. Still Zelensky often chooses to poke the bear. With thousands of Russian soldiers amassed on his border, Zelensky made open appeals for NATO membership. Now, with Russian boots on Ukrainian soil, he goads Putin to escalate his assault, even daring the Russia to carpet-bomb Kyiv. To paraphrase a famous saying about Vietnam, Zelensky may allow his country to be destroyed in order to save it.[104]

In the spring of 2021, Russia begins a buildup of military forces along the nation's border with an assembly of 140,000 troops.[105] Just before the end of the that year, intelligence sources from Washington and London were warning of the likelihood of a Russian strike. Most European nations as well as Zelensky himself downplayed whether

---

[102] Rogak & Gibbons, *Volodymyr*, 110.

[103] Derix & Shelkunova, *Zelensky*, 7-8.

[104] Urban & McLeod, Zelsnky, xi.

[105] Galeotti, *Putin's Wars*, 342-43.

Moscow would follow through with actual retaliation. They too easily dismissed what they believed as nothing more than Putin's saber rattling. On one occasion he made the remark to reporters: "You can say a million times, 'Listen, there may be an invasion.' Okay, there may be an invasion will you give us planes? Will you give us air defenses? 'Well, you're not a member of NATO.' Oh, okay, what are we talking about?"[106] As biographer Serhii Rudenko put it, "Zelensky insisted that everything was under his complete control and that foreigners were simply spreading unjustified panic."[107] No doubt Putin had been planning the invasion of Ukraine along with the annexation of Crimea in response to the Maidan Revolution. I will address the military and tactical details of the Russian invasion in greater detail in chapters three and four. On December 17, 2021, Putin and the Russian Federation drafted and delivered an agreement to NATO titled *Agreement on Measures to Ensure the Security of the Russian Federation and Member States of the North Atlantic Treaty Organization.*[108] The agreement includes a reference to the 1975 Helsinki Act and NATO relations. Article Six is referenced as follows: "All member States of the North Atlantic Treaty Organization commit themselves to refrain from any further enlargement of NATO, including the accession of Ukraine as well as other states."[109] According to the Brookings Institute Russia's draft agreement was rejected as a serious negotiating bid: "If the Kremlin is serious about negotiating and deescalates the situation near Ukraine, the West could engage on some elements of the drafts. Many, however, will go nowhere."[110] Some have criticized Russia as using the agreement's rejection as an excuse

---

[106] Plokhy, *The Russo-Ukrainian War*, 146.

[107] Rudenko, *Zelensky: A Biography*, 2.

[108] Russian Foreign Policy Archives, December 17, 2021. Source accessed on August 17, 2023, from https://mid.ru/ru/foreign_policy/rso/nato/1790803/ ?lang=en.

[109] Ibid.

[110] Steven Pifer, *Russia's Draft Agreements with NATO & the US: Intended for Rejection?* December 21, 2021, Brookings Institute Commentary. Source accessed on August 17, 2023, from https://www.brookings.edu.

for the invasion of Ukraine. Nonetheless, from Russia's perspective it validated their suspicions that the West was willing to encroach further upon its borders. Also, the culmination of incidents from the past decade of Ukrainian revolutions the Orange Revolution and the Maidan Revolution along with the new Zelensky administration only added fuel to the fire for Russian aggression. Although a few international intelligence agencies vocalized their concerns over the potential for a Russian strike on Ukraine, not all military experts believed that Putin would be so bold as to launch an attack. Mark Galeotti a scholar on Russian security affairs whose research I quote in this book even had his initial doubts: "To be honest, I must confess that until the beginning of February 2022, I was putting the chance of war as no more than 30-40%. The problem was that what looked like common sense to outsiders, clearly did not for Putin."[111] Putin would not only defy the conventional logic of international leaders and military experts alike, but he would also initiate a surprise attack upon Ukraine that not even Zelensky had anticipated.

Just before 5:00 am on February 24, 2022, Vladimir Putin made a state-televised public address that would be broadcast around the world. He began his address with a statement that "the People's Republic of Donbas appealed to Russia for help." Putin after referencing Article 51, part seven of the U.N. Charter citing the ratification of treaties for mutual assistance with the Donetsk People's Republic on February 22, 2022, issued the following statement: "I made a decision to conduct a special military operation. Its goal is to protect people who have been abused by the genocide of the Kyiv regime for eight years. And to this end, we will strive for the demilitarization and denazification of Ukraine, as well as bringing to justice those who committed numerous bloody crimes against civilians, including citizens of the

---

[111] Galeotti, *Putin's Wars*, 344.

Russian Federation."[112] Putin added that "our plans do not include the occupation of Ukrainian territories. We are not going to impose anything on anyone by force." Putin's speech would be denounced not only by Ukraine but by leaders of the international community especially on the following three claims: first, the request for assistance from Donetsk, second, the genocide of Donbas citizens at the hands of Ukraine, and third, the "denazification of Ukraine." The validity of these claims would be universally denied by world leaders and would become Zelensky's talking points of for months to come after the invasion. I will address the details of Putin's remarks in further detail in the third and fourth chapters, for now we will look at the specific events of the military operation that was announced in Moscow. Less than ten minutes after Putin's address, the Russian assault commenced on multiple fronts within eastern Ukraine. At 5:07 am Russian forces launched a series of missile attacks on multiple locations near Kyiv as well as long-range artillery attacks against the northeastern city of Kharkiv near the Russian border. The strikes continued to spread across central and eastern Ukraine with incoming blasts reported in the cities of Odessa, Dnipro, Mariupol, and Kramatorsk. Most of the confirmed targets were identified as military bases. At 6:48 am Zelensky announced martial law in Ukraine as military vehicles and troops were entering at border crossings in Belarus. Also, Russian helicopters landed at the Hostomel airport in northeastern Ukraine deploying hundreds of elite Russian Federation soldiers. At 7:00 am air raid sirens sounded in Kyiv and there was a mass exodus of civilians evacuating the major cities as well as the eastern regions. This was the beginning of what would be called the *Russo-Ukrainian War* that would elevate Zelensky into the international spotlight.

---

[112] Transcript from Sydney Morning Herald, February 24, 2022. Translated by Washington Post Journalist Mary Ilyushina. Source accessed on August 18, 2023, from https://www.smh.com.

The Zelensky Effect

Shortly after the beginning of the invasion, Zelensky appeared before the media wearing camouflage trousers and an olive drab t-shirt and speaking words of defiance to Putin and the Russian Federation. When asked by the US State Department if the Ukrainian president needed an airlift, he makes a reply that would be captured by the international media as a red badge of courage: "I need ammo, not a ride."[113] Zelensky's skills from his past life on the stage before live audiences and on television would now be channeled into his ability for powerful public rhetoric while the war was raging on the eastern borders of Ukraine. Although Zelensky's ratings and public opinion had waned considerably in his past three years in office, the war would now propel him into overnight international stardom. Now more than 90 percent of Ukrainians supported Zelensky as his approval ratings nearly tripled over those of December 2021, just before the Russian invasion. In the first two hundred days of the war, he would give eighty-one speeches to foreign dignitaries, international leaders, and the US Congress. Whereas most of the world had previously regarded the Russo-Ukraine conflict as something that was far-away and limited to the European continent, now the president of Ukraine would influence international opinion with the perspective that this was now everybody's war. This shift in public opinion with the spotlight on Ukraine would receive unanimous support from a globalist perspective At the U.N. General Assembly, Zelensky in stating his objectives for the end of the war, concluded: "That is why we need to the support of the world." At the Munich Security Conference, he would admonish attendees that a new world order needs to rise to the challenges of modern global security: "The architecture of world security is fragile and needs to be updated. The rules that the world agreed upon decades ago no longer work…It is

---

[113] Zelensky, *A Message from Ukraine*, xi.

too late to think about repairs. It is time to build a new system."[114] At the European Union, Zelensky would chide members, "This is not merely Russia's invasion of Ukraine. It is the beginning of a war against Europe." And the Ukrainian president would also make a powerful appeal to members of US Congress to ask for the enforcement of a no-fly zone: "For today, it is not enough to be the leader of the nation. Today it is necessary to be the leader of the world." Members of Congress, many wearing Ukrainian flag lapel pins, would respond with a standing ovation. Zelensky would directly address Joe Biden, "That's why today the American people are helping not just Ukraine, but Europe and the planet, to keep justice in the world…And so, as the President of my country, I am addressing President Biden. You are the leader of a great nation. I wish you to be the leader of the world. Being the leader of the world means being the leader in peace." Zelensky's speech to Congress resulted in more than $84 billion in weapons and security assistance given to Ukraine's military.[115] What will surprise most American citizens is that this is in addition to $45.4 billion given in assistance to Ukraine since the 2014 bloody Maidan Revolution and radical government overthrow. Also on September 8, 2022, $2.2 billion was made available through long-term investments under the Foreign Military Financing for the purpose of bolstering Ukraine and its NATO allies. This also includes an additional $42 million from the Global Security Contingency Fund, a joint program of the US Departments of State and Defense to provide military training, advisory services, and equipment to assist the Government of Ukraine to further develop the tactical, operational, and institutional capacities of its Special Operations Forces, and National Guard. You can find a very long list of military equipment purchased for Ukraine on the US State Department web site including air defense and missile systems, artillery and munitions, tanks, helicopters, grenade launchers, explosives, and satellite communications. This

---

[114] Zelensky, *A Message from Ukraine*, 43-44; 72-73.

[115] US Department of State. US Security Cooperation with Ukraine Fact Sheet, August 14, 2023. Source accessed on August 19, 2023, from https://www.state.gov.

was all granted by Biden's executive orders for what is known as an emergency "Presidential Drawdown Authority" that allows direct transfer of equipment from Department of Defense stockpiles. It gets better with almost no support from the Biden administration to assist with US border security, over $34.8 million has been provided to support Ukraine's border security in a program known as the "Export Control & Border Security Program." Wherever Zelensky went he was seen as an international hero standing against a powerful Russian Federation to raise his fist defiantly against Putin: "What will bring the end of the war? We used to say peace. Now we say victory."[116] To every nation that has given Zelensky an audience, he has made strong demands for military assistance. This has been met with an overwhelming response from the international military community and fifty NATO allies who have provided more than $13 billion to purchase multiple launch rocket systems, 178 long-range artillery systems, 359 tanks, and 629 armored personnel carriers. Zelensky's star status in the global community would earn him and Ukraine a full military arsenal and financial support to take to the bank. In December 2022, *Time Magazine* featured Zelensky as *Person of the Year* in an issue titled, *Volodymyr Zelensky & the Spirit of Ukraine*. This is Time's glowing tribute:

> Volodymyr Zelensky galvanized the world in a way we haven't seen in decades...Ukraine's President was everywhere. His information offensive shifted the geopolitical weather system, setting off a wave of action that swept the globe. In a world that had come to be defined by its divisiveness, there was a coming together around this cause, around this country that some outside it might not be able to find on a map...Ukraine's flag unfurled across social media; its colors, blue and yellow, lit up landmarks from Tokyo to Sandusky, Ohio. The spirit of

---

[116] Zelensky, *A Message from Ukraine*, 43-44

Ukraine was embodied by countless individuals inside and outside the country.[117]

Most US politicians both Democrat and Republican rallied around Zelensky with overwhelming support. Both Senators Mitch McConnell and Lindsey Graham called for ramping up military support for Ukraine. Only a few would refrain from lavishing praise upon Zelensky. Tucker Carlson, before he was terminated from Fox News, warned that the US should not be involved with the support of Ukraine. North Carolina Republican Representative Madison Cawthorn boldly commented: "Remember that Zelensky is a thug, remember that the Ukrainian government is incredibly corrupt, and it is incredibly evil, and it has been pushing woke ideologies. It is really the new woke world empire."[118] However, the mainstream media favored Zelensky and influenced public opinion worldwide. If there was ever a poster child for globalism, Zelensky would be preeminent and shining brightly. Nearly everyone embraced the international trend to proudly display Ukraine's flag and proclaim the motto "I stand with Ukraine." Putin and Russia did not stand a chance in public opinion against the world's praise for Zelensky; they would be vilified as the bad guys during the Russo-Ukraine War. Grant Farred stated: "Zelensky has made Ukraine a litmus test on global democracy…The world believes Zelensky."[119] While Ukraine was now rolling in the dough with billions of dollars in funding and military assistance, Russia would come under the most severe international sanctions known in history.

The EU adopted a three-pronged attack on Russia with economic sanctions that would be enforced by the international community: first, the blocking of Russian banking transactions through the electronic SWIFT network, second, the blockade of any industrial support for

---

[117] Time Magazine, December 26, 2022. *Person of the Year: Volodymyr Zelensky & the Spirit of Ukraine*. Source accessed on August 19, 2023, from https://time.com.

[118] Urban & McLeod, *Zelensky*, 33-34.

[119] Grant Farred, *The Zelensky Method*, Washington, D.C.: Westphalia Press, 2022, 11.

Russian oil refineries, air fleet technologies, and of any airport access for Russian business- oligarch flights, and third, the complete censorship of Russia's media: *Russia Today and Sputnik*.[120] The Biden administration announced on March 8, 2022, that all Russian oil and gas imports would be banned and Russian cargo ships would not be permitted access to any US ports. Both the US and the UK also joined the EU in freezing all financial accounts and assets belonging to Putin and his foreign minister Sergei Lavrov. International athletic organizations also followed suit as the World Athletics Council and the International Tennis Federation banned all athletes from Russian and Belarus from competition. Then came corporate bans from all over the world from McDonald's, Coca-Cola, Starbucks, Pizza Hut, Ikea, Nike, FedEx, Apple, Google, TikTok and KFC. Credit card and merchant account services such as Visa, Mastercard, American Express, and PayPal also banned Russian accounts. Cinema producers and music studios joined in with the ban on Russia: Netflix, Disney, Warner Brothers, and Universal Music. Nearly 300 corporations completely withdrew their business from Russia. While most EU nations have fully supported the economic sanctions against Russia, there are a couple of retractors who do not support a proxy war in Ukraine. Hungary's prime minister Viktor Orban, an EU member, met personally with Putin on October 17, 2023, to express that both nations have suffered because of the sanctions.[121] Hungary wishes to continue trade relations with Moscow because it is dependent upon Russia's supply of natural gas, oil, and nuclear fuel. Orban reported that Budapest blocked over $526 million in financial aid to Ukraine. Prior to Orban's meeting with Putin, in August 2023, in an interview with Tucker Carlson on X he warned that funding the war in Ukraine was a dangerous provocation of Russia and that Trump needed to be re-elected to achieve peaceful solutions by directly

---

[120] Urban & McCleod, *Zelensky*, 58-69.

[121] Justin Spike & Ken Moritsugu, *Putin Meets with Hungary's Prime Minister in Rare In-Person Talks with an EU Leader*. The Associated Press, October 17, 2023, source accessed on October 17, 2023, from https://www.msn.com.

negotiating with Putin. Serbia is also one to resist the popular movement of Western sanctions against Russia as it is moving away from EU membership and moving closer to Russia economically and politically. Despite the most aggressive sanctions in history, Russia remained defiant and continued their military operations against Ukraine. I will look at the military operations and key historical battles of the Russian Federation in the next chapter.

Chapter Three:

The Bear Provoked; Understanding Russia's History and Its Military

And behold, another beast, a second one, like a bear. It was raised up on one side. It had three ribs in its mouth between its teeth; and it was told, "Arise, devour much flesh." (Daniel 7:5)

Russia: A Brief History

The Rule of the Tsars (988–1917)

The subtitle here is a contradiction in terms of perspective the history of Russia as well as that of its European counterparts is anything but brief. Unlike the new Republic of the United States of America with just two centuries of history, Russian history spans over ten centuries. It is an amazingly complex story. Nonetheless, a summary overview will help readers to better understand the nation's culture and what drives its leadership in the eastern European realm. By the sixth century much of the Western Empire, formerly Rome, had dissipated into Germanic successor states. However, the eastern emperors with their capital at Constantinople, retained control of a vast region from the Balkans through Asia Minor. In addition to being more populous than western

Europe, the eastern empire had an important strategic a geopolitical advantage because it offered abundant resources and a buffer zone to repel attacks from the Germanic and Asiatic tribes. The unique characteristic of the eastern empire was its Byzantine government that was a synthesis of Roman government, Christian religion, and Greco-Oriental culture. The late author and historian C. Warren Hollister who was the American Historical Association's representative to the Congress of Historical Sciences in Moscow in 1970 described Byzantine society as follows: "To the Byzantines, their state was the ark of civilization in an ocean of barbarism the political embodiment of the Christian faith and as such it had to be preserved at all costs."[122] The orthodox Christians within the eastern empire regarded their rulers as more than a secular state sovereign; they were God's vice-regents who were also a protector of the Holy Church. Therefore, the Byzantine armies fought not merely for the empire but also for God and their faith which was closely aligned with their patriotism. I will show that this is a cultural value that was retained for centuries even to the present day in modern Russia regarding the Orthodox Church. Just as Constantine dominated the clergy at the Council of Nicaea in 325 A.D., so also the Byzantine emperors were closely aligned with the church patriarchs in Constantinople. The major difference between their Western counterparts, who had allegiance to the Church in Rome and its Popes, was that Byzantine religion and civilization was distinctly Greek and cherished their Hellenistic ecclesiastical heritage. In the ninth century the Byzantine empire began further expansion under the dynasty of the Macedonian emperors (867–1056) which flourished under a rich literary and artistic revival of eastern culture that was further advanced by Eastern Orthodox Christian missionaries. A surge in church missions under the Macedonian emperors shaped the cultural development of Eastern Europe for the next millennium. As a result, many of the Slavic peoples who converted to the Orthodox Church were the ancestors of the populations living in the Baltics, Eastern Europe, and Eurasia. Although

---

[122] C. Warren Hollister, *Medieval Europe: A Short History*, New York: John Wiley & Sons, 1978, 25 – 26.

the Orthodox Church was in the majority, there were also settlements of Muslims and Jews throughout the Byzantine empire as well. In the ninth century missionaries such as Cyril and Methodius who were called "the Apostles to the Slavs" invented the Slavonic alphabet and a Slavic vernacular Bible that later led the Balkans and Russians into Orthodoxy.

In the late ninth and tenth centuries the Byzantine rulers known as Tsars (or Czars derived from the Roman imperial title of Caesar) had economic and political interests on the northern shore of the Black Sea as trade flourished concurrent with the rise of Russia. The Black Sea was a gateway into the Eastern Empire providing access for the Norseman who served as mercenaries for the Byzantine emperors. In the tenth century Swedish Vikings ventured into Novgorod (a medieval state in northern Russia). Eventually Novgorod captured the Russian commercial center of Kiev which is the capital of modern-day Ukraine. The earliest known female regent of Kyiv was Princess Olga who succeeded her husband Igor I after he was assassinated by insurgents. Olga became the first Christian convert in Russo-Ukraine and was baptized in 957 in Constantinople. After her death, Olga was canonized a Saint by the Orthodox church and became known as a patron saint of widows and new converts. Olga's grandson Vladimir succeeded his grandmother Olga and became the prince of Kiev. The Macedonian emperor Basil II (976-1025), who ruled over the regions of Georgia, Armenia and the Balkans strove to maintain diplomatic relations with what became known as "Kievan Russia" (also referred to as Kievan Rus).[123] Basil received military aid from Prince Vladimir of Kiev and in turn pledged his sister in marriage to Vladimir. The intermarriage within the families of imperial rulers was an ancient diplomatic practice that united peoples and their cultures. The marriage of the Byzantine princess also led to the conversion of Vladimir to Christianity. The Kievan Russians in turn followed suit giving their allegiance to the patriarch of Constantinople. This allegiance established the Christian

---

[123] Joan Mervyn Hussey, Britannica, *Basil II: Byzantine Emperor*. July 23, 2023. Source accessed on August 29, 2023, from https://www.britannica.com/biography/Basil-II.

(Eastern) Orthodox Church in Russia. which later would be known as the Russian Orthodox Church. Mass baptisms were conducted for the inhabitants of Kiev. These baptisms were later chronicled in history as the baptisms of *Kyivan Rus*. This ancient history is preserved in records dating back to 1377 by the Kievan Orthodox monk Nestor in a work titled *The Russian Primary Chronical*. The *Chronicle* continues to this day as an important primary source for Russian history. To this day contemporary Russia has maintained that Ukraine has for centuries been part of the Russo-Ukraine identity, based upon this ancient history. Before the Maidan Revolution, Putin made a visit to Kiev July 27, 2013, to observe the 1,025th anniversary of the baptism of Kyivan Rus.[124] His speech to the Ukrainian people titled *Orthodox Slavic Values: The Basis of Ukraine's Civilizational Choice* about the baptism of the first converts, highlighted their shared heritage and spiritual tradition:

> Here at this site, at the baptismal site on the Dnieper River, a choice was made for our entire people. When I say 'for our entire people,' we know today's reality of course, know that there are the Ukrainian people and the Belarusian people, and other peoples too, and we respect all the parts of this heritage, but at the same time, at the foundations of this heritage are the common spiritual values that make us a single people...The Baptism of Rus was a great event that defined Russia's and Ukraine's spiritual and cultural development for the centuries to come. We must remember this brotherhood and preserve our ancestor's traditions. Together, they built a unique system of Orthodox values and strengthened themselves in their faith.[125]

---

[124] Plokhy, *The Russo-Ukrainian War*, 149.

[125] President of Russia; Events – *Orthodox-Slavic Values: The Foundation of Ukraine's Civilizational Choice*. July 27, 2013. Source accessed August 29, 2023, from http://en.kremlin.ru/events/president/news/ 18961.

While some secular historians accused Putin of romanticizing Russian history to "Russify" Ukraine, his address makes a strong appeal to the spiritual heritage shared by their people in the face of Western Europe's socialist advance upon traditional values. I will address in the next chapter the reason Putin regards Western ideology as corrupt and his concerns over the erosion of traditional values.

After the fall of the Byzantine Empire in 1453 with the Ottoman Turk's conquest of the Balkans, Moscow became known as the last citadel of Russian Orthodoxy and was referred to by some as the "Third Rome."[126] In 1547 Ivan IV, the grand prince of Moscow, was crowned *Tsar of all Russia* and sought to establish a Christian state based upon principles of justice. Ivan was a brutal and ruthless leader who earned the title *Ivan the Terrible*. Ivan's vision was to advance Russia beyond its borders into Europe. This vision was carried on by Peter I also known as Peter the Great. Peter I, was ambitious in learning trade and industry from other advanced nations and developed a Grand Embassy comprising 250 representatives who would gain skills such as shipbuilding from Great Britain and other European nations and incorporate them into Russia. By the eighteenth-century Russia's system of government under the tsars became more totalitarian through an aristocratic class that exercised authoritarian rule with specific class distinctions and system of a medieval serfdom. Alexander II (1855-81) was concerned over Russia's decline socially and intellectually in its place among the more advanced nations of the world. Therefore, Alexander initiated enlightened, modern reforms in education and emancipated the serf's who were regarded as commoners subservient to the aristocracy to farm the land and provide for the ruling class. Alexander also developed a vast railway that operated across 14,000 miles and brought extensive industrial and economic progress. This progress accelerated the growth of many cities with Kyiv becoming the seventh largest. Alexander also reformed the judicial systems of government moving away from the

---

[126] Britannica, *Tsar – Title*, Source accessed on August 29, 2023, from https://www.britannica.com/topic/tsar.

earlier authoritarian rule of previous tsars. The results that would follow from Alexander's reforms would be a grand renaissance of Russian culture that would produce some of the world's greatest authors and composers: Tolstoy, Gogol, Dostoevsky, and Tchaikovsky.

Despite the great reforms of Alexander II, Russia's imperial monarchy lacked a cohesive parliamentarian system that would rival those of nations like Great Britain, France, and Germany. By the 1900's autocratic flaws in Russian governance would create major instability. The conservatives wanted to adopt a constitutional model like the United Kingdom while liberal factions like the Marxist Mensheviks and the socialists wanted a revolution that would do away with the ancient dynasties altogether. The government deteriorated seriously under the inept rule of Nicholas II (1894-1917) who lacked the ability to adequately address the demands of the workers, peasants, and conscripts who were tiring of an out-of-touch monarchy.[127] Nicholas was introverted and lacked the skill to be the nation's leader. Rather, he followed the promptings of his wife Alexandra who influenced him away from his Orthodox faith toward the guidance of the mystic occult shaman Grigori Rasputin. Rasputin was known for his morally licentious life that later scandalized the imperial family. Rasputin became a personal advisor to Nicholas and was responsible for the appointment of incompetent cabinet members as well as undermining the ecclesiastical oversight of the Orthodox Church.[128] By this time the imperial monarchy was spiraling quickly in a downward descent and by February 1917, when local textile workers, armament factories, and soldiers went on strike, it became extremely difficult to restore control. Therefore, a provisional government was formed to provide order under the leadership of liberal Georgi Lvov in the cabinet. Policy reforms were announced until a constituent assembly could be elected. All this came too late

---

[127] Robert Service, *Comrades: A History of World Communism*, (Cambridge, MA: Harvard University Press, 2007), 58.

[128] John L. H. Keep, *Nicholas II: Tsar of Russia*, Britannica. Source accessed on August 29, 2023, from https://www.britannica.com/biography/Nicholas-II-tsar-of-Russia.

because the dark specter of revolution had been gathering strength during the decline of the Nicholas II imperial reign.

The provisional government was in shambles as a Petrograd Soviet had been elected by workers and soldiers as a rival to the monarchy cabinet. The most dangerous challenge came from the Bolshevik party, which was a wing of the Russian Social-Democratic Workers Party. The Bolsheviks had been in disarray until their central committee came under the leadership of Joseph Stalin (a follower of Karl Marx). The Bolsheviks became even more emboldened when Vladimir Lenin, through his proposal for action titled *The State and Revolution* introduced an action plan to transition the government to socialism under a state dictator. This plan was the opportunity Lenin had been looking for when he was in Helsinki studying the doctrines of Marx and Engels to develop a postulate for violent revolution. His argument was that twentieth-century military developments had set the stage for a socialist seizure of power as the only practical strategy. To accomplish this, Lenin claimed that the *bourgeois state* (the middle class between the peasantry and the aristocracy) had to be eradicated for the sake of the *proletariat* (the exploited working class) and in essence all class distinctions would be removed for the common sharing of wealth and resources through the authority of the state. The conditions after the February 1917 revolt of the workers in Russia against the provisional government were now ripe for revolution from the perspective of Stalin and Lenin. It was the "perfect storm" that they were looking for as citizens became fed up with the imperial monarchy and were ready for radical change. Capitalism was viewed as a failed economic system that could only be extracted through revolution. Lenin and the Bolsheviks convinced the far-left socialists to adopt their strategies. It was summed up by Robert Service, a Fellow of the British Academy and professor of Russian history: "The prophetic vision of Marx and Engels would be fulfilled...The Bolsheviks lived and breathed the desire to transform the world."[129] The revolution

---

[129] Service, *Comrades*, 63 & 65.

began on the evening of October 24, 1917, and by 10:00am on the 25th, Lenin issued the proclamation that the provisional government had been overthrown. Nicholas II had been detained by the provisional government prior to the revolution. The royal family was executed on July 17, 1917, and their bodies were burned. Nicholas II would be the last imperial monarch. The reign of the Tsars was over now the Union of Soviet Socialist Republics (USSR) would emerge as the iron boot of communism that would dominate most of eastern Europe for the next seventy-four years.

The USSR (1917-1991)

With the Bolsheviks in power, Lenin was now the supreme leader of the new state regime. His first order of business was to establish a security police force known as the Extraordinary Commission for Combating Sabotage and Counter-Revolution (known as Cheka). A state police force would be required for dealing with any opposition to the "dictatorship of the proletariat." The police state later under Stalin evolved into a formal Soviet order that would conduct mass surveillance upon every Russian citizen. As Russian historian Robert Service described it: "Theirs was a secular gospel which they intended to take to the willing and impose on the unwilling. They studied the French Revolution relentlessly; they were Jacobins with the telephone and the machine gun."[130] In addition to the Cheka, they quickly organized the Red Army which could rapidly deploy soldiers throughout the nation to fight any insurrectionists. Terror and brute force were the methodologies by which Lenin's dictatorship operated. Now all industry and farmland were the property of the state. Churches, synagogues, and mosques were either confiscated or destroyed. Priests, rabbis, and clerics were executed. Just before Lenin's death in 1924 (caused by health complications from a prior assassination attempt on his life), he managed

---

[130] Ibid, 66 & 71.

to lay the foundation for what would become known as the Union of Soviet Socialist Republics. The USSR was a one-party, one ideology state-driven totalitarian system that rained down terror upon the local citizens to make them subservient through a rigid system of indoctrination. The one man that had been at Lenin's side through the Bolshevik Revolution who would drive the USSR dictatorship for next 30 years in Russia would be Joseph Stalin.

Stalin was born to a poor family in the country of Georgia and was selected at a young age to enter seminary studies and become a priest in the Orthodox Church. However, Stalin had no interest in divinity studies but was fascinated by and studied voraciously, the works of Karl Marx. After dropping out of seminary, he determined that his life's calling would be to carry out the doctrines of Marx and Engels. After Lenin's death, Stalin pursued extensive collectivization of agriculture and industrialization programs to provide *bread and bullets* for the Soviet State. Millions perished due to famine in Russia and Ukraine caused by the farm collectivism, and the masses were oppressed under inhumane labor conditions in factories. If anyone dared to speak out against the Soviet regime, they were sent to the gulags in Siberia to endure forced labor and most often would perish. Stalin cultivated his own cult persona that became the iconic Soviet Premier who was wore a military style tunic and knee-length black boots.

By 1932, Stalin developed his statecraft into an instrument of cruel barbarism and in 1936 he instituted what would be known as the "great purge" of millions of anti-Soviet dissidents from Russian society. Passports were created for urban residents so that police could closely monitor the population's movement. The Main Soviet Administration ran an entire penal system through the Gulags for the state's rehabilitation program of anyone whose loyalty could be called into question to the state. A systematic campaign of arrests and executions were carried out by the Soviet police state known (in English translation) as the People's Commissariat for Internal Affairs (NKVD) that proved to be far more brutal than Lenin's Cheka. Every facet of life was to be subservient to the Soviet state. Members of specific trade occupations had to belong to unions, from the average factory all the way the physicists. Soviet guilds were established for writers and artists, and their works had to be closely scrutinized to ensure that they were compliant with Soviet doctrine. Hundreds of artists, writers, and intellectuals who did not comply were either arrested or executed. Phone lines were tapped, conversations were monitored, and personal correspondence was reviewed by the police. Even those who were close to Stalin were not exempt from interrogations as younger ambitious officers were encouraged to report any suspicious activities to the police; no one was safe from police surveillance: Communist Party administration, military officers, or the average housewife. The famous Russian author Alexander Solzhenitsyn, while serving as a commander in the Russian artillery, was arrested by the NKVD for sending a personal letter to a friend of his that was deemed critical of Stalin. Solzhenitsyn told of his story of being sentenced to the Gulag for eight years. Although the writer never used Stalin's name in the letter and was careful to refer to him only with pseudonyms, the NKVD thought police deciphered Solzhenitsyn's writing.[131] Historian Robert Service described Stalin's gulags: "From the mid-1930's there were always around two million convicts in the labor camps...They dug canals, sawed timber, mined for gold, and built new cities. Labor camps were set up in Siberia and north Russia wherever an economic purpose was served."[132]

The Communist Party was not content to remain within the borders of the USSR. The Communist Manifesto had a global vision for every nation in the world. The USSR was a purveyor of communist doctrine which had expanded its reach into the outlying eastern European nations: Ukraine, Belarus, Yugoslavia, and Georgia in the years following the Bolshevik Revolution. On June 22, 1941, Hitler pushed his forces into the USSR much to the disbelief of Stalin. This invasion

---

[131] Alexander Solzhenitsyn, *Solzhenitsyn: A Pictorial Autobiography*, (New York: Farrar, Straus & Giroux, 1974), 20.

[132] Service, *Comrade*, 152.

resulted in a massive Soviet counter-offensive that was maintained through the sacrifice of the Red Army as twelve million men were conscripted into service. The Second World War thrust the USSR into the western alliance and, along with the United States and the United Kingdom into what would be referred to as the "Big Three" because they shared a common enemy Nazi Germany. Stalin now partnered with Roosevelt and Churchill in this alliance. Fighting the Germans was brutal as the eastern front cities of Kharkov in Ukraine were captured. Stalin ordered his military that they were not allowed to retreat, and millions of soldiers were to fight to the death. After the war, Stalin belittled Russian prisoners of war publicly and even sent some of them to the gulag as punishment for being captured by the enemy. Stalin's Red Army prevailed and captured Berlin. This victory would later result in east Germany's inclusion in the allotment to the USSR. Amazingly given the reputation that the brutal dictator Stalin had in Moscow, he now came into the spotlight as a war hero. He was made Time magazine's Man of the Year for the second time in January 1943. Churchill and Roosevelt praised Stalin with much appreciation for his contribution to the Allied Forces. Yet, Stalin's victory came at a high price as twenty-six million Soviet citizens perished either on the battlefield or in concentration camps, and nearly 1,200 Russian cities were in ruins from his scorched-earth policy during the years of 1941-42.[133] In the post-war years, Stalin continued his brute force dictatorship and during 1949-50, he had many of his own political elite in Leningrad executed simply for personal distrust or suspicion. The USSR maintained its military and political superiority in eastern Europe during post-war rebuilding.

Soviet intelligence had been following the top-secret plans of the US Oppenheimer Project with great interest. After the first atomic bombs were dropped on Hiroshima and Nagasaki in 1945, Stalin demanded that Soviet scientists replicate the secret technology so that the USSR would have access to the world's most powerful weaponry. In 1949, the

---

[133] Service, *Comrade*, 224-28.

Soviets detonated their first atomic bomb to announce that they had arrived officially as a nuclear superpower. This heightened the concerns of the Western powers so the US, and the UK sent their intelligence agents into Albania and Ukraine to subvert communist power. Through the CIA Washington expended more than $65 million over three decades beginning in 1948 for Soviet surveillance and covert operations; this trend would continue into the development of modern-day Ukraine. The Stalin regime continued until his death in 1953. The Soviet Premier remained highly suspicious of everyone even in his own administration until his death. On the day of his death on March 5, 1953, Stalin's own bodyguards were too afraid to check on him when he did not awaken for his usual routine. By the time security consulted a physician it was too late Stalin died of a heart attack. Nikita Khrushchev would succeed Stalin. Khrushchev joined the Red Army in 1919 and had been a faithful supporter of Stalin and one of three provincial secretaries who would survive the mass executions of Stalin's Great Purge in the 1930's. When he became the USSR's supreme leader in 1957, he surprised everyone with his speech on the *cult of the individual* as he openly denounced Stalin's mass executions during the Great Purge. Khrushchev made a significant shift in what was known as the "de-Stalinization" of Soviet policy.[134] Millions of political prisoners were released from Gulag labor camps and the domestic political atmosphere became somewhat relaxed compared to Stalin's reign of terror. The new leadership was still committed to a communist state and began to focus more upon the Soviet Bloc in eastern Europe under the Warsaw Pact. He also began to encourage the development of new regional agencies. Khrushchev was more outgoing than Stalin and traveled to key diplomatic meetings. He met with President Eisenhower at Camp David in 1959 and later with John F. Kennedy in Vienna in 1961. Although the new Soviet Premier was more relaxed in his policies compared to Stalin, Khrushchev was quite forceful in his direct comments

---

[134] Service, *Comrades*, 311.

to the U.N. criticizing them for Western Imperialism and the USSR soon built the Berlin Wall. He secretly attempted to establish medium range missile bases in Cuba which escalated in the Cuban Missile Crisis during Kennedy's administration.

After Khrushchev died in 1971, he was succeeded by Leonid Brezhnev whose leadership would be marked by policies that enforced traditional communist dogma in eastern Europe as well as a more relaxed attitude in international relations. When the new leadership of Czechoslovakia attempted to liberalize its communist system, Brezhnev developed a concept known as the "Brezhnev Doctrine."[135] This policy endorsed the Soviet invasion of Czechoslovakia, and the Warsaw Pact allies for the purpose of protecting the interests of the USSR. Brezhnev also advanced the modern industrialization of the USSR, and the development of its space program and military. Much of this was done for the Soviets to keep up with other modern nuclear nations such as the US Because the USSR was prioritizing its modern industrial complex, it needed to be able to compete economically in world trade. For the Soviet economy to enter open trade cooperation it had to ease the Cold War tensions with the US through a period known as "Détente." President Richard Nixon and General Secretary Brezhnev entered into a dialogue to further détente-based foreign policy. These discussions also led the way for SALT I & II (the Strategic Arms Limitation Treaty) to pull back the reins on the nuclear arms race. Although détente helped to ease some diplomatic relations between the US and the USSR, there were still stress points with the Warsaw Pact allies and then later with the Soviet invasion of Afghanistan in 1979. Afghanistan was a hot button between the US and the USSR for years as the Soviets supported the secularized government whereas America supported the Muslim radical insurgency. The Russian military presence in the Middle East

---

[135] Britannica, *Leonid Brezhnev: President of Soviet Union*, August 7, 2023. Source accessed on September 5, 2023, from https://www.britannica.com/biography/Leonid-Ilich-Brezhnev.

would continue to clash with US military interests years later in other nations like Iran and Iraq in addition to Afghanistan.

Attempted Reforms and the Inevitable Collapse of the USSR

After Brezhnev's health began to decline, Mikhail Gorbachev who served as the General Secretary on the Central Committee for the Communist Party, eventually succeeded him. The Russian Soviets were now going through a significant period of reform that brought a stark contrast to the brutal Bolshevik Revolution and the ruthless reign of Stalin. This period of reform began with Khrushchev's "de-Stalinization" internal government reforms and later expanded through Brezhnev's détente resulting in more relaxed foreign policy relations with the US The cultural shift known as *glasnost* (the Russian word for "openness) brought about new trends toward the freedom of cultural expression in Russia. Gorbachev would take the new cultural reforms another step forward through *perestroika* (the Russian word for restructuring.) Under Gorbachev modest attempts were made toward the "democratization" of the Soviet Union that permitted secret ballot elections and limited free-market capital in the economy. In 1988, a new bicameral parliament was formed called the USSR Congress of People's Deputies, and Gorbachev was elected Chairman. Even the language began changing in Soviet government rather than the leaders being called Soviet premiers, they were called presidents in keeping with other modern nations. Although still a devout communist state, the USSR began showing some signs of lenient progress. Gorbachev had several key meetings with President Ronald Reagan. During Reagan's first term of office, he gave a blistering condemnation of the Soviet Union at a March 8, 1983, National Association of Evangelicals conference where he called them the *Evil Empire*. Now in his second term Reagan was encouraged to see Gorbachev's positive steps toward reform for the Russian people with the dismantling of ruthless totalitarianism. Gorbachev's efforts resulted in the reunification of East and West Germany after the fall of the Berlin wall in 1989. Not all were in favor of Gorbachev's reforms, communist hardliners were still loyal to the old regime and still presented challenges for positive reform efforts. Despite the progressive reforms of Gorbachev, the Soviet economy soon hit serious stagnation and recession that would lead to the eventual collapse of the USSR.

The détente era was at a time when many Europeans felt that the iron curtain of communism was beginning to loosen its grip. At least European communism in an institutional sense seemed to give way with the collapse of the Berlin Wall in 1989. However, this in no way removed the ideological foundations of cultural and political Marxism from Europe, as socialism was well entrenched into all the EU nations and their institutions at every level.[136] The decade of the nineties proved to be a period of excessive volatility for the Soviet Union because of instability within the Communist Party of Russia and strife in the ranks of its leadership. Some party leaders were wary of the perestroika reforms of Gorbachev. Boris Yeltsin supported Gorbachev's reforms while he was the mayor of Moscow. Gorbachev while on vacation at his resort in Crimea on August 18, 1991, was confronted by his chief of staff and the KGB head of security. They announced that power was being transferred to his vice president, Gennady Yanayev. Gorbachev and his family were soon placed under house arrest. The following morning Radio Moscow announced that the president was in ill health and that there would be a transfer of power with the signing of a new union treaty. Within hours tanks rolled onto the streets of Moscow to smash the attempted takeover and Boris Yeltsin climbed to the top of one of the tanks to denounce the political coup. Yeltsin, who served as the first secretary of the Communist Central Committee, was in line with the reforms and soon took the helm of leadership

---

[136] Author's Note: while historians think that Communism collapsed with the demise of the USSR and later with the capitalist reforms in China, it never left the scene and is alive and well in every nation on the face of the earth and flourishes in every institution: education, arts, churches, cinema, literature, etc. It might be recast as Democratic Socialism, but its end goal is always a Marxist regime of Communism.

after Gorbachev's resignation in late 1991. Yeltsin asserted his powers of office by meeting with the presidents of Ukraine and Belarus to establish a new Commonwealth of Independent States that would replace the USSR. But even for Yeltsin, this was no cakewalk because he would eventually be impeached, and the Russian Federation would face one upheaval after another with influences from gangsters and warlords who wanted to compete for leadership.[137] Economic and social reforms had come too late the Soviet Union was no more as the USSR collapsed.

Perestroika Becomes an Entrance Ramp to the New World Order

Meanwhile another incident was brewing in the Middle East with Iraqi invasion of Kuwait. President George H.W. Bush rattled sabers with his words of condemnation: "This will not stand, this aggression against Kuwait." The conflict led to the US armed response of Operation Desert Shield. Bush as Commander in Chief quickly deposed Saddam Hussein with military bombing operations.

After the Persian Gulf crisis, Bush focused upon his next geopolitical card in the deck–Russia. The season of perestroika was on the fast-track to international peace with talks of strategic arms reductions and non-proliferation. Yeltsin met at Camp David with Bush and later with U.N. Security Council members in early 1992. Bush promised to support Russia's admission to the IMF and the World Bank, and a joint declaration was signed proclaiming that "Russia and the United States do not regard each other as potential adversaries."[138] The US government further pledged $4.5 billion as a share of a $24 billion international program to support economic reform in Russia. I need to pause here to point out an important principle: the process of globalism the goal of international consolidation of power by relinquishing national

---

[137] Mark Galleotti, *Putin's Wars From Chechnya to Ukraine*, (New York, Osprey Publishing, 2022), 51.

[138] US Department of State Archive: US-Russian Summits, 1992-2000. Site accessed July 18, 2023, from https://1997-2001.state.gov.

sovereignty has been going on for decades. In our US government, both parties Democrat and Republican have leaders in Washington who are fully vetted with moving us toward a global one-world order. And the Bush dynasty was just another player in the field for this geopolitical master plan. Just a mere eleven years prior to 9/11, Bush, Sr. during the Persian Gulf crisis delivered a speech before a joint session of Congress on September 11, 1990, describing his vision for a "new world order." Here is an excerpt from that speech:

> Out of these troubled times, our fifth objective a new world order can emerge: a new era free from the threat of terror, stronger in the pursuit of justice, and more secure in the quest for peace. An era in which the nations of the world, East, and West, North and South can prosper and live in harmony. A hundred generations have searched for this elusive path to peace, while a thousand wars raged across the span of human endeavor. Today that new world is struggling to be born, a world quite different from the one we've known...This is the vision that I shared with President Gorbachev in Helsinki. He and other leaders from Europe, the Gulf, and around the world understand that how we manage this crisis today could shape the future for generations to come.[139]

Notice that Bush had discussions even with Gorbachev about resolving the Persian Gulf conflict and the need for a new world order. One thing about global elites, they will entice you with money if you play along with their agendas and plenty of funding was now flowing into Russia. With the collapse of the Soviet Union, the new Russian Federation

---

[139] The Other 9/11: George H.W. Bush's 1990 New World Order Speech; Out of these Troubled Times, A New World Order Can Emerge. The Dallas Morning News, September 8, 2017. Site accessed on July 18, 2023, from https://www.dallasnews.com.

looked like a prospective player in the development of globalism this was the chance to influence the Russian leaders to buy into the new world order through billions of dollars for their national reforms. Of course, there's always a catch in the geopolitical realm with receiving international funding you must be willing to do the bidding of the global elites. However, as mentioned in the previous chapter Russia was not willing to relinquish its national sovereignty. As a result the global community would raise a voice of opposition to the Russian Federation with calls for numerous international sanctions in opposition to Moscow's military actions. Bush, Jr. would also attempt to influence the Russian Federation shortly after 911 just as his father had tried to influence Gorbachev and Yeltsin.

During the upstart of the Russian Federation, geopolitical leaders within NATO and the EU soon wanted a sphere of influence in the nation's evolving development. However, in 1999 after the Czech Republic, Poland, and Hungary joined NATO, the Atlantic organization's expansion resulted in Russia's distrust of the West. This trust further deteriorated when NATO began their bombing campaign of Serbia which was condoned by the US government. Because the Russians shared a common heritage with the Slavic people, they identified with the Serbian Orthodox Christians, who were a minority among the Muslim populations in the area. Russia in turn broke off relations with NATO to protest American and U.N. intervention. With the given complexity of circumstances, Russian relations with NATO and the US would be off to a shaky start for the next decade. A nation with over a thousand years of history from imperialism to the collapse of the USSR was going to pose serious challenges for the new Russian Federation. I will cover this in more detail in the next chapter about this transitional phase. For now, the nations that had been in Russia's domain of Soviet influence began looking at opportunities for secession from the Russian Federation and to demand their independence. All of this added to a greater sense of vulnerability for Russia especially with tensions between NATO and the West. In the north the Baltic region nations of Estonia,

Latvia, and Lithuania are NATO members. Add to that Finland and Poland also holding NATO membership. Therefore, the last buffer zone between Russia and NATO comprises Georgia, Ukraine, and Belarus. This can be visualized in terms of living in the US, with Communist China moving in to occupy either Mexico or Canada. And not only that, but they also decided to set up missile launchers and military bases right at the backdoor of your US borders. So, one can see that Russian sentiment of being surrounded by hostiles are not exaggerated when they are facing the same prospects of potential threat from NATO on their borders. Because the nations of Georgia, Belarus and Ukraine have been in the sphere of Russian domain for centuries, the prospects of succession are not easily resolved from the perspective of the Russian Federation. Neither has it been an easy thing for Russia to reconcile the fact that there were more than 20 million ethnic Russians living outside the boundaries of the Federation throughout most of these nations.[140] Now, if one merely sees Russia as Reagan's *evil empire,* bent on domination of these nations, the other perspective is to argue for their independence no matter what the cost. Russia is dangerous and armed and can prove to be a hostile and formidable threat in many geopolitical contexts. In our foreign policy and diplomacy with Russia, we must avoid a one size-fits all or an all-or-nothing approach in dealing with Moscow. Those who are eager for the democratization of the former Soviet Bloc will poke Russia in the eye with a stick and pour billions of dollars of military assistance through NATO and the EU at the risk of provoking a nuclear conflict. This side of the argument believes that there is no problem because we are just providing these nations with freedom from Russia's authoritarian domain. But there is really a much bigger picture to see behind all of this and it is the agenda of the global elites. The proxy wars of the eastern European nation's independence from Russia are merely a straw man in this geopolitical chess game. The global elites are not really concerned about the independence of

---

[140] Galeotti, *Putin's Wars*, 69-70.

these nations as much as their goal for bringing about a new world order. Russia is most often seen as the obstacle to implementing the plan of the global cabal. Whether this means severely weakening the Russian Federation, overthrowing the government, forcing the removal of its leadership, or even the complete destruction of the nation Russia's power and influence in the geopolitical sphere must be removed if the Great Reset is to be fully implemented. Russia certainly has the potential to be a powerful adversary and cannot be trusted in world affairs. It is a force that must be reckoned with and that requires considerable precautions. Therefore, it is important to understand the history of the nation and its leadership.

Vladimir Putin Takes the Helm of the Russian Federation

After seventy-five years of communist domination under the Soviet Union, Russia as a nation had gone through a grand metamorphosis from Khrushchev's de-Stalinization to an epic reform movement of glasnost and perestroika under Gorbachev and Yeltsin. Communism proved to be a seriously flawed system that bankrupted Russia's economy and devastated its culture. Not only did the Russian people suffer greatly under the USSR but also many of the eastern European nations who were under the iron boot of communist oppression. This significantly contributed to the unrest in nations such as Ukraine and Georgia. After the demise of the Soviets the Russian Federation would had to rebuild their government. The new ruling order was one that would attempt retain some of its grand imperial heritage with the tsars and yet would also embrace a strong contemporary national identity. Such a task would not be easy, to say the least. Those who were experienced in government and exemplified strong leadership skills had mostly come out of the past Soviet regime. Former KGB and Soviet police remained in positions of influence and now operated as *Russian Maffia* financed by rich oligarchs who competed for power and control at every level of government. Therefore, it would be completely naïve to assume that the Russian Federation would morph overnight into a grand constitutional republic of sorts. Every government has deeply entrenched corruption and this would be a major character flaw for the Russian Federation as well. It is within this framework that after only six leaders who spanned less than a century in the Soviet order, Vladimir Putin would come to the forefront as the president of the Russian Federation. In this section I will briefly highlight Putin's political career and his rise to power. In the next chapter I will focus more on Putin's character, values and guiding philosophical presuppositions—and, more specifically, what drives him in his leadership.

In 1998, Yeltsin installed former KGB Officer Vladimir Putin as director of the Federal Security Service (FSB) which would replace the KGB. Later Putin was appointed to serve as prime minister in 1999 and publicly distinguished himself in organizing a successful military operation against separatist rebels in Chechnya. Because the military operation was a significant Russian victory, it propelled Putin into popularity and, after Yeltsin's resignation, he won the March 2000 election with 53 percent of the vote. Putin organized control over Russia's eighty-nine regions and republics by structuring them into seven federal districts with newly appointed representatives. After the 9/11 attacks on the US, Putin pledged Russia's assistance for the war against terror. With a prosperous Russian economy and with positive leadership ratings, Putin was re-elected in March 2004. His party, United Russia won an overwhelming majority of seats in the Russian parliament. Putin later stepped down temporarily from power when the integrity of the elections was questioned, and he chose Dmitry Medvedev as his successor. Later, May 7, 2008, Putin returned to office. In December 2013, he commemorated the 20th anniversary of the adoption of the Russian Federation's Constitution with the release of 25,000 individuals from Russian prisons. Putin was re-elected for a fourth term on March 18, 2018. We will now turn to Putin's contributions to the Russian Federation military and how it became a strategic fighting force as well as three significant Russian war campaigns prior to the invasion of Ukraine.

Modernizing the Russian Federation Military

Although it remained a large fighting force, the post-Soviet military, with its outdated equipment and lack of modern tactical training, had been in decline and lagged behind modern armies in comparison to NATO and the US. The aging military command structure was an antiquated remnant of the Second World War and needed improved tactical reorganization. When the USSR collapsed, scores of soldiers were in poverty and had limited rations to sustain themselves. The officer's corps were top-heavy and military leadership badly needed a significant overhaul. In 2003, a military after-action performance analysis based upon the Chechen war operations titled *Urgent Tasks for the Development of the Armed Forces of the Russian Federation* was submitted as an outline for military modernization. A lean and mean tactical force would emerge with the new Russian Federation reforms and become streamlined and mobile by shifting the basic army from 10,000 infantrymen to lighter brigades with fewer than 6,000 soldiers. Fighting forces were redesigned to support rapid deployment to areas in eastern Europe. Over two hundred generals were dismissed from military service, and sixty-five military schools were scaled down for efficiency to ten centralized military training centers. Outdated munitions and the Second World War era T-34 tanks had to be decommissioned and replaced. Beginning with the streamlined conversion of the Airborne Division, which was deemed successful in 2005, more units would be overhauled. Military Districts were folded into three regional groupings known as *Voyenny Okrugs* referred to as "VO's." The Western Command incorporated Moscow and St. Petersburg along with the Baltic and Northern Fleets and the Air Force Defense Command. The Southern Command covered the North Caucasus, the Black Sea Fleet, and the Caspian Flotilla. The remainder of the country would be supported by the Eastern Command to include the far eastern, Siberian and Pacific Fleets. The fifth Northern Artic Command was added in 2014. It included mechanized infantry and motor rifle brigades. These units could quickly deploy up to 80,000 troops within close proximity to US territories and were exercised in 2015 military training operations. Putin convinced the Kremlin that the extensive military modernization projects would require significant funding allocations, and between 2001 and 2007, the defense budget nearly quadrupled. Another significant aspect of the military reforms included cutting back on wasteful spending and the termination of High Command officers who were not deemed trustworthy with the financial accounting of budget expenditures. Spending to develop a modernized military would continue beyond the next decade under Putin's administration. By 2020 the Russian Federation National Defense Budget grew to $51.3 billion, — 2.7 percent of their GDP — making the nation the third largest military spender in the world behind the US and China. Also, Russia is the second largest global arms exporter (the US occupies the first place). The old Soviet regime had been reluctant to purchase foreign made equipment and weapons but under Putin there was an openness to acquiring new innovative weapons technology from outside sources. New T-90A tanks with advanced thermal imaging systems were acquired from French manufacturers. Also, Italian made FIAT-Iveco M65 light tactical vehicles were acquired as well as new amphibious assault ships and Israeli drones. By October 2010, the Russian Federation had developed a modernized army, navy, and air force. Shortly after the Maidan Revolution, the Russians rapidly deployed 40,000 troops to the Ukrainian border within seven days. This deployment was a record speed compared to 1999 when it took three times longer to activate a regional fighting force. The new *Ratnik* (Warrior) infantry combat fighting forces with their digital camouflage and modern body armor are the Russian soldiers of the 21st century. Media reported them as the "little green men" spotted on the Crimean Peninsula in 2014 who did not sport the traditional insignias. The Russian Federation armed forces now are estimated to number over 900,000 active-duty personnel. This also includes over 60,000 airborne and special forces. Russia's active-duty servicemen, and outsourced paid mercenaries complemented these forces. The Wagner mercenaries have been utilized since 2013 and have come to light recently in the war in Ukraine. Wagner's central commander Yevgeny Prigozhin, was nicknamed *Putin's chef* because of his love for fine cuisine, was a notorious thug, warlord, and troublemaker. The use of mercenaries is as ancient as warfare itself but can prove to be detrimental to the nation who employs them as they can be bought out by the highest bidder. Wagener can shift their loyalties to follow the money.

In addition to battle tanks and other armored vehicles, the Russian Federation has an impressive array of artillery and rocket launch systems. Their heavy multiple launch systems can easily engage targets up to fifty miles away. Their Iskander (SS-26) ballistic missile systems can deliver conventional warheads and electromagnetic pulse devices up to targets over 300 miles in distance. Also, the modern technology in their long-range supersonic and hypersonic missiles can sink enemy naval cruisers from long distances. A submarine fleet of over 13,000 can actively launch conventional and nuclear warheads on the high seas. This fleet includes ten nuclear- powered subs armed with a total of 656 warheads. Russia has one of the world's largest air forces with over 148,000 personnel, second in size only to the US. Their aircraft include a wide assortment of 1709 fixed-wing combat aircraft, 1500 helicopters, 800 MiG fighters, and more than three dozen bombers. The Russian Federation's most deadly arsenal is their stockpile of nuclear weaponry. From the USSR they inherited a full complement of over 40,000 nuclear warheads which can be launched as long-range ICBMs from rail carriages or underground missile silos. The deeply trenched missile silos northwest of Moscow has 320 rockets ready to deliver up to 1200 warheads. The nuclear option card to initiate either a first strike or counter strike is well played by Putin and should not be taken lightly if he is backed into a corner. The Russian Federation will do what it takes to defend their homeland and to protect their borders. The 2015 Victory Day parade, which had been a long-standing military tradition in Moscow with the Soviets was fundamentally different from past military marches. It was not only that the new Russian Federation uniforms were impressive, but also that a significant break from the old communist state became evident. Defense Minister Sergie Shoigu stopped his motorcade in Red Square and stood to face the church while making the sign of the cross. Shoigu one of the highest-ranking military command staff was showing his reverence for the Russian Orthodox Church a public display that would have been unthinkable during the days of atheistic USSR. Not only was there modernized military in the Russian Federation, but now there was also the rise of a new populist movement toward faith, heritage, and a national Russian patriotism. I will now turn to three significant Russian Federation wars that would enhance the nation's preparedness capabilities prior to the invasion of Ukraine.

The Georgian War (2008)

The events behind the Rose Revolution (discussed in detail in the previous chapter) helped to put Mikheil Saakashvili into power as president of Georgia. When Saakashvili began to make significant steps toward NATO and the EU, Putin was of course concerned by the aggressive pro-Western policies of Georgia's new president. The Russians suspected that the Rose Revolution had had inside support from the CIA, as well as the backing of George Soros through his Open Society Foundation. Saakashvili was defiant toward Russia and immediately increased Georgia's defense budget to 9.2 percent of the nation's GDP. This amount was five times the recommended NATO minimum.[141] The Georgian military increased in size from 28,000 soldiers to 37,000. soldiers. Saakashvili also saw to it that he would closely align himself not only with NATO but also the US as he provided 2,300 infantry soldiers to support the U.N. post-Iraqi Freedom peacekeeping force. In exchange the US provided training and military equipment to Georgia. All of this, with Georgia's bold move toward the West and the recent unilateral secession of Kosovo from Serbia further angered Russia. Another

---

[141] Galeotti, *Putin's Wars*, 123–24.

event which further provoked Putin occurred with South Ossetia — a Russian region in the South Caucasus. There had been prior conflicts between the Ossetians and Georgians. In August 2008 South Ossetians broke a ceasefire agreement with Georgia and began shelling local villages. In retaliation, Saakashvili ordered Georgian forces to bombard Tskhinvali the capital of Ossetia. Georgian forces then seized the capital and blocked the main tunnel with the Transcaucasian Highway. Soon an additional 12,000 Georgian troops were deployed to the region. The bombardment of South Ossetia continued as the Georgian artillery attacked with more than 100 mortars targeting strategic locations. This led to a confrontation when Russian peacekeeping forces and Georgian T-72 tanks exchanged fire. Later, the Russian compound was surrounded by Georgian troops. In response to Georgia's attacks, Russian airpower was mobilized to strike Georgian airbases and the Georgian military positions in the South Ossetia capital. Soon after the airstrikes, over 3,000 Russian troops were deployed to the region; however, Saakashvili was not willing to surrender. Unfortunately, Georgia's fighting force was pared down after troops were sent to Iraq. In desperation a request was made to the US for an emergency airlift to bring the Georgian troops back to the country to join the fight against Russia. But with more than 10,000 Russian troops in South Ossetia, Georgia would be forced to accept defeat after sustaining more than 2,000 casualties. Georgia also abandoned a large cache of military equipment that was seized by the Russians mostly US M16 rifles and Humvee vehicles that became trophies for the Russian Federation military. The newly modernized Russian Federation military had successfully proven their battle readiness with the victory in the Georgian war.

Crimea (2014)

Like the events of the Rose Revolution that provoked Russia in Georgia, five years later the Maidan Revolution in Ukraine would also prove to become a source of consternation. Putin viewed Ukraine as not only within its sphere of influence, but also through the lens of a very strong underlying national sentiment that identified with the millions of Russian citizens near the eastern borders. The Kremlin was alarmed at the removal of Yanukovich and the installation of a new Ukrainian president who would make significant steps toward NATO. This would put Russia's strategic positions in Crimea at greater risk with the possibility that the Federation's Black Sea Fleet could be replaced with NATO ships.[142] No doubt Putin had been looking at contingency plans for bringing Crimea back into the Russian domain to avert a NATO naval threat when things went from bad to worse in Kyiv. On the one hand, Ukraine had 22,000 military personnel stationed in Crimea. On the other hand, the Russian 510th Naval Infantry Brigade held defensive positions in the Black Sea. Russia made the decision to make an advance on Crimea around 4:30am on February 27, 2014. Russian Federation soldiers in camouflage uniforms and body armor took over the Crimean parliament building, hoisted a Russian flag over the municipal complex and set up an interim government. Over the next several days and weeks the Russians also blockaded the Ukrainian forces by closing off the neck of the peninsula. In the meantime, the Russian Federation engaged in what would be called *hybrid wars* as cyber-attacks paralyzed Ukraine's military communications. The transitional government in Ukraine could not act quickly enough to mount a counterattack in response to the Russian assault on Crimea as more Federation forces and artillery equipment were rapidly deployed. In a matter of weeks Crimea became a militarized Russian Federation zone with over 32,000 troops and reinforcements from the Black Sea Fleet. In Russia, Putin's approval ratings gained a massive popularity boost (from 60 to 80 percent) because of a successful military intervention to secure Crimea back into the Federation domain. What Russia called a legitimate annexation of Crimea to boost their own national security was quickly condemned as hostile aggression by the West. The US,

---

[142] Galeotti, *Putin's Wars*, 168-69.

NATO, and the EU all responded with economic sanctions. Ukrainian historian Serhii Plokhy has criticized Russia for being an ideological revanchist[143]: "In many ways, the current conflict is an old-fashioned imperial war conducted by Russian elites who see themselves as heirs and continuators of the great-power expansionist traditions of the Russian Empire and the Soviet Union[144]." Whether or not Russia is an aggressive advocate of revanchist foreign policy, one thing is certain Putin demonstrated to the West that its military was more than capable of retaliation against the anti-Russian color revolutionaries, and was ready to defend what they believed to be their domain.

Donbas (2014)

Spanning over 9,000 square miles the Donbas region is an industrial area rich in coal deposits that lies adjacent to the borders of southeastern Ukraine and southwestern Russia. After the Maidan Revolution of 2014 there was civil unrest between pro-Russian separatists and Ukrainian nationalists. With the annexation of Crimea, Russia had little interest initially in utilizing direct military intervention in Donbas. Likewise, earlier in the conflict, Ukraine did not deploy their military in the region either because they preferred to let volunteer militias do the fighting. This plan resulted in a messy, ill-defined conflict with fighting between Ukrainian militias and pro-Russian militias. Most of the militia groups were poorly organized and lacked a centralized chain of command. The primary pro-Russian militia leader Igor Girkin (but known by the name of Strelkov), was a former Russian FSB and artillery officer.[145] Strelkov was a renegade of sorts and an alleged war criminal with history in dirty civil wars ranging from Moldova and Bosnia to Chechnya. His militia tactics were often brutal and although

---

[143] Definition of *revanchist*: one who advocates or fights for the recovery of lost territory or status.

[144] Polkhy, *The Russo-Ukrainian War*, xxi.

[145] Galeotti, *Putin's Wars*, 180-82.

he was an outspoken critic of Putin, the Kremlin tolerated Strelkov as the leader of a proxy war in Donbas. In April 2014 Strelkov led a ragtag militia force into southeastern Ukraine, dodging both Russian and Ukrainian border guards. Fighting between the militias intensified and the international community became appalled by human rights violations committed on both sides of the conflict. The militia groups on both sides were known to harbor violent extremist groups. Some of the Ukrainian militias consisted of neo-Nazis known as the Azov Regiment who represented anti-Russian and extreme fascist political ideologies. The greatest tragedy occurred when one of Strelkov's militias shot down passenger jet Malaysian Airlines Flight, 17 killing all 298 passengers and crew aboard on July 17, 2014. The weapon fired turned out to be a Russian anti-aircraft rocket. Later an investigation was conducted by the international community but there was no evidence that Russian military commanders had authorized the attack. Evidently Strelkov's highly undisciplined irregulars were acting on their own accord and fired at what they perceived to be a Ukrainian military aircraft. Such military weapons could be easily acquired by militia forces on the black market and Strelkov could have easily brokered such a deal although some claimed that the Kremlin willingly supplied the weapon. The incident came as a complete embarrassment to Moscow, and they immediately disavowed any direct authorization for the attack. The corruption within the Kremlin combined with its renegade proxy militias proved to be deadly and costly. The tragic downing of a civilian aircraft demonstrated that the soldiers for hire are trigger happy and have little accountability to the Russian Federation.

    Tiring of the poorly organized militias Ukrainian President Poroshenko launched an anti-terrorist operation and began to deploy regular Ukrainian military troops to Donbas. When the pro-Russian separatists started losing ground to Ukrainian military forces, Moscow became concerned that the Donbas region would completely fall to Ukrainian control. Suddenly the conflict that the Russians had not wanted to be involved in all along could no longer be ignored. By early

August 2014, some 4,000 Russian troops including the airborne and T-72 tank brigades were dispatched to Donbas. As fighting continued Russia sent an additional 10,000 troops into the region. The war continued through 2021 resulting in 14,000 casualties with on and off again ceasefire agreements. The Donbas conflict clearly set the stage for the Russo-Ukraine war in 2022. The West began to focus on military capacity building missions in Ukraine as early as 2015, during the Donbas conflict, through a program called *Operation Orbital* that Great Britain launched to provide military training to Ukrainian military commanders. Russian military subject matter expert Mark Galeotti described how the Donbas conflict and the Western military support of Ukraine would later escalate into the 2022 Russo-Ukrainian War:

> The aim was to make Ukraine a tough enough enemy not lightly to be challenged. Perhaps that prospect was looking too real to Putin, though. In 2021, Russia began massing unprecedented forces around Ukraine, and after almost a year of escalating rhetoric, these were unleashed on Ukraine, in the all-out war that had been looming for almost eight years.[146]

This was exactly what happened after the wars in the Donbas region. Some military and international experts stated that the 2022 Russian invasion of Ukraine was merely an extension of the Donbas conflict that had been going on for eight years. Ukrainian historian Serhii Plokhy believes that the Russian invasions of Crimea, Donbas, and Ukraine demonstrate Putin's "flexibility in geopolitical and ideological thinking" in the overall context of Russia's ambitions for the Eurasian Union.[147] I will address Putin's vision of Eurasian conquest in more detail in the next chapter. However, Moscow did not sense a complete victory in

---

[146] Galeotti, *Putin's Wars*, 192 & 201.

[147] Serhii Plokhy, *The Russo-Ukrainian War,* 131.

Donbas as they had in Crimea but viewed it as a stalemate for both sides. If this is the true, then Russia may have decided that it was time for a checkmate move toward a complete victory in Ukraine.

The Russo-Ukraine War (2022)

Putin's Pre-Invasion Address

Just hours before the invasion of Ukraine on February 24, 2022, a prerecorded speech by Vladimir Putin was broadcast on all Russian networks. In his speech, Putin unveiled what he described as a "special military operation" whose purpose was to "demilitarize and de-Nazify" Ukraine as well as bring to trial those who perpetrated numerous bloody crimes against civilians, including citizens of the Russian Federation."[148] Although the demilitarization aspect of the operation is clearly understood, just what Putin meant by the de-Nazification of Ukraine has been a topic of considerable debate. Most of the conventional pundits simply dismiss Putin's statement as propaganda rhetoric while other viewpoints have suggested the actual presence of neo-Nazi ideologies within Ukraine. Zelensky has condemned Putin's claims for de-Nazification by referring to his own Jewish ancestry and remarking that it is part of a Russian propaganda tool as Nazi ideologies have no place in Ukraine.[149] While Zelensky's statements are admirable, the recent historical record shows otherwise. During the Orange and Maidan revolutions there was a national identity element present that embodied the Second World War anti-Soviet sentiment of the Third Reich. Germans and Russians were sworn enemies during the war and many Ukrainians with a strong anti-Russian sentiment readily identified with the Nazi war on Russia. Recall when Ukrainian President Yushchenko recognized the infamous Nazi Stepan Bandera as a national hero. Some

---

[148] Serhii Plokhy, *The Russo-Ukrainian War*, 152-53.
[149] Zelensky, *A Message from Ukraine*, 27.

historians have expressed that this was merely a symbolic gesture to affirm an anti-Russian independence identity for the nation of Ukraine. But are there actual neo-Nazis within the ranks of Ukraine? According to Russian military subject matter experts such as Mark Galeotti we do know for a fact that during the Donbas region conflict there were Ukrainian militias that had members of the Neo-Nazi Azov regiment.[150] This group represented extreme fascist ideologies and were actively involved in the war against Russian separatist militias. Of course, the pro-Russian separatist militias were certainly not saints in the least as they also harbored ideological extremists and war criminals. That is what made the Donbas Region conflict extremely precarious in the initial phases of the civil war. The other element which has come to light is that the controversial Nazi iconography has been seen on some of the uniforms of Ukrainian military.[151] NATO allies posted photos on social media with a few Ukrainian soldiers wearing the Nazi skull and crossbones patch that was worn by Third Reich concentration camp officers. Other photos featured some military personnel wearing the Black Sun symbol that was worn by Third Reich Commander Heinrich Himmler who led the Schutzstaffel (SS) officers. Some mainstream media maintain that these military patches are only meant to be symbolic, and their wearers are not true neo-Nazi practitioners because they represent contemporary expressions of patriotism and identity in the fight against Russian hostile invaders. It should be noted that these patches are not worn by all Ukrainian uniformed military but only a small minority of troops. Whatever the original intent with Ukraine's soldiers wearing these uniform patches whether symbolic or an actual ideological identity from an ethical point of view they are problematic in their historical association with Nazi Germany. And Putin's statements about

---

[150] Galeotti, *Putin's Wars*, 183.

[151] *Why Are Nazi Symbols Spotted on Ukraine's Frontlines? The Complex Issue Explained.* June 7, 2023, News 18. Source accessed July 12, 2023 from https://www.news18.com.

de-Nazification might also be an indicative reference to these military emblems worn by a few of the Ukrainian soldiers.

Putin also characterized the operation as Russia's response to a global struggle against hostilities from NATO and the West: "Focused on their own goals, the leading NATO countries are supporting the far-right nationalists and neo-Nazis in Ukraine, those who will never forgive the people of the Crimea and Sevastopol for freely making a choice to reunite with Russia…They will undoubtedly try to bring war to the Crimea just as they have done the Donbas, to kill innocent people as members of the punitive units of Ukrainian nationalists and Hitler's accomplices did during the Great Patriotic War. They have also openly laid claim to several other Russian regions."[152] Again, most of the international community have criticized Putin's remarks regarding Crimea and Donbas as purely fallacious propaganda. Others have asserted that these regions are the victims of the imperial atrocities of the Russian Federation and not the other way around. Whether you are on the Ukrainian side of seeing the invaders as deadly hostile forces that must be stopped at all costs or the Russian Federation side of protecting Eurasian security interests there are always two sides to the story. Yes, I believe that the Russian attacks on Ukraine were brutal and ruthless, and they must be called into account, however, I believe that there is also a third side perspective mentioned previously in the introduction and the first chapter. These are not simple black and white matters, rather, they have a greater complexity in the grand scheme of geopolitics. For now, I call your attention to a summary of the events in the Russo-Ukrainian War from 2022 to present day.

---

[152] Atlantic Council Blog, *Our Experts Decode the Putin Speech that Launched Russia's Invasion of Ukraine*. Source accessed December 19, 2023, from https://www.atlanticcouncil.org/blogs/new-atlanticist/markup/putin-speech-ukraine-war/.

The Initial Invasion and Key Battles

Just before 4:00am on February 24, 2022, Russian Federation forces invaded southeastern Ukraine's main regional centers.[153] Heavy artillery bombardment commenced upon multiple targets that included military installations, airfields, command and control centers and critical infrastructure as well as the capital of Kyiv. More than one hundred short-range ballistic missiles were launched from land and sea within the first few short hours of the invasion. Tens of thousands of Russian troops soon converged upon southeastern Ukraine. The first deployment of 30,000 Russian Federation troops went via the Chernobyl exclusion zone into Ukraine, and the lightly armed Ukrainian guardsmen surrendered because they were no match for the overwhelming number of Russian forces. Russian tanks and artillery soon advanced from the Belarusian border. The first major battle between the Russian Federation and the Ukrainian military took place at the Antonov International Airport just twenty-two miles north of Kyiv. The Russians wanted to gain control of the airfield for the landing of military equipment and personnel. However, the Ukrainians were able to hold off Russian forces with their artillery units. Although Russian commanders had a tactical superiority through the sheer numbers of personnel and equipment, there were several major logistical errors which prevented the initial battle from becoming a complete blitzkrieg. First, the Russian tanks had to maneuver through the narrow urban streets and had very limited turning radius to utilize their gun turrets. This made the Russian tanks easy targets for Ukrainian mortar fire attacks. In addition to lack of preparedness for the complexities of urban warfare, the second and most serious logistical error was that troops were deployed with limited rations that would only sustain them for three to five days. Russian command evidently thought that they would quickly secure the key areas in southeastern Ukraine and establish command and control centers

---

[153] Plokhy, *The Russo-Ukrainian War*, 135-215.

that would be immediately utilized for transport of fuel, supplies, and rations to the airfields. When the Ukrainian artillery was holding out in their positions on the airfields, Russian soldiers found themselves without sufficient supplies of food and water. In turn some Russian soldiers had to abandon their posts to obtain food in nearby villages. The airport battle went on for several months after the initial invasion began and was not over quickly as planned by the Russian Federation. Over the next several months tons of equipment and ammunition would come from the West and NATO allies. On the other hand, the Russian Federation had to abandon tanks and vehicles either because they ran short of fuel or were damaged by Ukrainian artillery fire. If the tactical goal of the Russian Federation was to capture Kyiv, their mission failed to accomplish its objective because some of the significant logistical blunders. Also, the Russians may not have anticipated that they would encounter as much resistance given that they planned for a surprise element.

By May of 2022, the Russian invasion of Ukraine had resulted in a mass exodus of more than eight million war refugees, mainly women and children. Whatever the Russian Federation lacked because of logistical errors in the first few months of the invasion, they were able to maintain military air superiority and short-range missile attacks. Russian forces took control of a major industrial center at the port on the Sea of Azov on May 16, 2022, and captured over 2,400 Ukrainian military. Afterwards, Russian troops converged upon Donbas which was now reinforced with Ukrainian artillery. The battle was fierce and Russian Federation forces started to gain some ground. However, as Russians had difficulty in replacing equipment, the US supplied advanced mobile rocket systems had an advantage of precision ranges up to fifty miles. These weapons allowed Ukraine to gain some tactical superiority in the Donbas region. The Russian Federation did manage significant gains in the Black and Azov Seas capturing Ukraine's third largest urban centers with a population of over a million. Also, south of the Chernobyl power plant the Russian Federation forces were able to take the region near the Dnieper River. In Crimea Ukrainian mines were set up along the area highways but they failed to detonate by the time Russian tanks and equipment entered the area. There was a significant three-day battle for the Antonivka Bridge. The Russians soon took control of the nuclear power plants in the area, including one of the largest in Europe with fifteen reactors. At the time I am writing this section, the Russo-Ukraine war has waged on for nearly eighteen months. Almost every day each side makes some small gains. What will be the outcome and which side will prevail? On the one hand, the Ukrainians maintain an advantage in terms of a steady supply of equipment and ammunition from the West and NATO allies but have a limited conscripted army. On the other hand, the Russians, although having greater numbers in terms of fighting forces, are now at a critical point with their supplies, equipment, and ammunitions because of the extensive economic sanctions.

One of the top reasons that Russia is dangerous is that they will resort to any means necessary to gain access to military resources. The shortage of arms, equipment, and ammunition has forced Putin to reach out to his Eurasian neighbors, China, North Korea, and other anti-Western nations, for assistance. This was also true in the Middle East on July 19, 2022, when Putin met with Iranian President Ebrahim Raisi in Tehran to discuss arms deals.[154] According to Israeli intelligence from Mossad, there were reports that the Russian Iran arms deal might attempt to broker nuclear materials for Iran in exchange for weapons. In April 2023, Putin met with China's defense minister to discuss foreign policy with an attempt to provide resistance to the influence of the US and NATO.[155] Xi Jinping has not criticized the Russian invasion of Ukraine, rather he has sided with Putin and blamed the US and NATO for provoking Moscow. Although there have not been talks of China

---

[154] Yonah Jeremy Bob, *Russia, Iran Weapon Supply Chain Puts Israel at Risk – Mossad Chief*, The Jerusalem Post, September 10, 2023. Source accessed September 15, 2023, from https://www.jpost.com.

[155] *Putin Meets with China's Defense Minister in Moscow*, AP News, April 16, 2023. Source accessed September 14, 2023, from https://apnews.com.

providing arms to Russia, options are certainly opened for economic and business exchanges that would provide Moscow with some relief from the burden of the economic sanctions. Back in 2014 there was a $400 billion gas deal that China made with Putin to obtain access to Russian energy. China has interests in developing its *Belt and Road* infrastructure projects to connect it with the economies of Europe, Africa, and the Middle East while recognizing Russia's dominant influence in Eurasia.[156] The two nations have shared interests in strategic military corridors with bases in Tajikistan near the Afghan border. This has become a concern for NATO—Secretary-General Jens Stoltenberg warned that China could have greater access to Europe through Russia. NATO has reason for concern over Russia-Chinese military alliances in 2018, the Vostok military exercises included over 300,000 soldiers, 36,000 tanks and 1,000 military aircraft with the participation of 3,200 Chinese military troops. China's vassal state, North Korea, enters the Russian alliance picture as well. On September 13, 2023, Putin met in Moscow with North Korean leader Kim Jong Un for a rare summit to discuss military matters.[157] Putin gave Kim a tour of his space rocket site and discussed the possibility of sending a North Korean into space. At a dinner Kim raised a glass to toast Putin's victory in Ukraine. Given that Putin senses he is backed into a corner by the West and NATO, he will utilize whatever resources he can muster to his advantage even if it means alliances with dangerous totalitarian regimes. He is an opportunist and remains determined to continue the fight in Ukraine and to hold out as long as possible. When Russia celebrated the 350th anniversary of Peter I, the czar known as Peter the Great, Putin stated the following at a Moscow ceremony: "Peter the Great waged the Great Northern War for twenty-one years."[158] Perhaps Putin like Peter the

---

[156] Galeotti, 337-39.

[157] Guy Faulconbridge & Soo-Hyang Choi, *Putin and North Korea's Kim Discuss Military Matters, Ukraine War & Satellites*. Reuters, September 13, 2023. Source accessed September 14, 2023, from https://www.reuters.com.

[158] Plokhy, *The Russo-Ukraine War*, 214.

Great may have the tenacity and the perseverance in continuing to wage the Russo-Ukrainian war. In the next chapter I will consider the various geopolitical scenarios and discuss more specifically Putin's ideology and the psychology behind the Kremlin.

Chapter Four:

Understanding Putin and Russia's Vision for Eurasian Foreign Policy

Everything that looks like Russia, isn't Quote from the fictional CIA character Jack Ryan in Tom Clancy's Jack Ryan; Season 3, Episode 7: *Moscow Rules*

To most individuals, Vladimir Putin has remained a private, enigmatic figure despite his prominence on the stage of global politics for over twenty years. The former KGB officer has remained completely private about details concerning his personal life and family. No doubt this has been ingrained firmly into Putin's consciousness through his former work in Soviet Intelligence as well as a deeply rooted self-preservation instinct where many enemies abound, and where no one can be completely trusted. Russian-born US intelligence expert Rebekah Koffler is realistic about the challenges to understanding the Russian Federation president: "Even for those American-born analysts who speak Russian, it is extremely difficult to estimate Russia's geopolitical intentions and predict Putin's behavior."[159] Mark Galeotti who is a prolific author on Russia and international security cautions us about over

---
[159] Koffler, *Putin's Playbook: Russia's Secret Plan to Defeat America*, (Washington, D.C.: Regenery Gateway, 2021), xxxiii.

analyzing Putin's psyche: "He is like a Rorschach inkblot test used by psychologists: the splash of pigment is deliberately ambiguous; what we read into it says more about what is going on in our heads than what is on the paper."[160] Regardless of the mystery persona around Putin it is necessary to achieve a basic understanding of what makes the Russian Federation leader tick, what's behind his reasoning, what are his values and beliefs. Like the ornamental *matryoshka* Russian nesting doll, we must begin by opening the larger exterior figure and continue opening each nesting doll to finally arrive at the inner diminutive figurine to get a glimpse of Putin's thoughts and intentions in the Eurasian geopolitical realm. The various opinions on the Putin persona usually fall into three interpretations especially regarding the war in Ukraine. The first is that most individuals completely vilify him as an evil character. This interpretation connects him to the former Soviet regime, who were bent on conquest and power, and thus he must be completely defeated or destroyed. Among this view's adherents is Gary Kasparov, chairman of the Human Rights Foundation, who calls Putin the leader of a "mafia state" as "Putin's Russia is clearly the biggest and most dangerous threat facing the world today."[161] In the second interpretation, some believe that Putin is misguided as he is dangerously attempting to restore Russia to its previous history of glorious imperialism by seeking violent conquest of the nations within his realm, and that he must be resisted whatever the cost. Neocons like Senator Mitt Romney and the late Senator John McCain represent this view, which is critical of Putin and Russia. Romney stated that Putin "without question is our number one geopolitical foe" and McCain stated that "Moscow must understand that it cannot enjoy a genuine partnership with the West so long as its actions at home and abroad conflict so fundamentally with the

---

[160] Galeotti, *We Need to Talk About Putin: How the West Gets Him Wrong*, (London: Penguin Random House UK, 2019), 3.

[161] Garry Kasparov, *Winter is Coming: Why Vladimir Putin and the Enemies of the Free World Must Be Stopped* (New York: Public Affairs, 2015), xi.

core values of Euro Atlantic democracies."[162] In the third interpretation, others believe that his vision for Eurasian foreign policy is either misunderstood or completely ignored resulting in the conflicts which have been transpiring for the past twenty years, and that to avoid future escalations and conflicts from occurring we need to achieve some sort of middle ground of diplomacy with Russia (and stop funding the war in Ukraine). The first two views (that Putin and Russia must be completely resisted or defeated) are the most widely accepted and supported by the international community. The third opinion — that we should arrive at some understanding and mutual consensus to deescalate conflict with Russia as well as to cease funding the war in Ukraine— is perhaps the least popular view. This view is espoused by such individuals as Senator Rand Paul who has been a vocal critic of funding the war in Ukraine: "The longer this conflict continues, the greater the risk that miscalculation or purposeful escalation draws the United States into direct conflict with Russia. Russia's military may have a bloody nose, but Moscow still maintains the largest nuclear arsenal in the world. Let's not pretend that American involvement in this war comes without risks."[163] Later towards the end of this chapter and in the last two chapters I will add a fourth theory regarding Putin within the context of the anti-Russian globalist geopolitical ideologies and the agendas of the grand liberal international order.

From the KGB to the Presidency

Vladimir Putin was born on October 7, 1952, in Leningrad (now known by its pre-Soviet, historical name St. Petersburg) just a year prior to Stalin's death. He was a street-tough kid who grew up in an impoverished neighborhood in a single-room, cramped, communal

---

[162] Plokhy, *The Russo-Ukrainian War*, 87.

[163] Dr. Rand Paul, *The Federal Government Should Not Be Held Hostage for Ukraine Funding*, September 20, 2023, site accessed September 25, 2023, from https://www.paul.senate.gov.

apartment without hot water or a private bathroom. At age twelve he began learning judo, not only based upon his interest in learning martial disciplines but also to protect himself from other juvenile rivals. Galeotti, who calls Putin a "scrappy kid whose childhood had been lived in the ruins of postwar Leningrad" describes his early disciplines in mastering judo as being formative of his geopolitical strategies:

> He does know judo, however a black belt, he has been honing his skills since starting as a teenager, and his approach to statecraft seems to reflect this. A judoka may well have prepared for a rival's usual moves and worked out countermoves in advance, but much of the art is in using the opponent's strength against him to seize the moment when it appears. In this respect, in geopolitics as in judo, Putin is an opportunist.[164]

The trademark characteristic known of Putin's political career is that he respects power and has made frequent analogies to strong fighters in martial arts having a superior advantage this would become his focused mentality for competing on the world stage. If Putin senses what he perceives as weakness in a world leader, he will not give them the time of day. This is why Putin got along with Trump so well. Russian collusion narrative supporters criticized Trump's relationship with Putin but in fact, the Russian leader tended not to escalate as many outright conflicts under Trump's watch. This is quite a contrast to Putin's total lack of respect for Joe Biden, whom he regards as mere a puppet handled by global elites. Thus, the Kremlin has been emboldened to invade Ukraine. A US president who does not resort to using proxy wars against Russia but is willing to use a direct meeting with Putin will be likely to have much more success. As a teenager Putin was impressed with the KGB and on a visit to their regional headquarters asked an

---

[164] Mark Galeotti, *We Need to Talk About Putin: How the West Gets Him Wrong*, 14-15.

agent how he could prepare himself for a career in their organization. Following the KGB officer's advice to get a degree in law, Putin enrolls at the Leningrad State University and after completing his studies, he joins the KGB in 1975. For the next seventeen years he would serve as a KGB agent and rose to the rank of lieutenant colonel. Russian historian Galeotti stated: "Putin still identifies strongly with the so-called Chekists. Many of his closest allies are veterans of the KGB and its successors, and he retains close connections with the security agencies."[165] Putin regarded General Yuri Andropov as his mentor, who was the head of the KGB from 1967 to 1982. Andropov was highly regarded as a brilliant intellectual, soldier-statesman, and devoted Russian patriot and was greatly admired by Putin. In 1985 Putin was assigned to the KGB offices in Dresden, East Germany, until the fall of the Berlin wall and was later transferred to Leningrad. Putting it into perspective, Putin grew up during the latter reformation era of Soviet history and witnessed its demise as well. As a child he experienced the de-Stalinization policies of Khrushchev and most likely heard about stories of the terror of Stalin's purge from his parents. Putin would attend the university while Brezhnev was president and experienced firsthand the early liberalization of Communism through détente. Later, at the height of his KBG career, he would witness the period of Perestroika and the ultimate collapse of the Soviet Union. Seven years later Putin would be installed by Yeltsin as director of the FSB which would replace the KGB. After that Putin is appointed to serve as prime minister in 1999 and publicly distinguished himself in organizing a successful military operation against separatist rebels in Chechnya. This set the stage for Putin to assume the office of President in 2000. Although Putin was a member of the Communist Party because it was a requirement for service in the KGB, he later completely disavowed communism. This was because of his disillusionment with the party and its ideological

---

[165] Ibid, 28.

system.¹⁶⁶ When he announced his platform to run for president, he criticized communist doctrine as leading to a dead end. Putin also blamed the Communist Party for causing the collapse of the Soviet Union and would later express that the demise of the USSR was one of the greatest tragedies in the nation's history. Even though Putin grew up in a socialist nation, he is a committed practitioner of capitalism and business enterprise through which he has bolstered the Russian economy compared to the financially destitute post-Soviet era during the 1990's. During Putin's early economic reforms, the hardcore communist adherents in the Kremlin accused him of "exploitative neo-liberal market economics."¹⁶⁷ As Galeotti stated, "Putin did not coin the phrase 'There is no such thing as a former KGB officer,' but he certainly lives it." The Russian Federation President worked as an agent during an era when enemies of the state would disappear during the night or would be assassinated. Therefore, Putin is well versed in using spy-craft tools for efficiently taking down enemy traitors. When former Russian FSB officer Aleksandr Litvinenko defected to England to work for British intelligence two Russian *Glanoye Razvedyuatelnyoe Upravlenie* (GRU) operatives killed him by lacing his cup of tea with radioactive polonium at a luxury hotel in London. Another assassination attempt via a nerve agent was made on a Russian double agent Sergey Skripal in 2018, who was working for MI6. When it comes to individuals who double-cross Putin through what he deems as acts of treason against the Russian Federation, he is not hesitant to have them assassinated. That is why US Defense Intelligence Agency specialists consider Putin as extremely dangerous. However, as a matter of perspective while most consider Putin ruthless, he has little tolerance for betrayal especially if he perceives it as a threat to national security. And if this is the case, diplomatic caution should be exercised with a world leader who has access

---

¹⁶⁶ Koffler, *Putin's Playbook*, 28-29; 61.

¹⁶⁷ Galeotti, *We Need to Talk About Putin*, 142.

to one of the world's greatest nuclear arsenals. I will address the military threat components later. For now let's consider Putin's nationalist views.

Putin's Perspective of Russian History and Nationalism

Putin came to power amid an unprecedented resurgence of Russian populist nationalism. His campaign was characterized by the promotion of a tough nationalist identity that sought to restore the past glories of imperial Russian history. Putin is a voracious reader of Russian history and an admirer of the biographies of Peter I, Catherine II, and Alexander II. Such history had been suppressed for seventy-five years because it was re-written by the Bolsheviks and the communists to support their party narratives. Now with a renewed interest in national history, those who sought restoration in the aftermath of the USSR's collapse idealized the rule of the Russian czars prior to the Bolshevik revolution as the golden era. Putin's passion for Russian history inspired his project to completely restore and revise the old Soviet exhibition square in Moscow to feature a massive national history multimedia center.[168] This center included specific sections covering Russian history from the early Byzantine Empire all the way through the czars to contemporary history. Putin encouraged Russian historical scholarship in academia and all educational institutions. In a generation that regards pride in national heritage as hyper-inflated egotism some have criticized Putin's passion for history and patriotism as primordial nationalism. He also modeled his administration after basic tenets of imperial history. Regarding this glorification of Russian Imperialism, Koffler states: "This sense of imperial exceptionalism, even during communism, was passed down through generations. Russia was the 'Third Rome,' successor to the Byzantine Empire."[169] This imperial history especially of the early 18th century,

---

[168] Galeotti, *We Need to Talk About Putin*, 46.

[169] Koffler, *Putin's Playbook*, xl.

was when Russian tsars had ascribed to three characteristics within their rule: orthodoxy, autocracy, and nationality. Current Russian polity mirrors these three historical characteristics in the Kremlin. First, orthodoxy was recognized generally within the ecclesial domain of Eastern Orthodoxy of the Byzantine tradition as opposed to the Roman Catholicism of the West. More specifically, orthodoxy that recognized the Russian Orthodox Church as part of its official religious heritage. Putin has expressed loyal allegiance to Russian Orthodoxy. Second, regarding autocracy, the monarchy of the tsars gave way to the post-Soviet Russian Federation and developed constitutional parliamentary elections representing five parties. These parties within the State Duma and the Federal Assembly under the elected president do not operate as a true constitutional republic but have retained some autocratic tendencies of rule within the Kremlin. Therefore, Russian Federation rule in comparison to conventional western democracy is inclined to be more authoritarian as a top-down government. Putin's presidency more closely resembles the system of a royal court complete with loyal servants than an actual presidential cabinet. Therefore, what Westerners see as Russian imperialism in Putin's leadership is not that far removed from his aspirations for a revival of the glorious empire of the czars. The third characteristic of the rule of the Russian tsars is also expressed in the values of the current Russian Federation and in Putin's presidency the supremacy of a strong Russian national identity. Putin is unapologetic not only of the heritage of the Russian people and culture, but also of what intrinsically constitutes their existence as a Russian nation set apart from all other nations. This identity as a patriotic Russian nationalist is what defines Putin's ambitions for a sovereign nation apart from the Western alliances in Europe and NATO. Putin is fiercely defensive of Russian nationalism and sees it as a form of exceptionalism that comes from a strength based on a thousand years of history. In his State of the Federation address in 2012, he stated that "to revive national consciousness, we need to link historical eras and get back to understanding the simple truth that Russia did not begin in 1917, even 1991...We have a common continuous history spanning over a thousand years, and we must rely on it to find inner strength in our national development."[170] This is one of the reasons that Putin and the Russian Federation does not play well with those who seek to forge a globalist union, they are quite protective of what they perceive as threats to their national sovereignty and historical identity. The role of history has also attributed to Russian hypervigilance in national security and any perceived threats from the West. The nation fought against various enemies through the ages from the Vikings of the ninth century, to the Mongols of the thirteenth century, the Swedes in the eighteenth century the French in the nineteenth century and the Germans in the twentieth century. While Putin drives the vehicle of the Russian Federation on the road ahead, looking through the windshield toward future geopolitical strategies, his strong inclinations of national self-preservation are always influenced through the rearview mirror of past historical enemies. Putin has stated: "To have a better understanding of the present and look into the future, we need to turn to history."[171] In a lengthy essay titled *On the Historical Unity of Russians and Ukrainians* he wrote:

> Russians, Ukrainians, and Belarusians are all descendants of Ancient Rus, which was the largest state in Europe. Slavic and other tribes across the vast territory – from Ladoga, Novgorod, and Pskov to Kiev and Chernigov – were bound together by one language (which we now refer to as Old Russian), economic ties, the rule of the princes of the Rurik dynasty, and after the baptism of Rus – the Orthodox faith. The spiritual choice made by St. Vladimir, who was both Prince of

---

[170] President of Russia Archives, December 12, 2012. *Address to the Federal Assembly.* Source accessed December 19, 2023, from http://en.kremlin.ru/events/president/news/17118.

[171] Ibid.

Novgorod and Grand Prince of Kiev, still largely determines our affinity today.[172]

Although many critics would argue that Putin is only interpreting history to suit his geopolitical objectives in Ukraine, the convictions guiding the Russian Federation are clearly driven by what they see as history.

Putin's Orthodox Views

In addition to the imperial era of the tsars, Putin also places a great deal of value on the history of the Russian civil war that developed in the aftermath of the Bolshevik Revolution. While Lenin's Red Army was imposing totalitarian martial law, rebel resistance forces, known as the White Army, arose for a short period of time before they were completely defeated.[173] Because Putin sees the Bolsheviks and the Red Army as the precursor to the Communist regime that destroyed the nation, he has a strong ideological affinity with the White Army resistance. Putin viewed the White Army as true patriots who fought for the vision of a united Russia that was one and indivisible. Putin was influenced by the works of Ivan Alexandrovich Ilyin, a prominent White Army political and religious philosopher. Ilyin was born in Moscow in 1883 into an aristocratic family and later embarked on a successful academic career in philosophy at the University of Moscow. He was a devout Russian Orthodox Christian and during the outset of the Bolshevik Revolution authored extensive polemics about the Bolshevik resistance movement to counter the popular views of Leo Tolstoy who promoted a pacifist position. In his most popular work, *On Resistance to Evil by Force*, Ilyin appeals to a Christian worldview by arguing that evil must be resisted

---

[172] Vladimir Putin, *On the Historical Unity of Russians and Ukrainians*, July 12, 2021. Archived at President of Russia site from http://en.kremlin.ru/events/president/news/ 66181.

[173] Plokhy, *The Russo-Ukrainian War*, 15.

at all costs: "It is the aggressiveness of evil and the need for it to pour out into external actions that make a counteroffensive necessary."[174] Therefore, using Biblical metaphors, Ilyin makes statements that the evil and atheistic forces of the Bolsheviks who were burning down churches and synagogues and executing priests and rabbis, must be fought against by those who are the righteous contenders for God and nation: "Let your sword be a prayer, and your prayer be a sword."[175] Ilyin was later exiled and died in Switzerland. After the collapse of the USSR, his writings had a tremendous resurgence in Russia and were widely read. Then in 2009 Putin negotiated for the return of Ilyin's remains to be buried in the Donskoy Monastery in Moscow. Ilyin's philosophical and theological views on resistance to evil made a considerable impact on Putin's worldview because he closely identified with Ilyin's Russian orthodoxy and patriotism. Therefore, his spiritual convictions could be defined in terms of being an Orthodox patriot resistance fighter who compares himself to Ivan Ilyin. Whereas Ilyin was fighting the atheistic Bolsheviks, Putin sees himself as holding off the forces of an evil and morally decadent western empire. Putin aligns himself with those who adhere to conservative traditional values and frequently confides in his close spiritual advisor Russian Orthodox Bishop Tikhon. The bishop is described as a Christian intellectual who is quite versed in Russian Orthodox history and has authored a best seller now translated into English *Everyday Saints and Other Stories*. Putin also played a role in leading the reunification of the Moscow Patriarchate with the Russian Orthodox Church abroad. The Russian Federation president viewed the liberal corruption of Western morality and the West's spiritual decline as existential threats to the purity of Russian values and conservative orthodoxy. Putin would maintain that Russian Orthodoxy predetermined the overall basis of the culture, civilization, and human values that unite the peoples of Russia, Ukraine, and Belarus. Putin is

---

[174] Ivan Ilyin, *On Resistance to Evil by Force*, Translated from Russian by K. Benois (London: Taxiarch Press, 2018), 153.

[175] Ibid.

a conservative traditionalist to the core and is unapologetic about his values and convictions on morality. He has zero tolerance for any individual or group that chooses to defy moral tradition. Gary Kasparov the chair for the progressive Human Rights Foundation (HRF) is a vocal critic of Russia's lack of tolerance for the LGBTQ community caused by what he calls their "unholy alliance with the Russian Orthodox Church."[176] When Pussy Riot, an all-girl punk rock group, entered a Moscow church to film anti-Russian protest documentaries, they were arrested and jailed for trespassing and for the desecration of a holy sanctuary. Russian-born Kasparov later went to Moscow to protest the group's arrest and was forcibly detained by police was but later released. Kasparov and the HRF blasted Moscow for heavy-handed authoritarianism and for being the world's greatest offender against DEI the sacred mantra of progressives. Putin and the Russian Federation aggressively defend Orthodox morality and traditional values over and against DEI doctrines. Although gay rights and transgenderism have carte blanche expression in American and European societies, they are regarded as degeneracy in Russia. With unanimous approval in the Russian Parliament, Putin signed bills banning medical procedures and surgeries used to change one's biological sexual orientation.[177] The changing of public records and personal identification to declare changes in gender are not legal including same-sex marriage licenses. In September 2022, the court in St. Petersburg upheld a prosecutor's appeal to declare that social media posts which condone or promote LGBTQ and transgenderism as socially acceptable norms are illegal in Russia.[178] Russia's imposition of moral law in most nations is outrightly

---

[176] Kasparov, *Winter is Coming*, 225.

[177] Dasha Litvinova, *Russian Lawmakers Move to Further Restrict Transgender Rights in New Legislation*, AP World News, July 13, 2023. Source accessed on September 28, 2023, from https://apnews.com.

[178] Human Rights Watch, July 15, 2023, *Russia: Trans Health Care, Families Bill Violates Rights: Intensifying Assault on LGBT Rights*. Site accessed on September 28, 2023, from https://www.hrw.org.

condemned for blurring the lines between the religious and civil affairs of society. Even in the US, secular critics of Christian political activists in the US marginalize them as deplorable Christian Nationalists. However, in Russia there exists an intrinsic element whereby church and state are regarded as inseparable. Although this offends the sensibilities of progressives who believe there should be a wall between religious and spiritual influence in civil government, it is largely status quo in Russian society. Former Defense Intelligence Agency Rebekah Koffler is disturbed by the growing trend among American Christians who are sympathetic to Putin's efforts to promote traditional conservative values.[179] Koffler believes that American people of faith have been influenced by Russian propaganda. While I am not gullible enough to believe that Putin is a righteous saint, the fact is that many American people of faith feel betrayed by their own government regarding religious liberty. With the decline of moral values in America, many religious citizens identify with Putin and Russia who appears to be actively combatting decadent liberal Western values. Putin's views of Russian history and Orthodox religion are powerful and influential components for shaping his geopolitical view. The second greatest arena of influence for shaping both the geopolitical views of Russia and the West is best understood in terms of a political science theory used to create doctrines regarding the use of military power and the shaping of foreign policy for the superpowers of the world. I will now examine one of the most important geopolitical components from both the Western perspective and the Russian-Eurasian. I will first cover the Western views (primarily the US, NATO, and the EU) of Eurasian policy. Then in the second overview I will cover specifics of the Russian version of Eurasian policy.

---

[179] Koffler, *Putin's Playbook*, 197-98.

Western Geopolitical Worldview through the Lens of Eurasian Theory

Geographically Eurasia constitutes one of the world's largest landmasses and is composed of the continents of Europe and Asia. Obviously, the greatest significance of Eurasia is not realized merely in terms of geography but in terms of its geopolitical importance for both Russia and the West after the collapse of the Soviet Union. Political scientists have varied their interpretations of what constitutes Eurasia largely from the perspective of their geopolitical interpretations and have debated what exactly are the actual borders regarding each sociopolitical entity. For example, the most simplified approach is to merely view Greater Eurasia as being made up of Russia, China, and Central Asia. Russia, however, has traditionally regarded its imperial history as defining a much larger context of Eurasia principally comprising central and western Russia, Belarus, Kazakhstan, Ukraine, Tajikistan, Turkmenistan, Uzbekistan, and part of the Caucasus regions.[180] The most significant development of nineteenth-century Eurasian political science theories came right around the two world wars in European history, when military powers swayed the balance of influence either from the perspective of Europe and its Western Allies or Russia. The most prominent Western geopolitical scholar on Eurasia during this period was Sir Halford Mackinder who began a distinguished academic career in London. His initial theories were developed in 1904 in a thesis titled *The Geographical Pivot of History*. This work pursued the purpose of a stable peace settlement during World War I and regarded interior Asia and eastern Europe as the "Heartland" which was a strategic center of the "World Island."[181] Pivot nations were key components of influence

---

[180] Britannica, *Eurasia*. September 27, 2023. Source accessed September 28, 2023, from https://www.britannica.com/place/ Eurasia.

[181] Gerald Roe Crone, *Halford Mackinder: British Political Geographer*. Britannica. Source accessed September 28, 2023, from https://www.britannica.com/biography/Halford- Mackinder.

in the Eurasian theory which could be influenced by more powerful military and industrial nations and their alliances to sway the balance of power. The pivot nations would be comparable to the outlying nations of Ukraine, Georgia, and Belarus in the dynamic of Europe versus Russia. Mackinder entered a political career in Parliament and was known for his strong views on British imperialism. Later, in 1919, he served as a high commissioner to southern Russia to unify the White Russian forces in their fight against the Bolsheviks. Prior to the Second World War, Mackinder developed a military theory based upon what he called the Atlantic Community that would be influential in offsetting the power of the Eurasian Heartland through Western Europe and North America. This political science theory which promoted a single community of nations became the precursor to NATO after the Second World War. This in turn led to Mackinder being recognized as the father of Western geopolitical theory and to one of the earliest known visionaries of a Western global alliance. Another prominent political scientist who provided some alternatives to Mackinder's theories was Nicholas Spykman a professor at Yale University. Spykman did not put as much emphasis on the significance of a Heartland as Mackinder did but emphasized a *Rimland Theory* that favored the power of the coastal areas as having the greatest geopolitical potential for military and industrial power. However, both political scientists Mackinder and Spykman played a significant role in developing nineteenth-century Eurasian geopolitical theory.

What follows is a summary of the key points of Mackinder's Heartland Theory in the context of the dynamic tension between Russia and the West. First, Mackinder believed that Europe's expansion was in response to geopolitical pressure coming from the center of Asia, known as the "Heartland."[182] The Heartland (Eurasia) was believed to be one of the most advantageous geopolitical regions, given that whoever dominated it would also be positioned for military and industrial

---

[182] A. Tsygankov, *The Heartland Theory, and the Present-Day Geopolitical Structure of Central Asia*. Corpus ID: 43319867. Published 2010 SilkRoadStudies.org.

control of the larger European continent and Eurasia combined (known as the "World Island.") Mackinder surmised that "Whoever rules East Europe commands the Heartland and whoever rules the Heartland commands the World-Island; and whoever rules the World-Island (Europe and Eurasia) commands the world."[183] Russia has maintained its belief that not only did it incorporate the Eurasian expansion of central and western Russia, Belarus, Kazakhstan, Ukraine, Tajikistan, Turkmenistan, Uzbekistan, and part of the Caucasus regions during its imperial history but also during the Soviet Bloc era to include eastern Europe. Russian political scientists argue that the Soviet Bloc since 1949 expanded the pivot area to include Poland, Hungary, Czechoslovakia, Romania, Bulgaria, Albania, and Yugoslavia within the Heartland. A more basic overview of Russian interpretation sees Central Eurasia comprising Central Europe, Central Caucasus, and Central Asia within the larger context of Europe and Asia (Eurasia). The pushback from the Western side of Eurasian theory is that Russia, after the fall of the USSR, lost control over many of the nations within its Soviet sphere of influence when these nations insisted on their own sovereign rule. The West and its Atlantic Treaty Organization asserts that Russia's Eurasian vision is hyper-inflated neo-imperial ego, and regarding eastern Europe, they need to "let bygones be bygones." This is an oversimplification of the two sides of Eurasian political science the Western and the Russian views. However, there is a greater component within Eurasian geostrategic foreign policy which must be addressed.

As mentioned in previous chapters the 1990's, with the fall of the Soviet Union brought significant US foreign policy trends were developed especially regarding Ukraine and other nations within Russia's sphere of influence. Polish-born American diplomat Zbigniew Brzezinski played a significant role in applying Mackinder and Spykman's Eurasian theories to American foreign policy. Brzezinski was a liberal idealist who held to the visionary globalist ideals fashioned in the spirit of Woodrow

---

[183] Ibid.

Wilson. Therefore, he was quite supportive of the U.N., NATO and the EU being instrumental in building a unified international order. Brzezinski was a foreign policy advisor to President Lyndon B. Johnson and later a national security advisor to President Jimmy Carter. Carter's foreign policy was one of the greatest disasters of the twentieth century especially with Brzezinski's support for the Iranian Revolution and the overthrow of Iran's pro-national prime minister who was replaced by a radical Islamic shah. From there the nation of Iran went further downhill contributing to further instability in the region under the Obama administration because they were allowed to have access to nuclear weapons technology and US funding for jihadist.[184] Brzezinski's geopolitical views, such as those on the Middle East and his policies in Iran were driven by a progressive ordering of world powers. He articulates his views on the liberal international order from the perspective of an analogy he made comparing Eurasia to a chess game:

> Eurasia is thus the chessboard on which the struggle for global primacy continues to be played. Although geostrategy – the strategic management of geopolitical interests may be compared to chess, the somewhat oval shaped Eurasian chessboard engages not just two but several players, each possessing differing amounts of power.[185]

This geopolitical chess game from the perspective of US foreign policy sees Russia as an "antagonistic Eurasian power" which must be held in check if America and its Western allies are to exercise global primacy. Brzezinski maintained that it is "imperative that no Eurasian

---

[184] Britannica, *Zbigniew Brzezinski: United States Statesman & Scholar*. September 18, 2023. Source accessed October 2, 2023, from https://www.britannica.com/biography/Zbigniew- Brzezinski.

[185] Zbigniew Brzezinski, *The Grand Chessboard: American Primacy & Its Geostrategic Imperatives*. (New York: Basic Books, 1997), 31.

challenger emerges" as he praised Woodrow Wilson's Fourteen Points global manifesto with emphasis upon European geopolitics reinforced by "American might." The Fourteen Points sought to justify American intervention in World War One with the objective "to vindicate the principles of peace and justice in the life of the world."[186] Wilson's theory which was delivered to a joint session of congress on January 8, 1918, outlined the obtaining of peace with "a new balance of power" and the formation of a League of Nations (the precursor to the United Nations). Brzezinski concludes that this plan was dominated by "fifty years of bipolar American-Soviet contest for global supremacy: "The geopolitical dimension could not have been clearer: North America versus Eurasia with the world at stake. The winner would truly dominate the globe.[187]" And when the Soviet Union collapsed, the United States and its western allies had the opportunity to emerge as the true global power. Brzezinski insisted that this Eurasian advantage over Russia would be maintained institutionally by NATO and its partnerships with the US to be a key player in intra-European affairs. He insisted that the US through its global web of international agencies with the IMF and the World bank would be a stakeholder in the international economy. Brzezinski emphasized the critical role of Eurasia for the US and NATO:

> For America, the chief geopolitical prize is Eurasia. For half a millennium, world affairs were dominated by Eurasian powers and peoples who fought with one another for regional domination and reached out for global power. Now a non-Eurasian power is preeminent in Eurasia – and America's global primacy is directly dependent on how long and how effectively its preponderance on the Eurasian continent is sustained.[188]

---

[186] US State Department Office of the Historian, *Wison's Fourteen Points, 1918*. Source accessed October 3, 2023, from https://history.state.gov.

[187] Brzezinski, *The Grand Chessboard*, 31.

[188] Zbigniew Brzezinski, *The Grand Chessboard*, 29.

Brzezinski was quite anti-Russian in his beliefs as he insisted that they were the "antagonist" threatening globalism in the Eurasian arena and that US primacy must play a crucial role in ensuring peace. To this end according to Brzezinski, "Eurasian geostrategy involves the purposeful management of geo-strategically dynamic states and the careful handling of geopolitically catalytic states through institutionalized global cooperation." Who are the strategic players in this global cooperation? Brzezinski defined these players as Ukraine, Azerbaijan, South Korea, Turkey, and Iran because they are the crucial geopolitical pivots: "Given the growing consensus regarding the desirability of admitting the nations of Central Europe into both the EU and NATO, the practical meaning of this question focuses attention on the future status of the Baltic republics and perhaps also that of Ukraine." Brzezinski saw Eurasia as America's geostrategic stake in Europe and an enormous factor in developing a globalist international order. There are a few political scientists who have made a more honest assessment of the dangers in driving US foreign policy with the Eurasian balance of power including Christopher J. Fettweis. Fettweis criticized the Clinton administration which established foreign policy precedents for Ukraine, as "running a foreign policy that is at best reactive and at worst rudderless and confused."[189] Fettweis's article for the US Army War College Quarterly mentions that individuals such as Brzezinski are not the only movers and shakers in US foreign policy that have been influenced by Mackinder's Eurasian principles: "From Harry S. Truman to George Bush, the overarching vision of US national security was explicitly geographical and directly traceable to the Heartland theory of Mackinder." Fettweis also mentioned Henry Kissinger and Madeleine Albright as envisioning a grand geopolitical chessboard strategy for Eurasia. These are the foreign policy makers who have dictated a globalist vision for the international progressive order both Democrat and Republican

---

[189] Christopher J. Fettweis, *Sir Halford Makinder, Geopolitics & Policymaking in the 21st Century*. US Army War College Quarterly: Parameters; Vol. 30, Number 2, Summer 2000; Article 3. Army War College Press.

alike. And the conflict with Russia is only further exacerbated with the preeminence of a Eurasian Western primacy. The greatest downside will always be the inevitable pushback from the other side of the Eurasian interpretation, that of Russia which will result in a costly conflict with nothing to be gained for the United States. Fettweis stated this quite well:

> The inability to understand the other's view is one of the greatest historical features of US foreign policy. We still are not able to understand that the quest for empire in Russian history is at least in part an attempt to bolster the insecurity that its position has always entailed. Russia's imperial outposts in Eastern Europe, Central Asia, and elsewhere provided buffer zones against the attacks that have periodically devastated Russian land. Central positioning has led to a state of permanent insecurity, which has poisoned Russia's relations with its neighbors...Some observers assume that Russian meddling in the affairs of the states on its periphery is an inevitable sign of neo imperialism, which is a permanent characteristic of its eternal national character. To head off any return to empire, many feel that the West must be firm in discouraging a growth in Russian influence in the new states. Thus, the United States is interested in projecting power into Central Asia in the belief that filling power vacuums is necessary to prevent the Russians from doing so, and to keep the Cold War from recurring.[190]

Therefore, much of the American foreign policy in contention with Russia has been driven by this theory of the Eurasian primacy of the West. This theory has also set the stage for events that transpired in

---

[190] Christopher J. Fettweis, *Sir Halford Makinder, Geopolitics & Policymaking in the 21st Century*, 6-7.

Ukraine in the last few decades as well. The events that are unfolding with the proxy war in Ukraine make a grand contest of western Eurasian geopolitical theory. The West and its allies believe that it should be in everyone's best interest to pour billions of dollars into the war machine in Ukraine, one of the most corrupt nations on earth to offset the balance of power toward a global new world order. Meanwhile, our borders are porous, our economy is in shambles, our military power is emasculated, and our nation is on a destructive course to further undermine our national sovereignty by bowing to the global elites. Having covered the Western geopolitical view of Eurasian policy, I will now turn to consider the Russian interpretations of their vision for a Eurasian Union.

The Russian Vision for Building a Eurasian Union

Russia has held to an extensive view of their Eurasian domain: western Russia, Belarus, Kazakhstan, Ukraine, Tajikistan, Turkmenistan, Uzbekistan, and part of the Caucasus regions during its imperial history and the pre-Soviet Bloc era of eastern Europe. It has also been quite protective of what it considers to be the buffer-zone countries of Ukraine, Belarus, and Georgia. One of Russia's most influential political scientists, Vladimir Karyakin has contributed to the development of Moscow's most prolific geopolitical views. He is a retired USSR military officer and has specialized in research for the Kremlin regarding strategic nuclear weapons deployment and is part of a Russian Federation geostrategic think-tank known as the Center for Middle Eastern Studies (Russian acronym–ORSAM). Karyakin is also critical of the philosophical framework of postmodernism in contemporary geopolitics which essentially rejects traditional values of rationality, objectivity, and universal truth by deconstructing conservative institutions such as nationalism, faith, and religion for the pursuit of globalism. He sees a major paradigm shift in the geopolitical construct with the demise of the Soviet Union: "The collapse of the USSR has been one of the most important developments of our modern history. After the collapse of the USSR and the Eastern Bloc, the world map was reconstructed, new countries emerged and took place on the aforesaid map, the bipolar world order turned into a unipolar world order, and countries started to face very different threats."[191] Here he reflects the conventional Russian-Eurasian political science opinions that the post-Soviet era of a unipolar world order (globalism) opposes to a bipolar one (from the perspective of competing nationalist states). This postmodern geopolitical shift according to Karyakin has resulted in a permanent crisis with regards to the color revolutions such as the Rose, Orange, and Maidan revolutions which were essentially anti-Russian. This problem within the Eurasian construct is what he refers to as a Third Wave" in international trends toward the transformation into a new global order. Karyakin insists that this Third Wave trend towards globalization results in poverty and injustice as nations relinquish their sovereignty. He also criticizes the theories of Brzezinski's geopolitical chessboard as an imperative which calls for Eurasia to submit to the West.

In addition to Russian political scientist Karyakin the second most influential Eurasian visionary is Alexander Dugin who is not only regarded as eccentric but is also highly controversial in the light of popular public opinion. Whereas Vladimir Karyakin is regarded as a milder representative of Russian political science with influence on Russian foreign policy, Dugin is like the wild *Mad Hatter* in the Russian version of the Eurasian theory. In addition to his position as the head of Moscow State University's Department of Sociology, he is an advisor to the Kremlin on geopolitical matters. Dugin is also considered the leader of the International Eurasian Movement and is a flamboyant and outspoken political commentator in Moscow. He launched the Center for Geopolitical Expertise in the Kremlin and works closely with the Russian Federation, and the presidential administration, where he has been a foreign policy advisor to Putin. Because of his importance in

---

[191] Vladimir Karyakin, *The Third Wave: Geopolitics of Postmodernism*, ORSAM Report No. 131; The Black Sea International Report Number 26, November 2012. The Black Sea International Center for Research & Dialogue, Moscow.

the Russian geostrategic realm and chiefly with the political dynamic of Eurasia, I devote considerable space in this section to examine Dugin's core position and worldview. If we want to understand Putin and the ambitions of the Russian Federation, I believe that understanding Dugin is key. Dugin's early academic life from his teens into college would not be easily forthtelling of a future political career. Although he was born into a distinguished military family as a son of a GRU officer, in his youth he lived an eclectic bohemian lifestyle prior to the fall of the Soviet Union. He enrolled in the Moscow Institute of Aviation in the early 1980's and was later expelled when the KGB learned that he had attended a party of free-thinking hippies in a painter's studio and played the guitar while singing anti-communist songs. The KGB reported that he was in possession of "banned political literature" which included the works of the exiled Alexander Solzhenitsyn.[192] Dugin's early student radical days on campus sounds more like a 1960's Berkley University hippy than that of a geopolitical analyst. After being expelled from the Aviation Institute he later got work as a street-sweeper but had access to the Lenin Library with a forged library card. Dugin had a voracious appetite for reading and was known to dabble in every subject from world philosophy, and mysticism, to neo-paganism in his early days. Later, after the fall of the USSR, he began to search for existential meaning in the context of Russian history, traditionalism, and Russian Orthodoxy. Dugin turned his focus to political science and developed conservative concepts for a new Russian nation in the context of Eurasian geopolitical principles. Although he has authored several books on politics, one of his most influential, written toward the end of the COVID-19 pandemic, titled *The Great Awakening vs. The Great Reset*. In this book Dugin sets forth his counterargument against the globalist manifesto of Davos elite Klaus Schwab, *COVID-19: The Great Reset*. His concept of a Great Awakening is an antithetical proposal to

---

[192] James D. Heiser, *The American Empire Should Be Destroyed: Alexander Dugin & the Perils of Immanetized Eschatology*, (Malone, TX: Repristination Press, 2014), 36 & 42.

the Great Reset which he defines as follows: "The Great Awakening is a kind of philosophical and metaphysical program, a manifesto that deals with the Great Reset as an absolute evil...The Great Reset is a kind of conceptual chariot of the Antichrist, and in order to fight against him, we need to have a spiritual weapon, not only a technical one...I think the Great Awakening should be an awakening of the spirit, an awakening of the thought, an awakening of the culture, an awakening of our almost-lost roots." The book is an interesting read and vocalizes many conservative opinions of Dugin which rail against a globalist world order reset which I highlight in the following bullet points:[193]

- "Nominalism laid the foundation for future liberalism, both ideologically and economically. Here humans were seen only as individuals and nothing else, and all forms of collective identity (religion, class, etc.) were to be abolished." (page 8)

- "In the 1990's, liberal theorists began to talk about the end of history...and the unipolar movement." (page 11)

- "The ruling elite's strategy of globalism triumphed – outlined in the First World War by Wilson's Fourteen Points, but at the end of the Cold War united the elite of both parties, Democrats and Republicans, represented mainly by neoconservatives." (page 11)

- "Gender politics, the transformation of the category of gender into something optional and dependent upon individual choice...Combatting conservatives and homophobes that is, defenders of the traditional view of the existence of the sexes, has become the new goal of the adherents of progressive liberalism." (page 12)

---

[193] Alexander Dugin, *The Great Awakening vs The Great Reset*. (London: Arktos, 2021)

- "The last step for liberals, who have traveled centuries toward their goal, is to replace humans, albeit partially, by cyborgs, artificial intelligence networks...This agenda is already foreshadowed by posthumanism, postmodernism, and speculative realism."

    "This is the context in which Biden's engineered victory in the US should be placed. This is what the Great Reset or the slogan *Build Back Better* means." (page 13)

- "Liberalism was increasingly resisted by Putin's Russia, which has nuclear weapons and a historical tradition of opposition to the West as well as a number of conservative traditions preserved in society." (page 14)

- "If Trump had kept his office, the collapse of the globalist strategy would have been irreversible. But Biden succeeded, by hook or by crook, in ousting Trump and demonizing his supporters. This is where the Great Reset comes into play." (page 20)

- "The globalist candidate, Hillary Clinton, recklessly called Trump supporters, i.e., the domestic enemy, deplorables...The deplorables responded by electing Trump. This was a disaster for the globalists. Until Trump was dumped by means of a color revolution, engineered riots, fraudulent ballot, and vote-counting methods." (page 19)

- "From now on, Trumpism, populism, the defense of family values, and any hint of conservatism or disagreement with the tenets of globalists in the US will be nearly equivalent to a crime to hate speech and fascism." (page 22)

- "The Great Awakening is the spontaneous response of the human masses to the Great Reset." (page 29)

- "The rejection of liberalism and globalization has become particularly acute in recent years, as liberalism itself has revealed its deeply repulsive features to Russian consciousness. This justified a certain sympathy among Russians for Trump and a parallel disgust for his liberal opponents." (page 39)

Many of Dugin's points read like those of a conservative American patriot with his outspoken opposition to globalism and the liberal international order. He covered a wide range of topics from an ultra-conservative perspective: traditional family values, gender politics, the conservative critique of *Build Back Better*, and even support for Donald Trump's conservatism. Dugin used very interesting metaphors as he called the one world globalist elites evil, even comparing them to an Antichrist and describes conservatives and traditionalists as being in a battle against a liberal regime. Being a paleoconservative[194] (see footnote) in my own personal political orientation, most of Dugin's points that I have listed do resonate with me. However, there are statements which he made in his book that I do have serious problems with. First, although he has a great distrust for the world banking institutions and their progressive trends toward a liberal economic order (and I share the same sentiment), Dugin's views on free market capitalism are rather jaded. He tends to throw the baby out with the bathwater by criticizing capitalism for having ties to the corrupt global economy. Whereas I agree that some institutional capitalist systems within companies like big tech and those that are in alliance with totalitarian states

---

[194] Paleconservatism is a movement within American conservativism that seeks to preserve the nation's Judeo-Chrisian heritage as well as the patriotic ideals of the 1776 Founders. Other values of a paleoconservative include the limitation and decentralization of federal government, restriction of illegal aliens, greater border security, free market capitalism, and an "America First" policy.

like Communist China can be used for corrupt purposes, I am firmly committed to free-market capitalism and see it as a defensive weapon against democratic socialism. The other point that I have contention with Dugin is his opinion that China and Iran are not players among the global elites regarding the new world order. He is favorable toward them as adversarial forces against globalism. I suspect that he takes this position first because China and Iran are within the outer periphery of Eurasia, and second, because Russia has demonstrated a willingness to turn to these nations as a friend in time of need with the given anti-Russian sentiment from the West. I will address this in more detail later especially regarding Iran and Putin's opportunistic use of the Middle East to serve his interests. I see Communist China and Iran as existential threats and do not view them with the same level of tolerance that Dugin calls for. The other aspect of Dugin's worldview that readers must understand is that he is difficult to pin down into one primary category of interpretation. Scholars such as Marlene Laruelle who have studied Dugin's literature extensively, consider him to be an intellectual enigma: "While Eurasianism and geopolitics are Dugin's most classic and best-known business cards for public opinion and the political authorities, his philosophical, religious and political doctrines are much more complex and deserve careful consideration."[195] He tends to be syncretistic in both his philosophical and religious views. For example, although he stakes a claim in traditional Russian Orthodoxy and frequently uses religious, spiritual, and even eschatological metaphors, he is influenced by a wide spectrum of belief, not only in the Christian religion, but also gnostic and neopagan mysticism as well. Theologians such as James Heiser have written extensive doctrinal and theological reviews of Dugin's beliefs. Heiser who is critical of Dugin's eclectic spirituality describes his blending of spiritual worldviews: "It would be our contention that Dugin's fusion of Traditionalism and Eurasianism has become

---

[195] Marlene Laruelle, *Aleksandr Dugin: A Russian Version of the European Radical Right?* Woodrow Wilson International Center for Scholars; Kennan Institute Occasional Paper #294. (Washington, D.C.: Kennan Institute, 2006), 6.

a 'gnostic mass movement' of the third type, 'activist mysticism.'"[196] For instance in some of his writings, Dugin describes the northern geographic regions of Russia with metaphysical overtones: "Thus, North in Tradition is a meta-historical and meta-geographical reality. The same can be said also about the 'hyperborean race' – a 'race' not in the biological, but in a pure spiritual, metaphysical sense."[197] With the limited space here my purpose is not to provide an in-depth examination of Dugin's religious, spiritual, and philosophical views, but rather to show the key influence he has on Putin and the Russian Federation especially with his views on Eurasia. For readers who wish to take a deep dive into Dugin's philosophical views I would recommend the research of Marlene Laruelle and for those who want to further understand his eclectic spiritual and religious beliefs I refer you to James D. Heiser. For now, I will examine the specifics of Dugin's Eurasian policy principles.

Alexander Dugin would fit in the context of the more contemporary views of Eurasianism known as neo-eurasianism. The classical nineteenth-century Eurasianists such as Mackinder and Spykman along with the 1990's US foreign policy views of Brzezinski looked at applying Eurasian geopolitical principles as a means for containment of the USSR through swaying the balance of power to the Heartland so it could dominate the overall World Island (Europe, eastern Europe, and Eursasia combined) through the Western global alliances (US, NATO and the EU). This western geopolitical chessboard theory is still maintained today with respect to the Russian Federation and events that are currently unfolding in Ukraine. On the other side is the neo-Eurasian counterview that Dugin has developed in Russia since the 1990's. Dugin described his vision for Eurasia in his book *The Great Awakening vs The Great Reset* in a section subtitled *Russia Awakening: An Imperial Renaissance*:

---

[196] Heiser, *The American Empire Should Be Destroyed*, 103.

[197] Ibid., 85.

> What does it mean for Russia in such circumstances to "awaken"? It means fully restoring Russia's historical, geopolitical, and civilizational scale, becoming a pole of the new multipolar world. Russia has never been just a country, much less just one among other European countries. For all the unity of our roots with Europe, which go back to Greco-Roman culture, Russia at all stages of its history has followed its own particular path. This also had an impact on our firm and unwavering choice of Orthodoxy and Byzantinism in general, which largely determined our estrangement from Western Europe, which chose Catholicism and later Protestantism. In the modern age, this same factor of profound distrust of the West was reflected in the fact that we were not so affected by the very spirit of modernism in nominalism, individualism, and liberalism.[198]

Here are the three primary neo-Eurasian principles which can be deducted from Dugin's statement. First, the great awakening is a new national patriotic vision that sets Russia apart and considers the sum of Russia's imperial history to be unique among other European nations. This Russian exceptionalism, according to Dugin is not only derived from the era of the czars, but recedes even further into its early Greco-Roman roots. Second, the emphasis upon the Byzantine Orthodox church is also unique in the sense that it is set apart from western Catholicism and Protestantism. And third, because western philosophy and spirituality have corrupted the spirit of modernism in nominalism, individualism, and liberalism is rejected. The common theme of Dugin's writings is that Russians have a profound distrust of the West because of its corrupt moral, spiritual, and philosophical values, and institutions. Not only is there an effort to bring about this grand

---

[198] Dugin, *The Great Awakening Vs the Great Reset*, 40-41.

Imperial Renaissance through an awakening of the Russian people, but also the neo-Eurasian principle suggests a continuity of preservation and defense from aggressors. According to Dugin:

> Genghis Khan was an important lesson for Russia in centralized organization of the imperial type, which largely predetermined our rise as a great power in the fifteenth century when the Golden Horde collapsed, and Muscovite Russia took its place in the space of northeast Eurasia. This continuity with the geopolitics of the Horde naturally led to the powerful expansion of subsequent eras. At every turn, Russia has defended and asserted not only its interests, but also its values... Empire has become our fate.[199]

Here Dugin stated that the Russian neo-Eurasian principle is based upon a historically conceived notion that Russia will continue to defend its interests and values in the face of any aggressor because this principle has been determined as the fate of the Russian Empire. Laruelle added that Dugin's of Empire is quite an ambitious one:

> Dugin calls for a restoration of the Soviet Union and a reorganization of the Russian Federation. He is the only Neo-Eurasianist to include in his political project not only the Baltic States, but the whole former socialist bloc. His Eurasia must even expand beyond Soviet space, as he proposes to incorporate Manchuria, Xinjian, Tibet, and Mongolia, as well as the Orthodox world of the Balkans: Euraisa would only reach its limits with geopolitical expansion to the shores of the Indian Ocean.[200]

---

[199] Dugin, *The Great Awakening*, 41.

[200] Laruelle, *Aleksandr Dugin*, 7.

In addition to an ambitious vision for a Russian empire, Heiser added that Dugin's Eurasian theories also tend toward a mystical concept of geography with Russia at the center of influence: "In his article *From Sacred Geography to Geopolitics*, Dugin makes it clear that he wholeheartedly subscribes to a Traditionalist interpretation of the world in which geopolitical realities have mystical meanings."[201] To conclude this overview of Dugin's Eurasian geopolitics, the following is a list of the most important principles that influence Putin and the Russian Federation:

- A renaissance of the Russian empire is the manifest destiny of the Russian Federation.

- The West and its allies have been corrupted by postmodernism and liberalism. Russia must resist the ideological corruption of the West at all costs by relying upon traditionalism and Orthodoxy.

- Russia will defend itself no matter what the cost from any perceived enemies or aggressors – a lesson learned from Russia's long history of military conflicts.

- Globalism is evil and Russian nationalism must rise to the occasion to resist the Great Reset agenda and to protect Russia's national sovereignty.

- Russia's geopolitical domain is Eurasia, and it must continue to assert its influence to hold back Western aggressors (US, NATO and the EU).

---

[201] Heiser, *The American Empire Should Be Destroyed*, 86.

These are the neo-Eurasian principles of Alexander Dugin that drive Russian Federation doctrine and geopolitical policies. After considering some of the key philosophical, religious, and geopolitical views of the Russian Federation and those of their leader Putin, it is important to address a balanced threat assessment. The predominant Western view is that if we simply resort to the cold war era containment strategies to keep Russia held in check, as we did with the former USSR, then Europe and its allies can build their international liberal order, envisioned since the days of Woodrow Wilson, in peace. There are some who even hope that Russia someday will turn from its nationalist and autocratic ways and become progressively enlightened enough to embrace a unipolar political dynamic. These lofty neoliberal views downplay the chance that Russia would ever resort to using the full force of its military weaponry and power if backed into a corner. They see Russia kept at bay by Ukrainian forces if Ukraine is supplied with a steady stream of weapons and ammunition from the Western international order. The optimistic and hopeful outcome is for Russia to eventually lay down their arms and back off from Ukraine in inevitable defeat as they are weakened by international economic sanctions and beaten as a military aggressor. Yet, (at the time of this writing) we do not know what the precise outcome of the Russo-Ukraine War will be. It could be a lengthy protracted war with no end in sight unless some extensive diplomatic solutions are brokered, but at what cost?

Why We Must Not Underestimate Putin and the Russian Federation

Given the current Western geopolitical game of chess that has been consistently demonstrated by US foreign policy, Russia has been and continues to be seriously underestimated. The cold war-era ideology of Soviet containment through the reinforcement of a NATO wall of resistance has failed to provide stability in Europe and has further eroded relations with the Russian Federation over the past thirty years. Pouring billions of dollars into the corrupt nation of Ukraine to fight a proxy war to achieve a liberal international order has put us on a dangerous path of collision with a nuclear state that will defend its place in Eurasia no matter the cost. There were two historical cold war events both in 1983, that nearly precipitated a nuclear strike between the West and Russia. The first event occurred on September 26, 1983, when Lieutenant Colonel Stanislav Petrov was the commanding night shift duty officer for the Soviet Air Defense Forces.[202] Petrov was called in to fill the shift for another officer who became ill. He was monitoring the Russian satellite warning systems when his alert panel lit up shortly after midnight. The system showed that an American ICBM had just been launched from the US and four more missiles were on the way. According to Soviet military defense protocols Petrov as the highest-ranking officer after confirming that an enemy attack had been launched, was in the command chair position to notify his superiors who would in turn order a nuclear counter strike. However, Petrov delayed based upon his suspicions that only five missiles would hardly constitute enough launches for the US to initiate an all-out strike, many more missiles would have to be deployed. Also, Soviet radar installations were not confirming any heat trail signatures that would be present during an actual launch. Fortunately, Petrov reacted based on his gut-instinct rather than conventional Soviet counterstrike protocols. He reasoned that there could have been a malfunction with the Russian satellites, and this explanation was later confirmed. Things might have turned out differently if Petrov who was later credited as the *Man Who Saved the World* was not on duty that night. Political science foreign policy subject matter expert Michael Anton recounted how a second near nuclear mishap had occurred in 1983 during the cold war when sixteen NATO states along with the US participated in a military exercise code named

---

[202] Dan McEwen, *Stanislav Petrov: The Man Who Saved the World*, History on the Net, Salem Media, 2000. Source accessed October 12, 2023, from https://www.history-onthenet.com.

"Able Archer."[203] Anton described the exercise as not merely military but also political in scope with major western heads of state represented, including Margaret Thatcher, Helmut Kohl, and Ronald Reagan. The exercise commenced on November 7, 1983, rolling out simulations that included NATO alert phases to move to DEFCON 1, which involved the deployment of nuclear weapons and NATO bombers in an attack on the Soviets. The exercise which was later declassified in 2015 had overlooked one essential element, the Russians did not know that it was merely an exercise and went to high alert status in anticipation of a retaliatory strike. Anton describes this harrowing near nuclear Armageddon with NATO and Russia as follows: "In 1983, both sides misunderstood one another. The Americans assumed that the Soviets knew that all those fly-bys, flyovers, fleet maneuvers, dummy warheads, and DEFCON escalations were just drills. The Soviets, for their part, knew no such thing. They really believed that it all might be prelude to a surprise first strike." This time it was an American who is credited with diverting a nuclear catastrophe, Lieutenant General Leonard Perroots.[204] Perroots was the intelligence officer in the US Airforce European Defense Division at Ramstein Airbase. When Perroots intelligence units confirmed that the Soviets had gone to counterstrike alert status, he immediately informed his superiors, and the Able Archer exercise quickly stood down.

Both events demonstrate the willingness of the Russians to exercise nuclear options against the US and NATO. Some would argue that the stakes are not as high as they were in 1983, given that we are now in a post-cold war/post-Soviet era. However, Anton makes the following comment that this reasoning is devoid of both logic and common sense as it downplays Russia's nuclear option capability regarding Ukraine:

---

[203] Michael Anton, *Nuclear Autumn* Claremont Review of Books; Volume XXII, Number 4, Fall 2022. Upland, CA. 39.

[204] Center for Arms Control & Non-Proliferation, *The Soviet False Alarm Incident & Able Archer 83*. Source assessed October 12, 2023, from https://armscontrolcenter.org.

The way in which the stakes are higher should be equally obvious. Unlike 1983, 2022 is defined by a hot war, in which Russia is a belligerent. This time the Kremlin isn't watching a bunch of troop movements wondering whether they're an exercise or the prelude to war. They *know* we're arming Ukraine, providing targeting information that's killing Russian generals, and using our power over the global financial system to try to strangle their economy – a far cry from merely banning Aeroflot for a few years. Moscow held back in 1983 in part because, at the decisive moment, we held back. That's not what we're doing now...Some especially ardent neoliberals insist that the risks are necessary to defend the "rules-based liberal international order."[205]

These same neoliberal talking heads who are willing to push us into nuclear annihilation also ignore the Eurasian geopolitical ambitions of Russia and the reality of their military doctrine. Former defense agency intelligence analyst Rebekah Koffler confirms the reality of Putin's willingness to play his nuke card when prompted:

> Putin's doctrine is focused on Russia's preparedness to fight a limited war – including with nuclear weapons – with the narrow objective of "defending" what Moscow views as its strategic perimeter. In other words, the nuclear option is not a theoretical doctrine. It has battlefield utility.[206]

Koffler also adds that Russian nuclear capabilities are not the only arsenal that they can utilize but they also have arsenals in all the

---

[205] Anton, *Nuclear Autumn*, Claremont Review, Volume XXII, No. 4, Fall 2022.
[206] Koffler, *Putin's Playbook*, 259-61.

domains of air, sea, land, space, and cyberspace. The Russians regularly practice simulated nuclear launch drills to maintain their readiness – this time there might not be a Petrov (*The Man Who Saved the World*) in the command center to delay a launch. Now the driving force of influence is not the old Soviet regime but a new Eurasian geopolitical order in Russia as captured in the words of Putin's geopolitical security advisor Alexander Dugin: "Liberalism was increasingly resisted by Putin's Russia, **which has nuclear weapons** (italics mine) and a historical tradition of opposition to the West as well as a number of conservative traditions preserved in society."[207] Rather than pouring billions of dollars into a corrupt nation with the idea that they will fight a corrupt Russian regime and prevail on behalf of a liberal international order there needs to be a serious critique of the disastrous foreign policies that have failed for the past several decades in Ukraine and in places such as the Middle East. Reform of our foreign policy is needed to arrive at working solutions for the Russo-Ukrainian war. Senator Rand Paul's remarks on the US Senate floor call for the need for such reforms: "As elected officials, we have an obligation to pursue a foreign policy that advances the security and prosperity of our country, funneling billions of dollars that must be borrowed into the meat grinder of eastern Ukraine does neither. The longer this conflict continues, the greater risk that miscalculation or purposeful escalation draws the United States into direct conflict with Russia."[208]

Putin, Hamas, Israel, and the Middle East

With the deadly Hamas attacks on Israel on October 7, 2023, questions have come to the forefront regarding Putin's Middle East foreign policy stance: Is Russia complicit in the terrorist attacks and what of

---

[207] Dugin, *The Great Awakening*, 40.

[208] Dr. Rand Paul, US Senator for KY, *Dr. Rand Paul Puts Congress on Notice, Opposes Ukraine Spending at the Expense of American Taxpayers*. September 20, 2023. Source accessed October 12, 2023, from https://www.paul.senate.gov.

their relationship with nations like Iran? To address these questions, I will need to consider the primary regions in the Middle East which are regarded as crucial for the Russian Federation to maintain an axis of power. Putin is an opportunist and will develop relations to gain access to international regions he considers beneficial to Russia's strategic interests. To the south of Eurasia, Russia considers the nations of Turkey, Syria, Iraq, Iran, and Afghanistan not only a gateway to the Middle East corridor for Russia, but they are also considered as pivots of influence that will provide advantage over the presence of the United States and other Western allies in Middle Eastern affairs. Putin has been known to negotiate with Middle Eastern nations that are under the influence of Islamic radicals in exchange for Russia to gain military equipment, supplies and regional access and he does so whenever he sees an opportunity to gain an advantage over the West. However, closer to the homeland of Russia he has zero tolerance for Islamic extremists. This is a strange paradox of sorts especially for a leader of the Russian Federation who can just as easily on the one hand sit at the same table with Middle Eastern leaders for geopolitical gain and yet on the other hand be ready to carry out deadly force against extremists in his own homeland. The Chechen wars highlight Putin's swift military operations upon Middle Eastern grown terrorists who infiltrate Baltic State regions. The Chechen government in the hands of Muslim moderates was in shambles and an easy prey for extremists to gain foothold. Saudi-born Thamir Saleh Abdullah fought against the Soviets in Afghanistan and later joined the Al-Qaeda ranks with 9/11 terror mastermind Osama Bin Laden.[209] Thamir illegally entered Chechnya under the guise of a journalist and began training and recruiting radicals who would actively declare jihad across the North Caucasus to drive out Christian Russia and to create an Islamic caliphate. In September 1999, jihadists from Chechnya bombed civilian apartment buildings in Moscow, the North Caucasus, and southern Rostov killing more than 300 residents

---

[209] Galeotti, *Putin's Wars*, 84-85, 91-92.

and injuring thousands. Putin assisted with the planning of special counterterrorism operations in response to the deadly bombings as he reassured Russian civilians that he would deal out certain retribution: "We will hunt the terrorists everywhere…If you'll excuse me, if we catch them in the toilet, we'll soak them in the toilet, if that's what it takes. It will all be finally sorted."[210] The Russian military deployed storm detachment units consisting anywhere from thirty to fifty soldiers trained in urban warfare. Russian Federation military vehicles and tanks were retrofitted with additional armor to withstand enemy shoulder- fired rocket attacks. Whereas most European nations had been considered soft on terrorist cells operating among growing populations of Muslim migrants because of relaxed security protocols, Russia delivered a swift and brutal military response. Therefore, when the West expressed outrage over Putin's so-called brutal tactics to subjugate Chechnya, he called their outrage out as hypocrisy saying that Washington waged their own global campaigns against Al-Qaeda however it saw fit but now criticized Russia for its counter-terrorism response. However, it should be noted that Putin is not beyond his own hypocrisy in the matter. Whereas he quickly defended Russia against militant Islamic attacks, he condemned Israel for their aggressive actions in Gaza against Hamas militants.[211] Putin also called for a cease-fire and for Israel to back off and support a two-state solution. The failed two-state solution has been on the table since 1993 when Israel gave into pressure from the international community to develop the Oslo Accords. This agreement gave the PLO terrorists carte blanche to occupy Gaza. Since then, Israel has had nothing but military conflict with Hamas terrorists and now it's time for the Israel Defense Forces to drive them out of Gaza. Therefore, Putin is seriously misguided in promoting the interests of Hamas terrorists over and against Israel's sovereignty.

---

[210] Ibid, 93.

[211] Reuters, *Putin Blames West for Gaza Crisis, Says US Needs Global Chaos*, October 30, 2023. Source accessed November 1, 2023, from https://www.reuters.com.

I will show that Putin is a strange contradiction that he promises support for world leaders but will undertake a contrarian course of action to preserve the self-interests of Russia. In the aftermath of 911 Putin was one of the first leaders to contact George Bush to offer help with counter-terrorism operations but because Washington's high level of skepticism based upon their previous years of engagement in Afghanistan and question of their underlying motives, the answer came with a polite but firm, Thank you, but no thank you. During the early years of the American global war on terrorism, Russia had managed to keep a low profile in the Middle East although they had always been lurking in the shadow of various Arab nation states. However, as the American invasion of Iraq unfolded, with the overthrow of Saddam Hussein on the suspicion that he was harboring weapons of mass destruction, Russia became more critical and outspoken against US military intervention in the Middle East. Russia's distrust for American intervention would come to a head with events in Syria. In 2011, when Syrian President Bashar al-Assad attempted to utilize aggressive force against the Arab Spring protesters, civil unrest exploded giving way to armed insurrections. Insurrectionists formed the Free Syrian Army (FSA) which consisted of Kurdish-Arab Syrian Democratic Forces (SDF) and the Islamic State of Iraq and the Levant along with several jihadist groups linked to Al-Qaeda.[212] By 2012 the US, the UK and France were financially supporting the FSA and in 2016 US Special Forces were covertly deployed to Syria to join their fight and to train their military. This further complicated the situation in Syria because Russia had been an ally and supporter of Syria's al-Assad. Russia provided supplies, funding, and weapons to fight the insurgents although the U.N. had been unsuccessfully trying to broker peace accords between Damascus and the rebel groups. Things became even more complex in Syria when Iran and the Lebanese Hezbollah also provided al-Assad with assistance. When Syria had fallen into the hands of various rebel groups, the nation's collapse

---

[212] Galeotti, *Putin's Wars*, 202-203.

seemed imminent. Russia was concerned that Syria might wind up like Libya, with the civil war and NATO airstrikes that led to the overthrow and execution of Gaddafi back in 2011. Russia also had grave concerns that a rebel coalition backed by the US would be reminiscent of the color revolutions in Georgia and Ukraine which also had underlying American and NATO support coupled with anti-Russian sentiment. Russia's chief concern was that if Syria fell into the hands of a radical Islamic state, then this might once again open doors for jihadists to strike the homeland as in the Chechen terrorist attacks. Reminiscent of his appeal to George Bush in the aftermath of 9/11 to assist with counter-terrorism operations, Putin made a bold proposal to the U.N. General Assembly for a joint operation in Syria which came to nothing. The day after Putin's failed proposal to the General Assembly in 2015, to most of the international community's surprise, Russia directly intervened in Syria, sending troops and a large complement of military equipment. Waves of Russian airstrikes and missile launches soon commenced against the Islamic State occupied territories, killing hundreds of rebel fighters. Russia further intensified their fight against Islamic State militants when terrorists bombed a Russian passenger jet flying from Egypt to St. Petersburg. Turkey soon joined Russia as they launched offensives against Kurdish forces in Syria. Seven thousand Russian soldiers engaged in extensive combat operations against the Islamic State and Syria (ISIS), joined by Iranian-trained militias and Wagner Group mercenaries, referred to as ISIS Hunters. The US eventually backed off its support of the SDF and pulled out American troops in Syria in 2019. Russia had proven its military capability for direct intervention in the Middle East. The Kremlin maintained that Assad's defeat would have had disastrous consequences for regional and global stability. The Russian Chief of General Staff reported that their intervention into Syria was necessary in the interest of his nation's security: "ISIS would have continued to gather momentum and would have spread to adjacent countries. We would have had to confront that force on our own territory. They would be operating in the Caucasus, Central

Asia, and the Volga region of Russia."[213] Russia had also grown impatient with the failed attempts to arrive at a diplomatic solution between the Syrian government and the rebel forces. The RAND Corporation an American nonprofit global policy think tank which engages in research and development projects over multiple government sectors and private industries also reported that between January 2014 and September 2015 there were over eighty-five diplomatic engagements from the US, the EU, and U.N. which had failed.[214] One thing is certain about Russia's intervention into Syria, they saw what they believed to be a threat to their national security and acted in the interests of their homeland. This determination to act explains why Russia is willing to sit at the table with Middle Eastern nations, although these very nations might harbor pro-Islamic radicals. It is all about Russia achieving leverage in the Middle East for the sake of their Eurasian geopolitical foreign policies. Now what about Israel, are they friend or foe to Russia in the grand scheme of Eurasian interests?

The relationship between Putin and Netanyahu developed after the Middle Eastern entrance ramp for Russia was once again opened through Syria. In the past the former Soviet Union alienated itself from Israel through its relations with Tehran the avowed enemy of Israel. But now the post-Soviet relations of the Russian Federation with Israel have not only thawed but are seen an essential asset for Russia to maintain a foothold in the Middle East. Russia also has vast stakes in the oil and gas energy markets as a significant producer and exporter along with the Arab nations. Whatever impacts the Middle East regarding crude oil production and export will also impact Russia in the energy sector as well. Therefore, it is in their best interest to extend diplomatic relations to Israel to insure stability in the Middle East. Also, Russia is quite competitive in terms of their Eurasian geopolitical ambitions in the Middle East and sees the US and the West as a force hostile

---

[213] Samuel Charap, Elina Treyger & Edward Geist, *Understanding Russia's Intervention in Syria*. RAND Corporation Research Report, 2018.

[214] Ibid.

toward these interests. Israeli Prime Minister Benjamin Netanyahu has developed a close friendship with Putin since 2015. One of the avenues of this relationship has come through an open visa program between Russia and Israel given that there is a very large ethnic population of Russian Jews.[215] As many as one in five Israeli citizens has Russian roots and is most likely fluent in the Russian language. The other component that has fostered a positive relation between Israel and Russia is the concessions Russia has made regarding Iran. Although Russia has maintained its relations with Iran on the one hand, on the other hand, they have reluctantly permitted Israel to conduct military operations in response to pro-Iranian militant attacks. This has been an eccentric, precarious on-again off-again relationship between Israel and Russia. Russia's balancing act on the tightrope with Israel and Iran along with the other Arab nations is jeopardized whenever there is an Islamic radical terrorist attack either from Hamas or Hezbollah and Israel retaliates. When Hamas launched brutal attacks within Gaza on October 7, 2023, there was speculation that Russia was behind support of the terrorist groups based upon Putin's relations with Iran. Although Russia no doubt enjoyed the brief parentheses of time when world attention turned away from the Russo-Ukrainian war to events in Gaza, to date at the time of this writing, there has been no direct evidence from intelligence sources to verify that Russia was working with Iran in the planning of the attacks on Israel. That doesn't mean that things could change, and Putin decides to engage directly in the conflict with Israel. On October 26, 2023, Putin had a meeting in Moscow with delegates from Hamas, including their senior member Moussa Abu Marzouk, to discuss the release of hostages in the Gaza Strip.[216] This is of key

---

[215] Eugene Rumer, *A Brief Guide to Russia's Return to the Middle East*, Carnegie Endowment for International Peace, October 24, 2019. Source accessed October 17, 2023, from https://carnegieendowment.org.

[216] Mikhail Japaridze, *Hamas Delegates Arrive in Moscow for Talks*, The Moscow Times, October 26, 2023. Source accessed October 27, 2023, from https://www.themoscowtimes.com.

interest to Russia because it was confirmed that there were Russian citizens among the hostages, and the Russian government is continuing dialogue with Israel. However, Putin has expressed criticism of Netanyahu's military operations in Gaza to counter Hamas. This is the contradictory nature of Putin who will offer the hand of friendship in one instance but turn against that friend in another situation because things are working against Russian interests in the Middle East. Some have claimed that the Wagner mercenaries were training Hamas militants to prepare them for the attack upon Israel. It has been confirmed that pro-Ukrainian groups were loading social media posts on X with these claims.[217] These claims lacked intelligence source confirmation and the false media accusations have no basis because Wagner has no verifiable presence in the Palestinian territories at this time. Israel is in a difficult spot because it acts as a mediator between both Russia and Ukraine, having a strong cultural connection to both countries. Dozens of Russian oligarchs from eastern Ukraine have sought refuge in Israel.[218] Although Israel has provided humanitarian support for Ukraine, it has withheld any direct military support knowing that this could jeopardize their relationship with Moscow. Shortly after the invasion, when Zelensky was publicizing his visit to Washington to rally American support for Ukraine, Putin called Netanyahu to congratulate him on his successful return to Israeli government. No doubt as the Russo-Ukraine war continues, Netanyahu will continue to feel that he is walking on eggshells with the pressure from the US and the West to affirm support for Ukraine while trying to strike a balance in Israel's relations with Russia. Israel is certain to take direct action against Hamas in the Gaza Strip and has already targeted proxy militias in Iran. As the war continues to escalate between Israel and Hamas, it will be interesting to see

---

[217] David Brennan, *Is Russia Behind Hamas Attack on Israel*, Newsweek, October 9, 2023. Source accessed on October 13, 2023, from https://www.newsweek.com.

[218] Elliott Abrams, *Why Israel Has Been Slow to Support Ukraine*, Council on Foreign Relations Middle East Program, April 8, 2022. Source accessed October 18, 2023, from https://www.cfr.org.

if Russia will maintain a low profile or becmone directly involved in the protection of its interests with Iran. Perhaps the presence of US Naval fleets in the Mediterranean will discourage Russian intervention. For now, Netanyahu has expressed his determination to root out the Hamas terrorists from Gaza. If Israel is successful in their military operations against Hamas, Russia might bolster more support directly for Iran and Turkey to fight their own proxy wars against Israel.

I close this brief section on the Russia's intervention in the Middle East with a little trivia from ancient Biblical texts within the context of eschatology. If this is something (to borrow a phrase from Dan Bongino) that is "not your bag of donuts" then feel free to move on to the next chapter! A Jewish priest from Judah living in exile in Babylon in the late fifth century BCE wrote an ancient prophecy (Ezekiel 38:1-2, 9): "And the word of the Lord came to me saying, Son of man, set your face toward Gog of the land of Magog, the prince of Rosh, Meshech and Tubal, and prophesy against him...You will go up, you will come like a storm; you will be like a cloud covering the land, you and all your troops, and many peoples with you." (NASV). The text describes a battle that takes place in the future (*in the latter years* – v.8) from a warrior people or nation far north of Israel. It mentions the "land of Magog" which happened to be a reference to the Scythians a nomadic people from ancient Persia (modern day Iran) from the ninth century BCE who migrated from Central Asia to southern Russia and Ukraine.[219] The mystery for many years was who is the "prince of Rosh?" There were no known Hebrew texts that contained "Rosh" until late 19th century research on Byzantine and Arabic writers discovered mention of an ancient peoples referred to as the variant of the Hebrew and Aramaic word for Rosh: *Rus* a people who dwelled in the ancient country of Tarus.[220] Experts on ancient semitic language believe that Rosh (*Rus*) could possibly refer

---

[219] Britannica, *Scythian – Ancient People*, Source accessed October 26, 2023, from https://www.britannica.com/topic/Scythian.

[220] C.F. Keil & F. Delitzsch, *Commentary of the Old Testament: Volume IX,* (Grand Rapids, MI: W.B. Eerdmans, reprinted 1983), 159-60.

to tribal populations living in the Black Sea region or, more specifically, Russia. The Ezekiel 38 passage addresses a time in the future when an army from the land of Magog (Central Asia and Eurasia) under the leadership of "the prince of Rosh" (Russia) will mount a military offensive in the Middle East. Russia comprised an ancient warrior people and a civilization with a long and complex history. This ancient late fifth-century Hebrew prophecy written by a Jewish priest referred to a time in the future when they will be regarded as a hostile military force of invaders who will have an impact upon the Middle East. To date there has been nothing that has ever occurred that would suggest a literal fulfillment of the Ezekiel 38 passage. However, is this event being set up through the unfolding of current events with Russia, Iran, and Israel and the ongoing Middle East conflicts? Regardless of whether you believe in the literal fulfillment of an ancient Hebrew prophecy, Russia is both unpredictable and dangerous, especially when there are escalating conflicts in the Middle East. I will now discuss the significance of the proxy war in Ukraine in our next chapter.

Chapter Five:

Proxy Wars, Russian Collusion, & Political Corruption in the Deep State

But understanding the vast, money-printing, influence-peddling, backstabbing, dog-eat-dog corruption of Ukraine would have helped the world understand why Donald Trump was having the conversation that set off the entire, absurd, impeachment charade. – Don Bongino, Follow the Money.

The Art of Proxy Warfare

Webster's New Collegiate Dictionary, the term "proxy" is defined as "the agency, function, or office of a deputy who acts as a substitute for another; the authority or power to act for another."[221] When it is applied to warfare, it is really nothing new, because proxy wars have been used for centuries by nation states to fight against a common enemy. From a global perspective proxy warfare has emerged as highly sophisticated statecraft that has the purpose of achieving specific geopolitical objectives and desired outcomes. The global policy think tank RAND Corporation (an acronym for "research and development") has

---

[221] *Webster's New Collegiate Dictionary,* (Springfield, MA: G & C Merriam, 1977).

been influential in influencing foreign policy for over seventy-five years through planning and consulting for the defense industry as well as large private sector international corporations. According to RAND, proxy warfare is a means to accomplish specific geostrategic outcomes through secondary or tertiary combatants giving it an advantage over traditional or conventional warfare:

> Geopolitical factors, including security and diplomatic concerns, are typically the primary motives for states that sponsor local proxies. Often major powers begin to engage in proxy warfare out of a sense of acute vulnerability to the actions of other states. As they develop their capabilities for this form of competition, however, they often begin to engage in proxy warfare on a much wider basis, often drawing themselves and other states into yet more such conflicts.[222]

Examples of proxy warfare include the Vietnam War (1954-75) where Communist China and the Soviet Union supported the Viet Cong with military equipment, arms, and ammunition in a fight against US military forces. The Chinese and the Soviets did not have to fight in North Vietnam because they equipped and empowered communist revolutionaries to do their bidding. Proxy wars are a way for larger global powers to avoid direct confrontation.[223] The US in the past few decades has utilized proxy warfare in the Middle East with the outsourcing of military operations to various guerilla militias and Islamic faction groups in Afghanistan, Iraq, and Syria. Because these proxy fighters are familiar with the language, local terrain, and the complexities of

---

[222] Stephen Watts, *Proxy Warfare in Strategic Competition: State Motivations & Future Trends*, RAND Corporation Published Research, March 9, 2023. Source accessed October 18, 2023, from https://www.rand.org.

[223] L. Sue Baugh, *Proxy War; Armed Conflict*, August 31, 2023, *Britannica*, source accessed October 19, 2023, from https://www.britannica.com/topic/proxy-war.

tribal and cultural entities, the US military equipped and trained them to accomplish certain military objectives.[224] Proxy war has high risks and costs associated with it because there could be serious repercussions. Given the regional instability of these nations, equipping and arming radical Islamic militias becomes a two-edged sword that can be used against our nation or innocent civilian populations when there is a regime change or when US troops withdraw. This is what former Secretary of Defense Christopher Miller calls Counterinsurgency Operations or COIN, which is a driving force behind today's defense industries and is influenced by financial gain: "As a result, major defense contractors quickly bought out a bunch of start-ups that provided interpreters, reconnaissance aircraft, intelligence analysts, maintenance personnel, information technology services, and civilian advisors to government...In the Pentagon, everything comes down to money. If you have money, you have power and influence."[225]

Regardless of the enormous risks involved or the staggering financial costs, proxy warfare is highly regarded as a valuable weapon in the hands of global elites. It is used extensively in covert operations and in the statecraft of intelligence agencies for overthrowing governments and toppling regimes. For decades the US Central Intelligence Agency (CIA) has been operating behind the scenes in espionage as saboteurs in nations all around the world wherever proxy war doctrine has manifested. Charles S. Faddis, who served for twenty years as a CIA operations officer, in an article for Hillsdale College titled *Why the CIA No Longer Works*, highlighted the "bureaucratization and politicization" that have led to the Deep State compromises within the agency. He further addressed the espionage element of the CIA: "At its heart espionage is a very old business...There is a reason intelligence officers talk about

---

[224] Daniel L. Byman, *Why Engage in Proxy War? – A State's Perspective*, May 21, 2018. Brookings Institute. Source accessed October 19, 2023, from https://www.brookings.edu.
[225] Miller, *Soldier Secretary*, 143-44.

tradecraft. Espionage requires innate skills."[226] These tools of tradecraft in proxy warfare are also described as Fifth Generation Warfare or 5GW which can be an effective means to accomplish geostrategic objectives through stealth or clandestine operations. The foundational principles for 5GW evolved from the work of two Chinese People's Liberation Army officers Qiao Liang and Wang Xiangsui who capitulated that "the first rule of unrestricted warfare is that there are no rules, with nothing forbidden…war will no longer be what it was originally."[227] Examples provided by the PLA officers range from biological weapons, cyber-terrorism and media disinformation campaigns. These new concepts in *Unrestricted Warfare* challenged centuries of conventional warfare dogma that had been developed by the 19th century Prussian military theorist Carl von Clausewitz.[228] Military theorist William Lind postulated that successive generations of warfare evolved from "qualitative shifts that make previous forms of military power obsolete."[229] These previous forms of military power include: 1GW (focus upon manpower), 2GW (focus upon firepower), 3GW (focus upon maneuvers.) Later in the early 2000's theorist Thomas Hammes proposed 4GW which focused upon the tactical art of insurgency. Theorist Robert Stelle soon developed the earliest concepts for 5GW from Hammes 4GW to include advances in technology that would empower individuals "to pursue ideological or personal objectives independent of nations but leveraging state-like capabilities."[230] David Axe another military subject matter expert connected the 5GW dimension of stealth principle to proxy warfare:

---

[226] Charles S. Faddis, *Why the CIA No Longer Works – and How to Fix It*. Imprimis, October 2023; Vol. 52, No. 10. Hillsdale College.

[227] Qiao Liang and Wang Xiangsui, *Unrestricted Warfare*, (Battleboro, VT: Echo Point Books, 1999), xvii-xviii.

[228] Armin Krishnan, *Fifth Generation Warfare, Hybrid Warfare, & Gray Zone Conflict: A Comparison*. Journal of Strategic Security, Vol. 15, No. 4; Article 23. (Greenville, NC: East Carolina University & Berkley Electronic Press, 2022), 15.

[229] Ibid.

[230] Ibid, 16.

"5G fighters, by contrast, remain 'subtle actors.' They may never wear a uniform or carry a rifle. Their weapon is the desperate population of a society on the brink; their major tactic is unrest; their goal is to undermine the established order in the interest of changing it, or just leaving it in ruins."[231] For global leaders who are working to achieve their ideal of a new world order, the unconventional warfare tactics of 5GW and proxy war is the means to shift the geopolitical equation in their favor. Daniel Abbot described this concept as follows: "War is no longer the sole purview of the nation-state. The convergence of ubiquitous networks with pervasive sensors can elicit tectonic shifts in geopolitics."[232] The Russo-Ukraine proxy war has the same objective to create the elicit tectonic shift that is referenced above by Abbot for the liberal international order. It is driven by the US, NATO, and the EU to fight Russia by supplying funding and military equipment to Ukraine. This war has proven to be a costly protracted conflict not only in terms of billions of dollars of funding but also in the catastrophic loss of human life on both sides. It comes at great risks with the provocation of a major nuclear power. Russia is perceived by the global elites as an obstacle to the *Great Reset* narrative. Therefore, the goal is to either completely weaken and subdue the Russian Federation or to annihilate it altogether. Russia has always been a convenient enemy and is usually the springboard for one of the greatest liberal hoaxes of the century, the Russian Collusion. As I will demonstrate, this collusion narrative has ties to Ukraine.

Russia Gate – Tales of Collusion

Up until the 2016 election season very few of the Democrat establishment thought that Donald J. Trump would pose a serious challenge. Not too long after Barack Obama had given full endorsement to Hillary Clinton, in her self-assured campaign victory, she was marginalizing

---

[231] David Axe, *Piracy, Human Security, & 5GW in Somalia*; from *The Handbook of 5GW*, Daniel H. Abbott, editor. (Ann Arbor, MI: Nimble Books, 2020), 152.

[232] Daniel H. Abbot, *The Handbook of 5GW*, 19.

the conservative populist movement as a "basket of deplorables."[233] Never mind that Clinton had some serious skeletons in her closet from her days as Secretary of State in the Obama administration with allegations that she was using her private server for security sensitive emails. In 2014 it was reported by the State Department that when Clinton handed over her work-related emails that some had been deleted from the server.[234] Eventually it was determined that over thirty thousand emails were deleted after being pressured by congressional investigators, Clinton had FBI Director James Comey vouch for her by claiming that only a handful of emails were classified.[235] Comey further asserted that prosecution was not warranted because the FBI found no evidence that any of the additional work-related emails were intentionally deleted in an effort to conceal them. Obama also maintained that she was innocent of any wrongdoing and made steps to ensure that she would not be prosecuted as he told reporters that the emails were of no harm to national security. Clinton was skating toward the presidential elections as she had the FBI director's backing and the executive privilege granted with Obama's sarcastic statement to the press, "There's classified, and then there's classified" claiming that there was nothing classified in those thirty-thousand emails dumped from Clinton's private server.[236] All of which was quite a contrast to events that would transpire six years later when the FBI raided Trump's Mar-a-Lago estate and confiscated what they claimed were security-sensitive documents that later led to a series of absurd indictments. Not a problem, the Democrats in the Deep State can become a law unto themselves whenever convenient

---

[233] Todd Starnes, *The Deplorables Guide to Making America Great Again*, (Lake Mary, FL: Charisma Media, 2017), xiii.

[234] ABC News, *Why Hillary Clinton Deleted 33,000 Emails on Her Private Email Server.* September 27, 2016. Source accessed December 20, 2023, from https://abcnews.go.com/Politics/hillary-clinton-deleted-33000-emails.

[235] Andrew C. McCarthy, *Ball of Collusion: The Plot to Rig an Election & Destroy a Presidency* (New York: Encounter Books, 2019), viii-x.

[236] Ibid.

and then turn the tables to take down a conservative president and his campaign team. After the Democrats exploited their control of law-enforcement to obtain a carte-blanche exoneration for Clinton, the next step would be to use the intelligence agencies to undermine Trump. The infamous collusion hoax would promote a Russian cyberespionage conspiracy claiming election interference and fabricate an intelligence document known as the Steele dossier along with other documents. The Democrats would manufacture scandalous accusations through an old cold war enemy, Russia. As Andrew McCarthy put it: "Turns out the Cold War isn't so last century. Since November 8, 2016, in ever-evolving Democratic dogma, Russia has gone from a quaint obsession of neo-con warmongers to an existential threat on the order of Climate Change!"[237] Russia is a favorite tactic for trying to undermine political opponents, remember Carter's National Security Advisor Brzezinski, who laid the framework for anti-Russian geopolitical strategies? Brzezinski was tasked with finding information linked to Russia that could be used against Reagan's 1980 campaign. While the Russians certainly have the capability to hack into election systems as well as other kinds of cyberespionage, and have used it in the past, to date there has been zero proof that the Russians interfered with the 2016 elections. What is interesting is that there are some who believe that there was Russian interference in the 2020 elections. Former defense analyst Rebecca Koffler believes that Russia hacked the 2020 election that put Biden in office: "Sabotaging US elections serves Russia's broader purpose of subverting, destabilizing, and if necessary, defeating our military."[238] I am skeptical of this, because I would ask what the Russians would have gained from helping to put Biden in the White House when he is clearly pro-NATO and puts billions of dollars into Ukraine? From Russia's perspective, it made more sense to keep Trump in office, because he is clearly not an EU fan or a NATO advocate. While I do question the integrity of the

---

[237] McCarthy, *Ball of Collusion*, 1.
[238] Koffler, *Putin's Playbook*, 213.

2020 elections, my position personally is that it was an inside job with ballot harvesting and corruption in key state polling precincts and not something that was pulled off by the Russians. Yes, I believe that the 2020 election was stolen, but this was because of internal fraud and not foreign interference. I proudly fall into the category of *election deniers* who stood in agreement with votes against congressional certification! Now back to the 2016 collusion narrative.

The establishment ranks knew that Trump's business dealings had ties to Russian oligarchs; after all he had fully disclosed them. Coupling this with Trump's criticism of NATO, an organization that was created for the purpose of Soviet containment during the cold war era, he was fair game for opposition from both the globalist left and neoconservatives who forever saw Russia as the "evil empire." On the campaign trail, Clinton blasted her opponent with remarks that Donald Trump wants to pull us out of NATO while insisting that she would not abandon the international community. Trump, however, believed that NATO's mission was obsolete, and that the US had been pouring billions of dollars into a cold war relic with nothing to show for it. The idea of a Trump presidency did not sit well with European elites either; they regarded him as a self-centered MAGA (Make America Great Again) nationalist. And to the ire of progressives, Trump stated his belief that maintaining diplomatic relations with Russia would be far more advantageous than provoking it. CIA Director John Brennan, along with Democratic Senate Minority Leader Harry Reid, produced allegations that Trump's campaign was tied to the Russian government. Brennan also chimed in claiming that Trump was an unwitting agent of the Kremlin. The irony of it all is that the CIA has been one of the greatest actors in election interference for decades. Loch K. Johnson, a subject matter expert on US Intelligence stated: "We've been doing this kind of thing since the CIA was created in 1947…We've planted false information in foreign newspapers."[239] After Clinton lost to Trump,

---

[239] McCarthy, *Ball of Collusion*, 3.

Russian cyberespionage was a convenient scapegoat of election interference for the Democrats who, during the Obama administration, rarely mentioned Russia or Putin in their conversations. Now, they would focus upon the mainstream media narrative of how an evil empire got Trump into the White House. The collusion narrative would not be the only weapon in the liberal media arsenal, there would soon emerge shocking allegations claiming to be from intelligence sources related to both Russia and Ukraine.

Fusion GPS and the British Claims of a Secretive Source: the Steele Dossier

Fusion GPS is a commercial research firm located in Washington DC that is tucked away in a tiny office (above a Starbucks and a secondhand clothing store) that specializes in open-source investigations as well as political candidate opposition research. The company was cofounded by two former Wall Street Journalists–Glenn Simpson and Peter Fritsch. On the morning of Super Tuesday (March 1, 2016), Fritsch sent an email to a senior official in the DNC simply listing the word "-Trump-" in the subject line with the message: "Ok he has to be stopped. We have done the most on him." [240] By this time Fusion had been gathering some candidate opposition research on Trump since 2015. Now, Fritsch made a decision to take a deep dive, sensing an upside for profit potential for Fusion. Fritsch's partner Simpson responded in an email likewise: "The only way I could see working for the HRC (*Hillary Rodham Clinton – author's italics*) is if it is against Trump. We should make sure [the Democrats] know we have a big book on Trump. Lest they try to buy it someplace else." Fusion knew that funding for the anti-Trump research would be lucrative as Clinton's PACs had raised over $1.2 billion for her campaign. Also, money was

---

[240] Glen Simpson & Peter Frtisch, *Crime in Progress: Inside the Steele Dossier & the Fusion GPS Investigation of Donald Trump*, (New York: Random House, 2019), 54-55.

pouring into the Clinton campaign from wealthy globalists elites like George Soros who provided $16 million.[241] Soros had bankrolled his Open Society Foundation, an international organization with over $32 billion, to build the infrastructure for a progressive new world order. Open Society's projects included everything from appointing ultraliberal judges and supporting left-leaning candidates in the US to helping stand-up socialist leaders in nations like Ukraine. Another group closely associated with Fusion was the Democracy Integrity Project (TDIP) that also received over $1 million from Soros. This research firm was founded by Daniel J. Jones, a former FBI analyst and staffer for California's Democratic Senator Dianne Feinstein, who paid over $3 million to Fusion's parent company Bean LLC. According to Simpson Bean's purpose was working with investigators around the world to expose Russian subversive operations in the United States and other western democracies. The net constructed by Fusion, their parent company Bean LLC, and the TDIP backed by significant funding streams from Soros and Clinton it was now ready to be cast at the most opportune time which was right around Trump's inauguration. After Hillary lost the election and her dreams of celebrating breaking through a glass ceiling had been dashed by the deplorables, media giants were eager to add more fuel to the fire of the Russian collusion narrative. There were claims that the FBI suspected that the Russian government had hacked into the DNC computer systems. If they could find a rabbit trail connecting the Russian collusion to Trump, then the media could drop an enormous bombshell. Simpson and Fritsch had been digging into every possible angle to uncover potential criminal activity related to Trump's business affairs in Russia. On January 4, 2017, Fritsch and Simpson claimed that they received a call from former *Washington Post* reporter Carl Bernstein who had exposed Watergate in the Nixon era and now was working with CNN. Bernstein revealed that he wanted to verify some information that might be a conclusive link between

---

[241] Dan Bongino, *Follow the Money: The Shocking Deep State Connections of the Anti-Trump Cabal*, (New York: Post Hill Press, 2020), 10-11.

Trump and Putin. This source of this link was from a London based intelligence research firm known as Orbis. Christopher Steele a former who specialized in Russian intelligence was the founder and director of Orbis. This no doubt was behind the comment that Brennan made to NBC on national television that "The FBI has a very close relationship with its British counterparts. And so, the FBI had visibility into a number of things that were going on involving some individuals who may have had some affiliation with the Trump campaign."[242] Although Steele claimed that his document was from genuine sources working closely with those on an inside track with Russia, his former MI6 superior was not as impressed and criticized the dossier as "falling woefully short of professional intelligence standards."[243] In addition to the fact that Steele claimed to have corroborated his document from various internet sources including posts from random individuals who could not be substantiated, it contained a host of errors, typos, and misspellings that looked more amateurish than genuine. Fusion hired Steele, as well as former CIA Russian analyst Nellie Ohr to supplement their research. Steele was eager to provide Fusion with the documents, referred to as a dossier, which claimed to link Trump not only to the Russian collusion but also to Putin and rich Russian oligarchs. Ohr during the dossier investigation had frequent conversations with the FBI and was married to Bruce Ohr, a Department of Justice (DOJ) official. Later it would be brought forth in senate inquires that Ohr's relationship with her husband and the DOJ would be a conflict of interest. Most interestingly the dossier was entrusted to moderate Republican Senator John McCain's longtime adviser David Kramer. Kramer spoke openly of his disdain for Putin and Russia. He was loyal to McCain who had the notoriety of breaking ranks with his party's conservatives had consistently leaned to the left on issues such as gun control, LGBTQ rights, and progressive civil rights policies. McCain not only resented

---

[242] McCarthy, *Ball of Collusion*, 145.

[243] McCarthy, *Ball of Collusion*, 155.

Trump because of some very harsh criticisms that were made in the past but also was quite vocal in his support of the Russian collusion narrative. Now with his hands on the Steele dossier, sweet revenge was in sight for McCain who sent copies to FBI Director James Comey. It wasn't long before CNN in a live broadcast on January 10, 2017, just ten days away from Trump's inauguration broke the story on the dossier. Per the protocols of executive transfer of power in Washington the dossier was included in briefings to both the incoming and outgoing presidents. This prompted Obama to order a massive investigation of Russian interference into the election. Obama realized that he had to set the precedent for ongoing investigations not only of Trump but also of his campaign staff in the months after he left office and throughout the Biden administration. To accomplish this, several Federal agencies would have to be weaponized to take down Trump and his accomplices: the Foreign Intelligence Surveillance Act (FISA) under the force of law through its court systems (FISC), the FBI, the CIA, and the DOJ. It is as National Review editor, Andrew McCarthy surmised: "Welcome to intel, the Obama way. It is the author of the Trump-Russia narrative."[244] Trump and his team would not be the only casualties as the emergence of an authoritarian police state would have the means to turn on ordinary citizens as well. Trump captured this in his remarks after his federal indictments, "In the end, they're not coming after me. They're coming after you and I'm just standing in their way."[245]

A Weapon for Violating Constitutional Rights: Federal Surveillance

Before Obama left the White House, he was the architect of a system that would call for a series of investigations, indictments, and arrests for Trump's team. Ultimately, Trump would come into the crosshairs with calls for his impeachment. This would give the Russian collusion

---

[244] McCarthy, *Ball of Collusion*, 55.

[245] Matt Dixon, *Trump Delivers Fiery Post-Indictment Speech*, NBC News, June 10, 2023. Source accessed on October 23, 2023, from https://www.nbcnews.com.

allegations added ammunition, especially with the Steele Dossier and a list of endless accusations to come. Regardless of what one thinks about Trump, everything that was put into place was not only a travesty for what they could do to a former US President but also an abuse of power in our court systems and the highest law enforcement and intelligence agencies in the nation. One of the chief surveillance tools that was created by Democratic President Harry Truman to decipher coded communications in the Second World War was the National Security Agency (NSA). The NSA operated within the US Department of Defense and became one of the nation's largest intelligence agencies operating along the CIA in countries around the globe. Although the NSA is meant to monitor the communications of bad-guy terrorists and spies, it has pushed the envelope regarding mass data collection on ordinary US citizens. This came to the forefront in 2013 when Edward Snowden, a former NSA intelligence contractor, discovered data mining operations known as metadata on millions of private citizens during the Obama administration.[246] When Snowden approached his superiors about concerns over privacy violations of citizens and was ignored, he became a whistleblower and released thousands of documents under classified surveillance to journalists. When authorities sought his arrest on charges of treason and criminal espionage, he fled the country to Hong Kong and later took asylum in Moscow where he was eventually granted Russian citizenship. Before the Obama administration was using surveillance, a Democratic Congress enacted FISA in 1978 under the executive signature of Jimmy Carter. In the post 9/11 years since then, the FISA court, FISC, broadened its authority through the Patriot Act. This act allowed for FISA warrants to be issued on the suspicion that an individual is acting as a clandestine agent of a foreign power giving the FBI the authority to monitor communications through wiretaps or other covert means and to use email addresses and phone numbers of American citizens for database searches.

---

[246] National Whistleblower Center, *Edward Snowden*. April 8, 2018. Source accessed on October 23, 2023, from https://www.whistleblowers.org.

The conditions that led to this environment of hyper-surveillance came through a major ideological shift in counterterrorism operations after 9/11. This tectonic policy shift was massive and yet so subtle that it flew under the radar of everyday American citizens. I remain in touch with intelligence and law enforcement colleagues that I knew in my former line of work in bioterrorism surveillance. A close friend of mine who worked as a special agent in FBI counterterrorism operations shared with me how he was broadsided by the Deep State in his agency when political correctness completely overhauled their field work. Initially his work included profiling jihadist extremists and doing surveillance on radical Islamic groups in the US such as the infamous Muslim Brotherhood that played a role in financing terrorists and other potential sleeper cells. The agency from the top down began conducting sensitivity trainings on Islamophobia and how it was prejudiced to discriminate against Muslims. Now I realize that there are dangers of racial and religious discrimination, but what we are talking about is a major redefining of the terrorist threat potential. There are certainly dangers of racial and religious discrimination, but the policy shifts reported by my friend, the former FBI agent, represented a major redefining of the terrorist threat potential. He mentioned that this shift started under George Bush, Jr. but gained momentum under Obama. This came to light during the deadly siege of Benghazi in 2012 on the eleventh anniversary of 9/11. American military personnel were killed, and four US state officials were brutally murdered including Christopher Stephens, the ambassador to Libya. Secretary Hillary Clinton issued a public statement portraying the violence not as a terrorist attack but as a response to an anti-Islamic video.[247] Later reports replaced the words *attacks* with the word *demonstrations* (all of which sounds vaguely familiar to when Antifa and BLM were burning down cities in what were called peaceful protests). The after-action reports on Benghazi removed any references to Islam and to al-Qaeda because they were completely whitewashed

---

[247] McCarthy, *Ball of Collusion*, 56-57.

with politically correct jargon. The very core of counterterrorism doctrine was radically changed with Obama's appointment of CIA Director John Brennan to become the top White House adviser for counterterrorism. Brennan who had voted for Communist Party candidate Gus Hall in the 1976 presidential elections started his career under Bill Clinton in the National Security Council and was a committed Deep State intelligence agency progressive.[248] Under Brenan and Obama, the new metric for counterterrorism would be known as Countering Violent Extremism (CVE). In CVE, jihadist terror was a thing of the past because the new threats would be defined by the Department of Homeland Security as *Rightwing Extremism*. According to McCarthy, Brennan was the perfect fit for the jihadist-friendly CVE doctrine and had once stated: "In all my travels, the city I have come to love most is al-Quds." *Al-Quds* is used by Brennan as the Arab name for Jerusalem that is preferred by Hamas and Iranian radicals; he would not dare use the name *Jerusalem* because that would mean showing favoritism to the Israeli "Zionists."[249] It was Brennan who called out American officials who were critical of funding terrorists in Iran saying that "we must cease Iran-bashing and tolerate and even…encourage greater assimilation of Hezbollah in Lebanon's political system."

Who are considered as the "rightwing extremists in CVE doctrine?" The list includes religious conservatives, anti-abortion activists, Second Amendment supporters, immigration opponents, and antigovernment protestors (those who want to limit big government overreach), to name a few on the new terror watchlists. Although Islamic extremists are forbidden under the new CVE counterterrorism doctrine because it is considered religious profiling of Muslims, there was certainly no political correctness exercised when conservative Catholics were targeted

---

[248] Ronald Radosh, *CIA Director John Brennan Proudly Acknowledges that He Once Voted for the Communist Candidate for President*, Hudson Institute, September 23, 2016. Source accessed December 20, 2023, from https://www.hudson.org/national-security-defense/cia-director-john-brennan.

[249] McCarthy, *Ball of Collusion*, 64-65.

by watchlist profiling. An FBI document was leaked that the bureau's Richmond division launched an investigation into "radical traditionalist" Catholics and their possible ties to "the far-right white nationalist movement."[250] The document singled out conservative "traditional" Catholics (those who believe in the traditional Latin Mass) as having potential to be linked to violent extremist groups. The new CVE doctrine of terrorist surveillance would also include the prime minister of Israel, Netanyahu as well as pro-Israel supporters in the US. Under DHS CVE parameters, the Obama administration would exploit its counterintelligence surveillance powers to spy on Americans who were suspected of being part of the Russian collusion narrative.

Crossfire Hurricane

These spy craft surveillance tools were utilized by the FBI in what they claimed to be a counterintelligence investigation conducted from July 31, 2016, to May 17, 2017, under the code name *Crossfire Hurricane*, into alleged connections between Trump's campaign and Russian collaborators to interfere with the 2016 presidential election. On the other side of the ocean, anti-Trump sentiment ran deep in Europe because he was perceived as a hostile threat to NATO and the liberal international order. The British equivalent to the NSA: GCHQ (Government Communications Headquarters) also began monitoring what they deemed as suspicious communications between Trump associates and suspected Russian agents.[251] This was also expanded to intelligence agencies in Germany, France, the Netherlands, Estonia, and Poland. CIA Director John Brennan also agreed to provide information gathered from foreign intelligence to FBI informants. Also, during the Crossfire investigation, the Justice Department was reviewing the

---

[250] Tyler Arnold & Joe Bukuras, *FBI Retracts Leaked Document Orchestrating Investigation of Catholics*, February 9, 2023, Catholic News Agency. Source accessed October 24, 2023, from https://www.catholicnewsagency.com.

[251] McCarthy, *Ball of Collusion*, 102-105.

Steele Dossier. Starting with the low-hanging fruit, Carter Page, a petroleum industry consultant would be the first target of Crossfire. Page who served as a foreign policy advisor on the Trump campaign team by coincidence conducted business that specialized in Russian and Central Asian oil and gas. Even though the Annapolis graduate and former naval intelligence officer had a squeaky-clean boy scout-worthy record, not only did his business interests in Eurasia immediately put him on the radar but also his pro-Russian diplomacy views were considered highly suspicious by the leftist investigation gestapo. Page was quite outspoken in his criticism of failed foreign policy and held that anti-Russian sanctions were counterproductive, causing a deterioration in Russian American relations which he said was "misguided and provocative through its hypocritical ideas such democratization, inequality, and corruption along with regime changes." I agree wholeheartedly with Page because his comments accurately depict the impact of the color revolutions that completely exacerbated the conflict with Russia and put us on a collision course with a nuclear power. He was also on target for criticizing the Obama State Department for inciting the deadliest of these revolutions, Euromaidan that set the stage in Ukraine for Zelensky. The other item that FBI Director Robert Mueller and his staff of Democratic partisans would bring to focus regarding Page would be his 2016 commencement speech at Moscow's New Economic School (NES). Commencements at the Moscow NES were not controversial in the past because they invited both Democrat and Republican guests from the US and even Obama spoke there in 2009. However, what singled out Page's presence at NES were his conversations with the Russian Deputy Prime Minister Arkady Dvorkovich, who expressed his support for Trump's campaign and his hopes that the two nations could work together. Since the Steele Dossier had also mentioned Page that was all that it took for Mueller to order a FISA application for surveillance on his emails and phone calls to further add to the Russia Gate narrative. However, as the investigation continued, they could not find any conclusive evidence that linked Page to involvement with Russian spies or any of the collusion narrative. It was later revealed that FBI attorney Kevin Clinesmith had deliberately altered an email that referred to Page that was submitted to the Justice Department as one of the documents in support of a call for surveillance.[252] Clinesmith got off easily with a mere slap on the wrist with probation from the Obama-appointed US District Judge in DC. With the lack of concrete evidence on Page, the FBI would now turn its attention to others in the Trump circle. Roger Stone, a Republican political consultant for the Trump campaign, would be the next target of the Mueller investigation. Mueller perceived that Stone, who had worked on campaigns for Ronald Reagan, Bob Dole, and George Bush prior to working for Trump was perceived as noncompliant with the investigation. After Stone was indicted by a federal grand jury on charges of obstruction of justice, the police state swung into full operation with an FBI raid on his residence. Twenty-nine FBI agents stormed into Stone's home in the early morning hours of January 25, 2019, placing the then 66-year-old consultant under arrest after searching his home.[253] Although the investigation yielded no conclusive evidence of ties to Russian collusion, the federal system was determined to make Stone pay the Justice Department would sue Stone for over $2 million based on tax evasion charges.[254]

The next target of Mueller's Russia Gate probe was retired Army Lieutenant General Michael Flynn. Flynn was promoted to lead the Defense Intelligence Agency (DIA) by Obama in 2012. Because Flynn was one not afraid to speak his mind on issues, he started to question Obama's political correctness policies on counterterrorism strategies,

---

[252] Eric Tucker, *Ex-FBI Lawyer Given Probation for Russian Probe Actions*, January 29, 2021, AP News. Source accessed October 25, 2023, from https://apnews.com.

[253] Brooke Singman, *FBI's Show of Force in Roger Stone Arrest Spurs Criticism of Mueller Tactics*, January 25, 2019, Fox News. Source accessed October 25, 2023, from https://www.foxnews.com.

[254] Jill Colvin, *Justice Department Sues Roger Stone Over $2M in Unpaid Taxes*, Breitbart, April 16, 2021. Source accessed October 25, 2023, from https://www.breitbart.com.

especially on Iran. Because of this Flynn came to be treated with disdain by the administration and members of the Deep State intelligence community.[255] The FBI also had considerable bias against Flynn because he stood up for an agent who claimed that she was subjected to sexual discrimination under Deputy Director Andy McCabe.[256] Flynn who by now was on the Deep State blacklist with the Obama administration, FBI, and intelligence agencies was eventually fired by Obama. Flynn would later describe his tenacity for telling the truth which would make him a public enemy in eyes of the Deep State cabal:

> I believed that it was my duty as a military officer to tell the truth to the American people and to their representatives on Capitol Hill...I spoke my mind, sharing a table with three senior officials who would later come to play a part in my persecution story – James Comey (Director of the FBI), John Brennan (Director of the CIA), and James Clapper (Director of National Intelligence). You probably won't be surprised to hear they were unhappy that I told the American public the truth."[257]

After Trump came into office, he admired Flynn for his straightforward and no-nonsense approach towards the establishment politicians. Although Obama directly counseled Trump not to hire him for top level administration, the new president named Flynn his national security advisor. Later Flynn and his colleagues had a discussion on the impact of the Russian sanctions on foreign policy matters and were advised to contact the Kremlin's ambassador to the US Sergey Kislyak. Flynn simply cautioned Kislyak to avoid any actions that could further escalate matters which would complicate US – Russian relations. Unknown

---

[255] McCarthy, *Ball of Collusion*, 314-15.

[256] Ibid.

[257] Michael Flynn, *A Letter to America: The Time to Fight for Your Faith & Family is Now*, (Tulsa, OK: Reawaken America, 2021), 21-22.

to Flynn, FBI counterintelligence was monitoring his communications with the Russian ambassador. This was all part of the Obama Russian collusion surveillance that had been in place. And now Flynn would come under the Mueller investigation tribunal. As McCarthy described it: "The Flynn investigation was a vindictive farce...The FBI opened an investigation on the decorated thirty-three-year-old combat veteran of the US Army on suspicion that, yes, he was an agent of Russia engaged in clandestine activity against the United States."[258] Shortly thereafter, because of conversations between Flynn and Vice President Mike Pence, Flynn was dismissed from his position as security advisor as a result of allegations that he lied through inaccurate descriptions of his conversation with Kislyak. Because the Mueller team knew that what they had was flimsy, they made obscure reference to the Logan Act of 1799 that criminalized negotiations between unauthorized Americans and foreign governments. The Logan Act originally designed to target those who were providing information to British spies was now being used to prosecute Flynn's phone conversation with Russia's ambassador. I believe that Flynn was set up by the Deep State cabal because he was a threat not only to the police state powers of the FBI, but also to the intelligence agency regimes. Later, this would come out through House Intelligence Committee Republicans who contended that Comey himself had stated that Flynn did not lie.[259] Another casualty in the collusion narrative was Senator Jeff Sessions, the Attorney General in the Trump Administration who also had communicated with ambassador Kislyak. The accusations were made that Sessions deliberately withheld disclosure of his communications with the Russian ambassador although the Senate Intelligence Committee had called the accusations as "appalling and detestable."[260] Sessions refused to answer any further questions

---

[258] McCarthy, *Ball of Collusion*, 316-17.

[259] Ibid, 321.

[260] Gregory Lewis McNamee, *Jeff Sessions: United States Senator & Attorney General*, Britannica, September 18, 2023. Source accessed October 27, 2023, from https://www.britannica.com/biography/Jeff-Sessions.

about his conversations with Trump saying that it would be inappropriate. The Crossfire team were delighted to pressure Sessions to resign because he was such a vocal opponent of Obama's Affordable Care Act, same-sex marriage, and liberal immigration policies. More members of Trump's team would be taken out by Mueller. Trump's personal attorney Michael Cohen was sentenced to three months in prison for claims that he had made false statements to Congress. George Papadopoulos one of Trump's foreign policy advisors was arrested and jailed for two weeks on accusations that he had withheld information about his correspondence with Russian government officials. After their successive victories in going after Page, Stone, Flynn, Sessions, Cohen, and Papadopoulos, the Mueller investigation would now look for someone on the Trump team that would be the object of a massive take down. This target for the Mueller investigation had ties to Ukraine and Russia and would not only be indicted and prosecuted but also sent to prison.

The Political Consultant Who Knew Too Much About Ukraine–Manafort

Paul Manafort was a conservative political consultant who had worked on the Ford and Reagan campaigns and had been a partner with Roger Stone. Because of his extensive experience he became Trump's campaign chairman. Big ticket political consultants run and promote their services as businesses. They are not limited to US candidates, but are also available to candidates in foreign countries. This was not highly unusual as both Democratic and Republican political consultants have been known to render their services to foreign clients. After the collapse of the USSR in 1991, the former Soviet Bloc nations opened a lucrative business field for political consulting. Part of this was based on the premise that these nations were great prospects for American democratization. The other aspect was that rich oligarchs were eager to either run for public office or to promote their own parties for the benefit of their business interests. This was especially true in Ukraine and the Baltic States, where wealthy Russian oligarchs had a lot of influence. Unfortunately, the downside included corruption with mafia-style crime bosses who also wanted a piece of the action. Both Russia and Ukraine were no exception regarding the influence of rich and powerful business elites and international criminal organizations. In 2008, Ukraine's Party of Regions reached out to Manafort and entered a contract for political strategy consultation. Manafort described his work as follows: "I had worked for the Party of Regions for almost ten years. I had managed the campaigns of three successful parliamentary elections in Ukraine, one presidential election, and multiple local elections. Part of what I did in Ukraine was to organize the best American political consulting talent and manage their services."[261] Recall from chapter two that the Party of Regions was the more conservative pro-Russian party compared to the liberal pro-Western Orange Party. When Yanukovich and the Party of Regions reached out to Manafort, he saw it as an opportunity to encourage stability in Ukraine by arriving at a middle ground consensus between the pro-Western sympathizers and those who considered themselves loyal to Russia in the eastern part of the nation. Manafort was not only aware of the tensions in Ukraine but was quite knowledgeable about the geopolitical dynamic behind 2004 Orange Revolution: "I was not involved in the controversial 2004 Ukrainian presidential election but came to understand that it was really a proxy election of Europe and the US against Russia. The European candidate Victor Yushchenko was elected president over Yanukovych in an election that had significant charges of fraud by all sides."[262] Yanukovych and the Party of Regions won the elections in 2010 but their success abruptly ended in the aftermath of the deadly Euromaidan revolution. Through pro-Western, NATO, and EU radical activists, along with the support of the US State Department the government was overthrown in 2014, which prepared the way for Zelensky to eventually come to power in

---

[261] Manafort, *Political Prisoner*, 104-105.

[262] Ibid.

another five years. When the Russian collusion narrative was spun and Obama launched Operation Crossfire Hurricane, Manafort was all too easy a target especially with him receiving compensation from wealthy business oligarchs who were pro-Russian and anti-EU-NATO. Manafort explained that as a lead on the consulting team his usual practice was to bill for his services, in turn be paid a lump sum and then pay his staff. He mentioned that it was common procedure for his company to receive payment through conventional bank-to-bank wire transfers. Shortly after Manafort became the campaign chair for Trump, there was a story of a so-called "black ledger" that was released by a pro-Western whistleblower at a press conference in Kyiv who claimed that Manafort was paid with large sums of cash.[263] The story was absurd because Manafort never received cash; rather, he received payment for services through electronic bank transfer that he fully disclosed. When the story hit the New York Times, there were accusations about illegal cash from Moscow. The conspiracy story later exploded with the Steele Dossier along with the mysterious black ledger on major media and social media outlets and happened to complement the Russian collusion narrative. Manafort who saw the handwriting on the wall, promptly submitted his resignation as campaign manager for the Trump team.

Another reason that Manafort was targeted by the Deep State is that he was one of the few who had the insight into the geopolitical ramifications of Ukraine for global elites:

> After five or six months of research, I concluded that what interested me in Ukraine was its geopolitical importance…I found that in eastern Ukraine there was an undercurrent that Yanukovych was the only national political figure who was viewed as able to protect Russian culture, language, and heritage. This was a growing issue in 2005 in Ukraine. Yanukovych's rivals,

---

[263] Manafort, *Political Prisoner,* 105.

President Yushchenko and Prime Minister Timoshenko, were trying to delegitimize Russian culture in Ukraine to rid the nation of feelings that they falsely claimed as uniting the country.[264]

If the campaign chair for Trump had this insight into foreign policy, no doubt international progressives saw that it could sway the balance of power away from the EU and NATO and upset the applecart of the progressive international order. Therefore, Manafort had to be stopped at all costs, he was also aware that this was orchestrated by Deep State operatives: "From the very beginning I suspected some involvement by the Deep State, which would stop at nothing to destroy Trump's credibility, devaluate his victory, and delegitimize his presidency. I was never so right in my life."[265] In the aftermath of the radical government overthrow of Manafort's consulting clients in the Party of Regions and of President Yanukovych, regime socialist Poroshenko came to power in 2015 and helped to establish the National Anti-Corruption Bureau of Ukraine (NABU). It is ironic that NABU, an anti-corruption agency was not only established under the socialist Ukrainian president Poroshenko, but also operated in a nation with a proven track record of corruption. NABU receives funding through such progressive agencies as USAID (United States Agency for International Development) that was an active sponsor of the Wuhan level-four biolab and gain-of-function COVID research. NABU also entered a counterintelligence-sharing partnership with the FBI and soon opened a political case against Manafort. Ukrainian deputy prosecutors, a special anti-corruption prosecutor, the NABU director and a self-proclaimed "whistleblower" met with the FBI to discuss Americans who were associated with the Party of Regions.

---

[264] Ibid, 120.

[265] Manafort, *Political Prisoner*, 125.

The multi-pronged attack on Manafort would include not only NABU, but also the Ukrainian embassy along the FBI and Obama's Crossfire Hurricane team. During the trials, mainstream and social media were going after Manafort likes sharks smelling blood in the water. He gave the following description of the scenes that unfolded on the federal courthouse steps: "During my trial, George Soros was funding groups to have people stand in front of the Federal courthouse holding signs that said 'Traitor, Go Back to Russia,' and 'Puttin Puppet.'"[266] During the course of the investigations, Manafort was scheduled to appear before the Senate Intelligence Committee on July 26, 2017, but the hearing was called off without explanation. Then, the following week at 6:00am, more than a dozen armed FBI agents raided Manafort's home while he and his wife were in bed. For over ten hours agents searched through every area of Manafort's home seizing information from all electronic equipment.[267] Although Manafort had been compliant with all aspects of the investigation, Mueller issued the search warrant on grounds that it was necessary to conduct the raid on the suspicions of criminal activity and interactions with hostile foreign agents. Over the next two years, Manafort faced a series of indictments and charges in two federal courts. Eventually, he was declared guilty on a host of trumped-up charges, everything from income tax returns, failure to disclose foreign bank accounts, to failure to register as a foreign agent. Manafort was sentenced to four years in prison. Trump would grant Manafort a full pardon just before he left office. All throughout Trump's time in the White House, there would never be anything that would prove the Russian collusion narrative. Furthermore, the greatest source document behind the Mueller investigation and Russia Gate, the Steele Dossier would be proven bogus.

---

[266] Manafort, *Political Prisoner*, 142.

[267] Catherine Herridge, *FBI's Manafort Raid Included a Dozen Agents, Designed to Intimidate*, Fox News, August 24, 2017. Source accessed October 27, 2023, from https://www.foxnews.com.

The Awkward and Embarrassing Truth of the Bogus Steele Dossier

Although too late in the process, much of the damage that had been done to innocent conservatives was based on the highly erroneous dossier fabricated by Steele and his colleagues through Fusion GPS. Everything behind Fusion, Orbis, and the fake dossier was a plot of Hillary Clinton to add fuel to the Russian collusion narrative and to damage and discredit Trump and his team.[268] First, Steele never went to Russia and instead drew upon various internet sources he claimed had legitimate intelligence on Russian agents who were operatives with Trump and Putin. Investigative researcher, Daniel David Elles wrote: "Steele never went to Russia for research included in the dossier. Instead, he relied on a source network of questionable contacts that provided Steele with DISINFORMATION."[269] At a hearing Simpson on behalf of Fusion would reveal that Steele never met his confidential sources in person. When asked why he did not go to Russia to meet directly with the sources, Simpson replied with the lame response that Steele did not want to blow his cover and put himself in danger. Really, the courageous whistleblower and former British MI6 intelligence officer would not be willing to risk his life for something that he regarded as the absolute revelation for the Trump-Putin narrative? Yet, he certainly had no reservations about peddling the fake dossier to Fusion. Even Simpson himself would later back pedal his belief in the authenticity of Steele's dossier in a Senate inquiry: "We're going to present to you things that we think come from credible sources, but we're not going to warrant to you that this is all true."[270] Simpson was now saying that he was hesitant to vouch for the accuracy of the Dossier that was given to the FBI and would be used as substance for the Mueller investigations? The dossier made serious allegations into the story on Russian collusion

---

[268] McCarthy, *Ball of Collusion*, 125.

[269] Daniel David Elles, *The Steele Dossier: What the Mainstream Media Won't Tell Us*, (Detroit, MI: Tiber Publishing, 2018), 26-27.

[270] Ibid, 30.

and how Trump worked with foreign agents to interfere with the elections. Other dossier allegations are simply far-fetched such as: *The Orthodox church is an arm of the Russian state. The Kushner's are ethnic Russian, and they have relationships in the Russian capitol. Trump had connections to a lot of Italian mafia figures, and then gradually during the nineties became associated with Russian mafia.* The dossier is such an amateur compilation of information supposedly derived from professional intelligence sources that it is incredible that the FBI did not properly vet these sources initially. Now they are distancing themselves from the dossier and much of the mainstream media has gone silent on the intelligence document of the century. Paul Gregory wrote, "In intelligence circles, the credibility of sources is the first question asked. Are they who they say they are? Can we trust what they are telling us? Do the sources have a hidden agenda? On all counts, Steele's sources fail."[271] Later, in a Senate Judiciary Committee meeting, Chairman Grassley would state: "But there is substantial evidence suggesting that Mr. Steele materially misled the FBI about a key aspect of his dossier efforts, one which bears on his credibility."[272] And remember Nellie Ohr the Russian language expert hired by Fusion GPS? Ohr's husband by coincidence also works for the Justice Department and claimed to have exchanged hundreds of encrypted email texts regarding Trump's connections with Russia in collaboration with Steele. This claim was later followed by the highly acclaimed but fake videotapes of prostitutes who were paid by Trump to urinate on the bed where the Obama's stayed at the Ritz Carlton's presidential suite in Moscow. The infamous *Pee Tapes* were claimed by Steele and Simpson to be used as blackmail recorded by the Russian FSB (kompromat).[273] This most outrageous claim also lacked

---

[271] Paul R. Gregory, *Why Was the Steele Dossier Not Dismissed as a Fake?* February 3, 2020. Hoover Institution. Source accessed October 27, 2023, from https://www.hoover.org.

[272] Elles, *The Steele Dossier*, 31.

[273] Andrew Prokop, *The Pee Tape Claim Explained*, April 23, 2018, Vox. Source accessed October 27, 2023, from https://www.vox.com.

any verification or authenticity and was as fallacious as the whole dossier. As for the so called "black ledger," just like the Steele Dossier, it was never substantiated. No one in the Party of Regions ever referenced the use of such a ledger for accounting purposes. Furthermore, one of the ledger documents sent to the media had a forged signature that claimed it was Manafort's. According to Manafort: "The Ukrainian who had released the "black ledger" at a press conference in Kyiv was not very sophisticated. His participation in this ruse was not something he would have thought up one morning. I reasoned that there was something larger and more sinister going on."[274] What Manafort was alluding to as "being sinister" is the entire fiasco of Russian collusion narrative along with the falsified documents of the Steele Dossier and the black ledger that would be used by Deep State operatives. Obama's Crossfire Hurricane and the Mueller investigation would take down good conservative patriots and then under the Biden administration Trump would become the ultimate target through a series of indictments and two impeachments. All of this would be carried out part of the greatest hypocrisy of the leftist political establishment ever because the left had its own trail of criminal activity in Kyiv.

The Brazen Hypocrisy of the Deep State Democratic Socialists in Ukraine

The progressive-leftist Deep State ties to Ukraine get interesting. When Manafort first appeared on the radar screen of the Mueller investigation, it was through the influence of Alexandra Chalupa, a Ukrainian-American who was a Democratic consultant for Hillary Clinton. Chalupa had ties to Kyiv that included Serhiy Leshchenko, a Ukrainian legislator who worked in the opposition Bloc to defeat Yanukovich. Leshchenko is a Ukrainian billionaire who gave generous donations of millions of dollars to the Clinton Foundation. Therefore,

---

[274] Manafort, *Political Prisoner*, 104-105.

it is no surprise that the wealthy Ukrainian oligarch also was quite vocal in his opposition to Trump: "A Trump presidency would change the pro-Ukrainian agenda in American foreign policy. Trump was a pro-Russian candidate who can break the geopolitical balance in the world. That is why most Ukrainian politicians were on Hillary Clinton's side."[275] It also turned out that Leshchenko was a direct source for Fusion GPS.[276] Ironically there would be conservatives in the Ukrainian parliament who would accuse Leshchenko of trying to interfere with the US elections! McCarthy sarcastically called this a reversed case of Russia collusion but this time around it was the Dems with Ukraine: "*Clinton Campaign Collusion with Ukraine*.[277] Ukraine and its corruption became a vortex for another collusion narrative all on its own. It was in this context that NABU investigators and Ukrainian prosecutors traveled to Washington to meet with the Obama administration, the FBI, and the Justice Department to discuss Manafort's ties to the Party of Regions. Under the Obama administration, Vice President Joe Biden pressured President Poroshenko into firing top prosecutor Viktor Shokin, who was investigating the Ukrainian natural gas company Burisma (that incidentally had his son Hunter on the board of directors).[278] Biden, in return for Shokin's firing authorized the IMF to grant Ukraine's government a $17.5 billion loan package. The vice president later boasted of using the loan as leverage to get the chief prosecutor fired. Meanwhile Burisma compensated Hunter's law firm with more than $3 million that was paid out over an eighteen-month span.[279] In addition to Hunter Biden profiting from Burisma, subpoenaed bank records were released revealing direct monthly deposits over

---

[275] McCarthy, *Ball of Collusion*, 119.

[276] Ibid, 120.

[277] McCarthy, *Ball of Collusion*, 118-121.

[278]

[279] John Solomon, *Joe Biden's 2020 Ukrainian Nightmare: A Closed Probe is Revived*. The Hill, April 1, 2019. Source accessed December 20, 2023, from https://www.congress.gov/116/meeting/house.

$24 million through over twenty shell corporations that included Joe Biden as recipient as well.[280] This was nothing compared to the $1.5 billion with Hunter's joint investment fund with China. However, when Trump later called Zelensky on July 25, 2019, to inquire about the role that Joe Biden had played in the firing of Shokin, the US House initiated impeachment proceedings against Trump on the grounds that he abused his power by attempting to solicit a foreign government for information that would influence the 2020 election.[281] The hypocrisy is astounding that the leftist regime has been using Ukraine as their virtual operations center for the liberal international order as well as to put cash into their own pockets without any accountability. Yet, it has been also weaponized against conservatives such as Trump, his campaign team and staff members included. Dan Bongino described Ukraine as a money-laundering operation for the Deep State: "Ukraine is a giant, twenty-four-hour ATM. A broken slot machine that spewed out money to greedy politicos, lobbyists, and yes, a son of the Vice President of the United States."[282]

I want to include an important side note concurrent with Israel's war on Hamas. We must put the brakes on full-stop to funding the proxy war in Ukraine and assist our friend Israel. With the recent conflicts escalating between Israel and Hamas, there is significant pressure calling for a "combination funding" package for both Israel and Ukraine. Democrats are comparing Israel's battle against Hamas terrorists with Ukraine fighting against Russia. Although Russia is certainly a hostile power to be reckoned with, it is faulty logic to compare the proxy war in Ukraine with Israel's war on the Hamas terrorists. The war in Ukraine

---

[280] Committee on Oversight & Accountability, *Comer Releases Direct Monthly Payments to Joe Biden from Hunter Biden's Business Entity*. December 4, 2023. Source accessed December 20, 2023, from https://oversight.house.gov/release/comer-releases-direct-monthly-to-joe-biden.

[281] The Post Millennial, August 27, 2023, *Former Ukrainian Prosecutor Viktor Shokin CONFIRMS He Was Fired After Joe Biden Demanded it*. Source accessed October 30, 2023, from https://thepostmillennial.com.

[282] Bongino, *Follow the Money*, 4.

is a protracted conflict that has a voracious appetite for billions of dollars from the US with no end in sight. There's no accountability from the Ukrainian government to show where our money is going and no plans for strategic or objective military outcomes. Whereas most of the GOP is weary of the insane funding of billions of dollars for this proxy war in Ukraine they do have a vested interest in assisting Israel. I sincerely believe that we should direct funding to Israel and not Ukraine. Ukraine is an enormous cavern of corruption and throwing more and more money into it for the last thirty years has not yielded any tangible results. Israel, however, has been the friend of the US since 1948 when it became a nation. They are in the hotbed of Islamic extremism, literally surrounded by hostile enemies and will accomplish the greatest results in the fight against terrorism. Because the Democrats and establishment Rino Republicans want to continue funding Ukraine, they see the conservative GOP interest in assisting Israel as an opportunity for another cash cow for Kyiv. Some of the establishment Republicans like Mitch McConnel (R-KY.) are pressuring other GOP members to cave into approving dual funding packages for both Israel and Ukraine.[283] Going forward this money laundering corruption at the "epicenter of the Ukrainian vortex" must be exposed and brought into the forum of public accountability. The criminal offenses must be fully prosecuted and the attacks upon good patriot-conservatives by the Deep State swamp must be stopped. There is some light on the horizon as public reports that expose this corruption in Ukraine are being released in Senate Committee hearings. The earliest and most substantial of these is an eighty-seven-page report that was released in 2020 through the efforts of Republican Senators Chuck Grassley from Iowa and Ron Johnson from Wisconsin. Their report is worth examining because it is an important start for an investigation process, and I have summarized its key elements in the following section.

---

[283] Sareen Habeshian, *Mitch McConnel Doubles Down Support for Ukraine Aid*, October 30, 2023. Axios Politics & Policy News. Source accessed November 1, 2023, from https://www.axios.com.

Subcommittee Investigations on Hunter Biden, Burisma & Corruption

Senator Ron Johnson (R-Wis.) is the ranking member of the Permanent Subcommittee on Investigations and Senator Chuck Grassley (R-Iowa) is the ranking member of the Senate Judiciary Committee. Together, they have released over 220 pages of critical foreign documents and banking records in support of a criminal probe on the Biden family.[284] The records regarding the Biden criminal investigation examine Hunter Biden's lucrative business dealings not only in Ukraine and Russia but also in Communist China while Joe Biden was Vice President in the Obama administration. The findings of Johnson and Grassley are fully detailed in their US Senate Committee report titled *Hunter Biden, Burisma, and Corruption*. Shortly after the violent Euromaidan revolution in Kyiv, on April 16, 2014, Vice President Biden met with his son Hunter's business partner Devon Archer at the White House.[285] Within a week of this meeting Archer joined Burisma's board of directors. The Executive Summary of Grassley's also mentioned that at the same time of the White House meeting British officials seized $23 million from the London bank accounts of Burisma's owner and corrupt Ukrainian oligarch Mykola Zlochevsky. Hunter soon joined Burisma's board and not only received millions of dollars from corrupt Ukrainian oligarchs but received a cushy $50,000 a month salary in addition to Secret Service protection services for his business travel to Ukraine, Russia and China at the expense of American taxpayers.[286]

---

[284] Ron Johnson US Senator for Wisconsin, *Senators Johnson, Grassley Share Investigative Material with Prosecutors in Hunter Biden Criminal Probe*. October 26, 2022, Press Release. Source accessed October 31, 2023, from https://www.ronjohnson.senate.gov.

[285] *Hunter Biden, Burisma & Corruption: The Impact on US Government Policy and Related Concerns*, released on September 23, 2020, by US Senate Committee on Homeland Security & Governmental Affairs & the US Senate Committee on Finance. (New York: Cosimo Reports, 2020), 3.

[286] Ibid, 5.

He also received other benefits like $142,300 for a car granted through his business partner Archer the same day that his father appeared in Kyiv to discuss Russian actions in Crimea. The Obama administration was fully aware of Hunter Biden's position on the board even though it was perceived as a conflict of interest with the execution of foreign policies in Ukraine. In 2015 the former Acting Deputy Chief of Mission, George Kent, at the US Embassy in Kyiv voiced his concerns about this perceived conflict of interest: "Furthermore, the presence of Hunter Biden on the Burisma board was very awkward for all US officials pushing an anticorruption agenda in Ukraine."[287] Specifically, what Kent was referring to was the same NABU anti-corruption team and the FBI that was weaponized against Paul Manafort. Now they had to hypocritically turn their eyes away from Biden's involvement with corrupt oligarchs as if it were not a problem if the VP's son is involved. Zlochevsky paid a $7 million bribe to staff officials serving the Ukraine prosecutor general who were working with NABU. The attacks which were made upon Trump's business relations in Russia were hypocritical excuses for the Russian collusion narrative as Hunter had corrupt business deals in Moscow. None of these concerns over an apparent conflict of interest prevented Hunter's lucrative business relations with Burisma because it was reported by the US Senate Committee report that he received a $3.5 million wire transfer from Elena Baturina, the wife of the former mayor of Moscow.[288] Shortly after that Hunter also opened a bank account to fund a $100,000 global shopping spree with James and Sara Biden. There are even financial transaction records where Hunter paid Russian and Eastern European women who were linked to prostitution and sex trafficking rings. The report also mentions the incident regarding Ukrainian prosecutor Victor Shokin who was investigating Burisma's owner Zlochevsky, and how Vice President Biden threatened to withhold $1 billion in IMF loans if Shokin was

---

[287] Ibid, 4.

[288] *Hunter Biden, Burisma & Corruption*, 5.

not fired.[289] The Burisma energy company had direct ties to Ukraine's involvement with the Municipal Energy Reform Program (MERP). MERP is a cash cow program funded by USAID for the implementation of renewable energy projects in Ukraine. USAID is the same entity that streamed funding for the COVID gain of function lab in Wuhan, China. MERP's key goal is to "reduce the consumption of conventional energy in Ukraine and cutting greenhouse gas (GHG) emissions" to meet EU compliance.[290] How convenient to have green ecology U.N. sustainability doctrine at the core of Burisma's values to make sure that Hunter's business leaves no nasty carbon footprint on the environment. This might be good PR for the ecosystem and for the Bidens although the atmosphere was already foul and polluted through their involvement with wealthy Ukrainian oligarchs.

---

[289] Ibid.

[290] USAID *Municipal Energy Reform in Ukraine*, January 2014 Municipal Energy Reform. Award No. IDIQ#AID-0AA-1-13-00015, Task Order: AID-121-TO-13-00006.

Chapter Six:

Conclusion: Getting America Back to the Vision of Our Founders After Decades of Foreign Policy Disasters

Herein lay the rationale behind the American diplomatic practice of standing aloof, so far as possible, from conflicts that occurred in Europe. The two most famous articulations of this theme – Washington's Farewell Address (1796) and Jefferson's First Inaugural Address (1801) – argued that a foreign policy of non-entanglement should be pursued in order to mitigate the threat posed by internal divisions. – Jay Sexton, *The Monroe Doctrine*

The Monroe Doctrine – The Founder's Intent

To understand how our foreign policy has shifted towards the support of a liberal international order and the funding of proxy wars in Ukraine, it is crucial that we look at how far we have moved from the original intent of our Founding Fathers. How did America shift so drastically from having a government *for the people and by the people* that once valued its sovereignty to a progressive authoritarian government that advocates an open border global society? Once we realize how far our nation has strayed from sensible and conservative foreign policy through the entirety of its historical progression, then we can retrace our steps back to making America great again. Our nation did not arrive at endless foreign policy disasters that fund proxy wars in nations like Ukraine in support of a new world order overnight. Just as history is able to bring us back to the ideals that built this great Constitutional republic, history can also provide us with valuable lessons to help us to chart the course back to a foreign policy that puts America first. The vision of a strong constitutional republic (not a democracy) promoted secure borders and a strong military to defend citizens from enemies both foreign and domestic. It promoted an America first policy and was careful not to relegate our interests to be subservient to a liberal international order. The nation's founders laid the framework for this America first foreign policy which was later clearly articulated during the administration of James Monroe. Monroe before he became the fifth president of the US was an American statesman with an impressive record in both domestic and foreign affairs. At the age of sixteen he enlisted to fight in the American Revolution and as a lieutenant crossed the Delaware with General Washington. Monroe was quickly promoted to the rank of captain and later shared in the hardships with his fellow troops during the cruel winter at Valley Forge.[291] In 1780, after resigning his military commission, he pursued the study of law under Thomas Jefferson when Jefferson served as the governor of Virginia. Jefferson was quite influential in Monroe's political career. Monroe was elected to the Virginia House of Delegates in 1782 and later served in Congress. In 1794 Washington nominated Monroe to serve as minister to France. After his first tour of foreign service in 1797 he was the author of a five-hundred-page report entitled *A View of the Conduct of the Executive in the Foreign Affairs of the United States*. In this extensively detailed work, Monroe addressed the fragile situation in Europe in light of the French

---

[291] Samuel Flagg Bemis, *James Monroe: President of the United States*, Britannica, October 18, 2023. Source accessed November 9, 2023, from https://www.britannica.com/biography/James-monroe.

Revolution and why it was in the best interest of the US to avoid direct engagement of international military conflicts:

> Examine next the external relations of France. The foreign ministers except the minister of the United States, had fled. The alliances against her were multiplying; the enemy numerous; their object to erect a military government; the empire of Great Britain on the brink of being uncontrolled. The French army was undisciplined... Every political motive dissuaded us from war, for we were without obligation to enter into it as a party. [292]

This work served as the catalyst of thought for Monroe's foreign policy development in later years.

In 1799 Monroe became the governor of Virginia and was elected twice serving until 1802. Later when Jefferson was president, Monroe was appointed to serve as envoy and minister to France in 1803. During the time of the Louisiana Purchase, many individuals were concerned that the continental US would be subject to territorial acquisitions from European nations such as France, Spain, and England. Monroe became involved with negotiations in Paris until after the Louisiana Purchase was completed. In 1805, Monroe traveled to London where he became involved with negotiations to address the forced recruitment of naval service personnel. Monroe was later assisted by William Pinkney of Maryland in these negotiations with the British. The Royal Navy would board US vessels by force to search for British deserters and this became the basis of heated confrontation with England. After his second tour of foreign service was completed, Monroe was elected president of the United States in 1817 and became the chief architect of the earliest foreign policy document, known as the Monroe Doctrine in response to national security concerns. Six years later Monroe met with his cabinet in the autumn of

---

[292] James Monroe, *A View of the Conduct of the Executive in the Foreign Affairs of the United States*, 1797. Digital Reprint Copy. (Miami, FL: Hard Press Publishing), 306.

1823 to respond to increased concerns that the European powers would recolonize the new independent states of Spanish America.[293] This doctrine that came as the result of the cabinet's discussions stated that "the Western Hemisphere was no longer open to European colonization and political intervention" and that "the American continents, by the free and independent condition which they have assumed and maintain, are henceforth not to be considered as subjects for colonization by any European powers."[294] The chief concern addressed was American opposition to European colonialism. Monroe had been influenced by both George Washington and Thomas Jefferson who advocated a policy of non-entanglement for the nation. They realized that involvement in foreign wars that were not a direct threat to our national security or did not serve our domestic interests were not in the best interest of the American people. Washington wanted to encourage trade relations with foreign nations as long as it was not a conflict of interest to the values of our constitutional republic: "The great rule of conduct for us in regard to foreign nations is in extending our commercial relations, to have with them as little political connection as possible."[295] Today's foreign policy interests runs against the grain of Washington's admonition from both parties. We see a progressive element that is more concerned with the political democratization of nations with the interests of promoting a global society. And even worse both parties have encouraged open trade and commerce with Communist China, an enemy driven by global conquest. Some have criticized the Monroe Doctrine for being too narrow in its scope of application considering the complexities of modern world events. Also, a mere eighty years after Monroe constructed his foreign policy statement, it was seriously challenged and even characterized as being out-of-date with the times.

---

[293] Jay Sexton, *The Monroe Doctrine: Empire & Nation in the Nineteenth-Century America*, (New York: Hill & Yang, 2011), 3.

[294] Ibid.

[295] Sexton, *The Monroe Doctrine*, 29.

The 19th Century Progressive Shift: The Roosevelt Corollary to the Monroe Doctrine

Until the early nineteenth century the American way of life was more focused upon domestic business at home rather than direct engagement with international affairs abroad. The industrial revolution and the development of railroads catapulted simplistic agrarian and pioneer society into a rapid continental urbanization. The advent of modern sea-faring vessels and the development of passenger aircraft brought the continents of South America, Europe, and Asia within much quicker reach. International trade and commerce, encouraged by the early founders, was now envisioned as an expanding enterprise with transatlantic travel in sight. In the era prior to vast technological progress was made in international travel (i.e., ocean transit and transatlantic passenger flights), America had little interest in direct intervention with foreign powers. This all began to change when the US became increasingly involved with Latin America and, in 1888, Congress appropriated funds for the first Pan-American Conference in Washington also called a hemispheric conference. The Spanish-American War of 1889 followed shortly and was the first conflict to begin the transformation of ideas shaping American foreign policy and intervention. Americans sympathized with the poor humanitarian conditions that Cuban citizens endured as they struggled for their independence from Spain. When the US Navy sent the battleship USS Maine into Havana's port to patrol the waters and to protect US citizens in Cuba, it sank on February 15, 1898, because of a massive explosion that killed all the crew on.[296] Newspaper journalists immediately claimed that the navy vessel was sunk by a Spanish torpedo; although this was never confirmed it helped to mobilize the US into war. Republican Theodore Roosevelt, who was the Assistant Secretary of the Navy, led the charge with the

---

[296] *Spanish-American War*, Britannica. Source accessed November 6, 2023, from https://www.britannica.com/event/Spanish-American-War/Fighting-in-the-Philippines-and-Cuba.

famous Rough Riders, a volunteer calvary brigade. After several key battles over a brief span of nearly six months, the Spanish armies surrendered on August 12, 1898. Riding on the wave of popularity with the Rough Riders, Roosevelt was elected as a Republican vice president in 1898 along with President William McKinley. After McKinley was assassinated, Roosevelt assumed the powers of the executive office on September 14, 1901. During this time, he delivered speeches aimed at raising public consciousness about the nation's role in world politics because he saw the Spanish-American War as an ending to American isolationism. Roosevelt also tended toward a more moderate political view compared to other Republican conservatives. When European nations began to become directly involved in Latin America to collect debts, he was even more motivated to influence American foreign policy to adopt measures inclined toward direct intervention. To accomplish this Roosevelt realized that the Monroe Doctrine would need to be expanded beyond the initial intent of the Founders and other early American statesman. In 1904 he framed the first significant revisions to Monroe known as the Roosevelt Corollary.

Roosevelt viewed the Monroe Doctrine in a new light capable of moving from a focus only upon national interests to the "larger interests of the true interests of Western Civilization." Jay Sexton described Theordore Roosevelt's aspirations for broadening the Monroe Doctrine into a more inclusive foreign policy approach: "Roosevelt went to great lengths to emphasize the advantages it yielded to the broader constituency of civilization...It compelled the United States, despite its tradition of nonentaglement, to promote its values and political practices to putatively less civilized peoples."[297] Because US concerns over foreign involvement in the Latin American countries, Roosevelt contended that the Monroe Doctrine needed to have a broader sphere of influence. Therefore, in 1904 Roosevelt announced the new Latin America policy that became known as the Roosevelt Corollary to the Monroe

---

[297] Sexton, *The Monroe Doctrine*, 216-17 & 229.

Doctrine.[298] This was paired with Roosevelt's "Big Stick" policy, which asserted that US domination in foreign nations is legitimate whenever, it is "considered as a moral imperative."[299] These changes resulted in the Big Stick proverb that became a favorite of Roosevelt's advocacy for foreign intervention: "Speak softly and carry a big stick; you will go far."[300] On the other hand, those who affirmed an America first sentiment and saw that domestic interests should be a matter of priority without interference in the affairs of foreign nations were called "isolationists." On the other hand, those who held to a more progressive approach toward international engagement were deemed as "interventionists." Sexton added that the result of the Roosevelt Corollary brought about a unification of nationalism and internationalism and that this convergence prepared the way to shift American foreign policy away from traditional isolationism to a greater openness toward interventionism. The interventionist ideas promoted by Theodore Roosevelt as Sexton surmised would also include broadening US powers beyond the American continents: "Roosevelt declared, 'may in America, as elsewhere, ultimately require intervention by some civilized nation, and in the Western Hemisphere the adherence of the United States to the Monroe Doctrine may force the United States, however, reluctantly, in flagrant cases of such wrongdoing or impotence, to the exercise of an international police power.'"[301] This would later evolve into a larger application of the US role as an international police power in the Second World War under the administration of Franklin Delanor Roosevelt.

---

[298] *The Roosevelt Corollary; United States [1904]*, Britannica. Source accessed November 10, 2023, from https://www.britannica.com/event/Roosevelt-Corollary.

[299] Ibid.

[300] Ibid.

[301] Sexton, *The Monroe Doctrine*, 229.

The Development of 19th Century Progressivism

As the conflicts in Europe during the First World War began to invoke feelings of anxiety among Americans, public opinion held that it would be in the best interest of the nation not to become involved via direct military intervention. It was one matter to be involved with the affairs of America's back door neighbors in Latin America under Theodore Roosevelt who led the charge of the Rough Riders in Cuba, but the idea of sending American soldiers to fight on the other side of the Atlantic was not popular at the time. Roosevelt sought reelection in 1912 but took a more progressive position in opposition to conservative Republicans and formed his own independent party known as the "Bull Moose Party."[302] This resulted in a split in the Republican party with William Taft representing most conservatives. Democratic contender Woodrow Wilson was elected with only 42 percent of the popular vote and a landslide victory in the electoral college, winning 435 votes to only 88 for Roosevelt. Wilson was a professional academic prior to running for political office and served as president of Princeton University. Although he was popular for his Ivy League persona, Wilson's ideological construct was steeped in racism. One might be surprised that such an enlightened academic as Wilson could be influenced by prejudiced beliefs. However, early 19th century progressivism was challenging every institution in science, literature, religion, and politics. I will purposely digress here as I believe that it is not only important to understand the historical context in which liberals like Wilson paved the way toward moving our priorities from traditional nationalism toward progressive globalism, but we must also realize the huge ideological paradigm shifts as well. This ideological revolution was also cast by such radical liberals as Charles Darwin, Karl Marx and Frederich Engels, who paved the way for the prevailing 19th century progressive enlightenment. Globalism and the new world order that drives foreign policy

---

[302] *Bull Moose Party*, Britannica. Source accessed November 13, 2023, from https://www.britannica.com/topic/Bull-Moose-Party.

in Europe and more specifically in Ukraine and with current events around the world is best understood in the context of liberal influence of foreign policy. Liberalism has invaded every institution on the face of the earth – government, education, media, arts, entertainment and religion. I will address in greater detail the philosophical world view of globalism at the end of this chapter, but for now individuals such as Darwin and Marx were among the *Apostles of Progressive Ideology* that laid the foundation for the Great Reset. Darwin's *Origin of the Species* postulated an evolutionary theory which claimed that simple biological organisms through millions of years of adaptation transcended into more complex life forms through a "survival of the fittest."[303] Darwin's theory was quickly embraced by Marx and Lenin who applied it to their theories of class struggle in their early foundational tenets of communism.[304] Far beyond a biological evolutionism, they saw a greater "social evolution" that would transform not only politics but all of society as a whole: "Communism abolishes eternal truths, it abolishes all religion, and all morality, instead of constituting them on a new basis; it therefore acts in contradiction to all past historical experience."[305] This radical progressive ideology which challenged every traditional institution found itself in major universities such as Princeton where Wilson spent much of his career before entering political service. Samuel Zipp describes Wilson's era of progressive enlightenment as follows:

> Social Darwinism, eugenics, and other popular theories of biological determinism were fashionable and influential, masquerading as common sense and giving an imprimatur of scientific authority to the racial hierarchies endemic to American society...These were, at their heart, theories of biological difference marked by race;

---

[303] Service, *Comrades!*, 18-19.

[304] Ibid.

[305] Karl Marx & Frederich Engels, *The Communist Manifesto*. Reprint of 1888 translation (Miami, FL: Savage Publishing, 2019), 35.

the savages were the inevitably dark-skinned peoples 'over there.'[306]

Darwin's "survival of the fittest" theories became the focal point for white progressive intellectuals to assert such preposterous ideas as the advancement of the Aryan races, which was found in Hitler's Third Reich and Nazi self-determinism world views. But their origin was influenced by such individuals as Francis Galton a devout follower of Darwin, who became the "father of Eugenics" and the progenitor of modern human gene editing. These transhumanism evolutionary concepts are widely supported by Great Reset global elites such as Klaus Schwab, the architect of the *Fourth Industrial Revolution*. Eugenics as mentioned here, is the "selection of desired heritable characteristics in order to improve future generations, typically in reference to humans."[307] Margaret Sanger the founder of Planned Parenthood widely promoted applied principles of eugenics and abortion as a means of population control within African American populations. Sanger promoted her progressive ideas in her magazine *The Woman Rebel; No Gods, No Masters,* as early as 1914 and extensively supported racial eugenics in some her other published works, such as *The Pivot of Civilization* and the *Negro Project*.[308] Is there doubt that the Democratic party, the party of racial tolerance and inclusiveness would promote funding for the murder of unborn babies in the womb as "women's health care" given the troubling racist legacy it has? These ideas were promulgated extensively by progressive elites in the 20th century and continue to trend among liberal leaders and their political platforms today.

---

[306] Samuel Zipp, *The Idealist: Wendell Wilkie's Wartime Quest to Build One World*, (Cambridge, MA: Harvard University Press, 2020), 30-31.

[307] Philip K. Wilson, *Eugenics: Genetics*, Britannica. Source accessed November 13, 2023, from https://www.britannica.com/science/eugenics-genetics.

[308] Abigail Shivers, *Margaret Sanger: Ambitious Feminist & Racist Eugenicist*, September 21, 2022, The University of Chicago. Source accessed November 13, 2023, from https://womanisrational.uchicago.edu.

Woodrow Wilson's League of Nations and Emerging Trends in Global Idealism

By the time Wilson assumed Executive Office in 1912, very few raised issues with his inclinations toward racism as it was already espoused by other progressive elites of the day. As a staunch believer in white supremacy, he was led by the idea that Europe and the United States should run the new world body: "The East is to be opened and transformed whether we will it or not: the standards of the West are to be imposed upon it; nations and peoples which have stood still the centuries through are to be quickened, and made part of the universal world of commerce and ideas which has so steadily been a-making by the advance of European power from age to age."[309] He set forth one of the earliest American concepts of international democratization that would gain momentum for decades to come. Wilson, during his first term of office, made sweeping progressive overhauls granting the Federal government greater powers of authority (a popular Democratic goal for building big government): the Sixteenth Amendment to the Constitution creating a national income tax, the creation of the Federal Reserve System, the Clayton Antitrust Act that regulated business competition and granted labor unions greater protections, and the creation of the Federal Trade Commission which regulated private business practices. With the First World War on the hearts and minds of the American people, Wilson was at first cautious about committing the nation's military overseas. On May 7, 1915, when a German U-boat sank the British liner Lusitania killing more than 1,100 people on board including 128 Americans, there was a lot of talk about retaliatory US military action.[310] Wilson was re-elected in 1916, winning on the rhetoric of his campaign slogan *He kept us out of war* along with his

---

[309] Zipp, *The Idealist*, 70-71.

[310] John Milton Cooper, *Woodrow Wilson: President of the United States*, Britannica. Source accessed November 13, 2023, from https://www.britannica.com/biography/Woodrow-Wilson.

progressive views on labor issues. It is during this time that Wilson began making speeches about "peace without victory" and the call for a league of nations to prevent future wars. However, as Germany ramped up their U-boat operations and with the ever-increasing threat of hostile blockades in the Atlantic, Wilson made a declaration for war before Congress on April 2, 1917, stating that "the world must be made safe for democracy." The enactment of the Selective Service Act assured that plenty of Americans would be recruited to support the war efforts in Europe. On January 8, 1918, Wilson proposed his goals for a postwar peace settlement known as the "Fourteen Points."[311] In his address to a joint session of the US Congress he called for open covenants of peace and open international trade relations. By the time of the Armistice of November 11, 1918, there had been over 40 million casualties from all sides combined in what would be known as the first modern conventional war. The American public was at this time war weary and wanting to move on. Wilson continued to push for his League of Nations to call for international peace until his death in 1921, but it did not gain enough support in Congress because of conservative push-back. After Wilson's death, foreign policy would swing back to the isolationist side for at least another twenty years much to the dismay of interventionists. However, Wilson's legacy would live on to see an emerging era of global idealism. Following Wilson's death, a group of progressive civic leaders and businessmen would unite to keep the flame of Wilson's vision burning by establishing a club in 1921, known as the Council on Foreign Relations (CFR). The club was officially chartered on July 29, 1921, with the goal of promoting, through invitation-only membership "a continuous conference on international questions affecting the United States."[312] The CFR elected the following as its first officers: Elihu Root (US Secretary of State and a moderate Republican), John Davis

---

[311] *Fourteen Points: United States Declaration*, Britannica. Source accessed November 13, 2023, from https://www.britannica.com/biography/Woodrow-Points.

[312] George Gavrilis, *The Council on Foreign Relations: A Short History*. (New York: Council on Foreign Relations, 2021), 9.

(a Wall Street lawyer), and Edwin Gay (the former dean of Harvard's School of Business). Just two years prior to the Second World War the executive director of the CFR contacted the State Department to offer their services as an advisory group for American foreign policy.[313] The foreign policy consultation project was titled "War and Peace Studies" and according to CFR executive director Mallory: "The men of the Council proposed a program of independent analysis and study that would guide American foreign policy in the coming years of war and the challenging new world that would emerge after."[314] Note the phrase "the challenging new world" which would be the earliest ideological basis for the new world order that would be later refined by Presidents Bush senior and junior. This collaboration project between the CFR and the State Department was kept confidential from the public during the war because of concerns that there would be criticisms with the US government working with an independent think-tank organization. Over the next five years, the Rockefeller Foundation provided $350,000 to fund one hundred personnel for the CFR project. The foreign policy collaboration between CFR and the State Department would continue after the war according to Bart Kessler: "In the spring of 1943, Armstrong, and Norman H. Davis (a Council Director) proposed a plan to Secretary of State Hull for a 'supranational organization' based on the Wilsonian ideals of liberal internationalism." Twelve presidential committees that addressed foreign and military policies between 1945 and 1972 were led by members of the CFR. The CFR would steer American foreign policy toward progressive internationalism through its prominent members who served in future presidential administrations: George Bush, Zbigniew Brzezinski, Henry Kissinger, Dick Cheney, Willaim Cohen, and Alan Greenspan. What seems like a conspiracy theory to many individuals regarding a progressive think tank that would influence American foreign policy was questioned by only a few conservatives.

---

[313] Bart R. Kessler, *Bush's New World Order*, 6-7.

[314] Ibid.

One of the few conservative voices that questioned the global ambitions of the CFR was Republican congressman Carroll Reese who headed a special committee on tax-exempt foundations in 1954. Reese's final report included these comments about the CFR:

> They have to a marked degree, acted as direct agents of the State Department...What we see here is a number of large foundations, primarily *The Rockefeller Foundation, The Carnegie Corporation of New York, and the Carnegie Endowment for International Peace,* using their enormous public funds to finance a one-sided approach to foreign policy and to promote it actively, among the public by propaganda, and in the Government through infiltration.[315]

Wilson laid the foundation for globalism and the new world order for the next generation, and the CFR perpetuated this vision as they received funding through wealthy progressive elites. Oxford history professor Jay Sexton summarized Wilson's enduring vision of peace through an international order: "Woodrow Wilson believed that American principles would transform global politics...Wilson hoped to use his nation's newfound power as leverage for the construction of a new world order... Wilson's rhetoric made him an instant global celebrity. Anti-colonial nationalists within Old World empires were particularly drawn to his promise of a new world order."[316] Modern historians such as Sexton maintain the belief that the Monroe Doctrine had outlived its usefulness in the advent of twentieth-century American foreign policy:

> By the early twentieth century, the Monroe Doctrine had become a national myth that stood alongside the

---

[315] Bart R. Kessler, *Bush's New World Order*, 15.

[316] Sexton, *The Monroe Doctrine*, 241-44.

other foundational symbols of American history...The power of the mythic Monroe Doctrine was so great that objective attempts to assess its origins and growth, such as that of Perkins, only reinforced its status as a national dogma...Bingham wrote in 1913," Old ideas, proverbs, catchwords, national shibboleths die hard."[317]

Sexton goes even further criticizing the Monroe Doctrine as "proclaiming national exceptionalism." Although progressives see the Monroe Doctrine fading into oblivion as a national myth and the ghost of past patriotic nationalism, I believe that this historic foreign policy doctrine truly embodied the intent of our nation's Founders that America should remain strong, nationalist, and sovereign. Our American exceptionalism should stay intact as a reminder that our great constitutional republic should not be entangled with the liberal international order. However, as the Second World War loomed on the international scene, Wilson's vision for a new world order would be energized by both Democrats and Republicans alike.

Laying the Foundation for Globalism

Republican President Calvin Coolidge (1923-29) was a vocal opponent of the League of Nations.[318] Herbert Hoover (1929-33), the next Republican who followed Coolidge into the White House tended to lean toward progressive views. Hoover alienated most conservatives in his party by openly supporting Wilson's League and increased government regulation in the newly formed industries of radio broadcasting and commercial aviation.[319] Hoover's progressivism was evident when

---

[317] Ibid, 244.

[318] *Calvin Coolidge: President of the United States*, Britanica. Source accessed November 14, 2023, from https://www.britannica.com/biography/Calvin-Coolidge.

[319] *Herbert Hoover: President of the United States*, Britannica. Source accessed November 14, 2023, from https://www.britannica.com/biography/Herbert-Hoover.

he served under Wilson as the US Food Administrator and supported food shipments to Russia during the Bolshevik Revolution by justifying it as a humanitarian effort. With the Stock Market crash in 1929 followed by the Great Depression, Hoover's administration was in freefall through disastrous public opinion. This provided the Democratic Party with a landslide victory in 1932 and the election of Franklin Delano Roosevelt (FDR). Although foreign policy interventionism had been on a brief pause for two decades after Wilson's presidency, in the aftermath of the Great Depression and the international complexities of the Second World War, America would forever be thrust into the forefront of global affairs. FDR was from a wealthy aristocratic family who owned estates in New York and resorts in Europe. While a student at Harvard, in addition to being a big supporter of Woodrow Wilson, FDR's role model was his fifth cousin President Theodore Roosevelt whom he admired greatly for his progressive policies.[320] Interestingly, FDR wound up marrying Theodore Roosevelt's niece Eleanor. As FDR went on to win a third and even a fourth presidential term, events with the Second World War soon challenged non-interventionist policies.

FDR and the Global Idealists

Congress passed the Neutrality Act of 1935 to prohibit the export of US arms to foreign nations at war.[321] Although FDR went along with the act in the outset of his administration, he stated that he was adamant about revising the Neutrality Act as it would keep Americans isolated from the existential reality of such world dictator regimes in Germany, Italy, and Japan. Therefore, at an address in Chicago in 1937, he proposed taking actions of "quarantine" against

---

[320] Frank Freidel, *Franklin D. Roosevelt: President of the United States*, Britannica. Source accessed November 14, 2023, from https://www.britannica.com/biography/Franklin-D-Roosevelt#ref23940.

[321] Department of State Office of the Historian, *The Neutrality Acts, 1930's*. Source accessed November 14, 2023, from https://history.state.gov.

hostile aggressors. Later in 1939 FDR called Congress into special sessions to revise the neutrality acts to allow for Britain and France to purchase American arms on a cash and carry basis. The tensions between the isolationists who were mostly conservatives and the interventionists who were mostly progressives continued to be an uphill battle during FDR's administration. Just before the war the political landscape would change incrementally, resulting in conservatives shifting their support toward interventionism. Two individuals who played significant roles in this political shift who were relatively unknown throughout much of American history were Wendel L. Willkie and Arthur Vandenberg. Wilkie was a lifetime Democrat and progressive who saw an opportunity to rally moderate Republicans in the 1940 presidential campaign. Willkie left the Democratic Party to become a moderate Republican and ran against FDR. In his campaign he called for rescinding the Neutrality Act. Samuel Zipp an historian at Brown University who has done the most extensive biographic work on Willkie summarized his foreign policy aspirations as follows: "Most galling for the Republican old guard, however, was Willkie's long-standing internationalism. He'd never lost his belief in the ideas behind Wilson's League of Nations, a faith that nauseated the midwestern Republican leaders whose brand of insular nationalism everyone called isolationism."[322] After his loss in the election, Willkie envisioned himself to be a public spokesman, calling fellow Americans to abandon their primordial nationalism and to convert to what he considered the greater good of globalism. He came up with the idea that he would venture a flight around the world in an epic 175 days in an international good-will campaign. FDR enthusiastically supported Willkie's international diplomatic travel tour and even provided him with a sealed letter to deliver personally to Stalin in the Soviet Union. In 1942 Willkie boarded a military prop plane and traveled to nations in the Middle East, Turkey, Russia, China, and the U.K. After his world-tour, in 1943 he published the story of his travels

---

[322] Zipp, *The Idealist*, 42-43.

in a book which became the best seller of his time: *One World* in which, through evangelistic fervor and zeal, he promoted his vision of a global new world order:

> America must choose one of three courses after this war: narrow nationalism, which inevitably means the ultimate loss of our own liberty; international imperialism, which means the sacrifice of some other nation's liberty; or the creation of a world in which there shall be an equality of opportunity for every race and every nation. I am convinced the American people will choose, by overwhelming majority, the last of these courses.[323]

Although Willkie would run again unsuccessfully against FDR in the 1944 presidential campaign, his vision for the creation of a liberal international order would impact many within the Republican party to shift their support toward interventionism especially during the war. One such Republican convert to internationalism was Arthur Vandenberg through his work in Congress toward the end of the war. Vandenberg, a senator from Michigan had been a staunch isolationist during most of FDR's administration. However, Vandenberg delivered an address to his fellow Republicans on January 10, 1945, in what was called "the speech heard around the world," calling for the full support of the US in international affairs, especially with the European allies.[324] He influenced many Republicans toward supporting the U.N. and was appointed by FDR as a delegate to the U.N. conference in San Francisco. Vandenberg later became chair of the Senate Foreign Relations Committee from 1946-48 and was later instrumental in supporting the Truman Doctrine during Truman's administration. This doctrine supported the provision

---

[323] Wendell L. Willkie, *One World*, (New York: Simon & Shuster, 1943), 202-203.

[324] United States Senate Classic Senate Speeches, *Aurthur H. Vandenberg: American Foreign Policy*. Source accessed November 15, 2023, from https://www.senate.gov.

of military aid to foreign nations that were considered vulnerable to Soviet influence[325]

Declaration of the United Nations

After Britain had sustained heavy losses of destroyer fleets to the Germans over a ten-day period, Winston Churchill made direct requests to FDR for assistance. Therefore, on March 11, 1941, after greatly heated congressional debates, FDR was able to pass the Lend-Lease Act a system that would allow the US to lend or lease war supplies to "any nation deemed vital to the defense of the United States."[326] This provided fifty destroyers to Great Britain in exchange for ninety-nine-year leases on British bases in the Caribbean and Newfoundland. The ultimate game-changer for shifting American opinion away from neutrality in the war came with the Japanese attack on Pearl Harbor on December 7, 1941, resulting in the deaths of 2,500 military personnel. The very next day, FDR prompted Congress to declare war on Japan and just three days later Germany and Italy in turn declared war upon America. FDR would meet directly with Churchill in a series of war planning conferences that would also include the Soviet Union along with the Western Allies. At a conference held in August 1941, FDR and Churchill met aboard a naval vessel off the coast of Newfoundland, Canada to draft the Atlantic Charter which specified a united allied front against Nazi Germany.[327] This directly led to the formation of the United Nations on January 1, 1942 when representatives of twenty-six nations at war with the Axis powers met in Washington to sign

---

[325] Britannica, *Truman Doctrine*. Source accessed December 21, 2023, from https://www.britannica.com/event/Truman-Doctrine.

[326] National Archives, *Lend-Lease Act (1941)*. Source accessed November 14, 2023, from https://www.archives.gov.

[327] FDR Library & Museum, *The Atlantic Charter*. Source accessed November 15, 2023, from https://www.fdrlibrary.org/atlantic-charter.

the "Declaration of the United Nations."[328] At this meeting there was unanimous acceptance for endorsing the Atlantic Charter. Another important meeting was the Yalta Conference in February 1945, at which Roosevelt, Churchill, and Stalin discussed plans for the final defeat and occupation of Germany and for an international court would try war criminals at Nurnberg.[329] This would be the very first structuring of an international tribunal to expedite a legal system of justice in history. It created the uncomfortable alliance with Stalin and the Soviet Union. Toward the end of the war because of declining health FDR would not complete his term and passed away in April 1945.

The Marshall Plan and the North Atlantic Treaty

Although I addressed the role of NATO and the UN in the first chapter in relationship to the geopolitical aspects of Ukraine and Europe, here I will look at the place of these organizations in contributing to the larger context of the progressive international order. Harry Truman succeeded FDR and although he had little foreign policy experience at the time, he completed the late president's international ambitions above and beyond his executive duties.[330] The first of these accomplishments was the final approval of the U.N. Charter at a conference in San Francisco between April and June 1945 with forty-six nations represented, and 850 delegates in attendance. Collectively with their respective advisors and staff there were over 3,500 attending with

---

[328] US Department of State Office of the Historian, *The Formation of the United Nations, 1945*. Source accessed November 15, 2023, from https://history.state.gov/milestones/1937-1945/un.

[329] *Yalta Conference: World War II*, Britannica. Source accessed November 15, 2023, from https://www.britannica.com/event/Yalta-Conference.

[330] Alfred Steinberg, *Harry S. Truman: President of the United States*, Britannica. Source accessed November 14, 2023, from https://www.britannica.com/biography/Harry-S-Truman.

media coverage from more than 2,500 press, radio, and newsreel staff.[331] The U.N. officially came into existence through the signatures of various national heads of state on October 24, 1945. Although Woodrow Wilson's vision for the League of Nations never became reality during his lifetime, it took the Second World War and the momentum from progressive idealists of both the Democrat and Republican Parties to birth the vision into reality through the formation of the U.N. Truman also provided oversight of the development of the atomic bomb during his administration and ushered us into the nuclear age with the bombing of Hiroshima and Nagasaki. After Stalin reneged on his promises to deliver democratic elections for east Germany and with communism making significant advances in Europe, the immediate concern was over the containment of the Soviet Union. However, postwar European nations that had been devastated economically in the aftermath of the war and would be vulnerable to Stalin's advances. On June 5, 1947, Secretary of State George Marshall in a speech at Harvard University proposed that European nations create a plan for their economic reconstruction and that the US should provide funding and assistance. This prompted Truman to set forth Marshall's proposal to Congress on December 19, 1947. The approval of Congress led to the formation of the Marshall Plan which was passed through the Economic Cooperation Act of 1948.[332] Over the next four years, Congress appropriated $13.3 billion for European nations. In essence, Truman was the first Democratic president to commit American taxpayer dollars to European nations and this trend would continue with the formation of NATO. After Czechoslovakia came under Communist control in March 1948, the US and the Western Allies began to take steps toward an organized consolidation of military defense. In April 1949, the North Atlantic Treaty was drafted and signed by the US, Canada, Belgium, Denmark,

---

[331] United Nations, *The San Francisco Conference*. Source accessed November 15, 2023, from https://www.un.org.

[332] National Archives, *Marshall Plan (1948)*. Source accessed November 16, 2023, from https://www.archives.gov.

France, Iceland, Italy, Luxembourg, the Netherlands, Norway, Portugal and the U.K. Truman in his speech at the historic signing declared: "By this treaty, we are not only seeking to establish freedom from aggression and from the use of force in the North Atlantic community, but we are also actively striving to promote and preserve peace throughout the world."[333] What truly gave international force to the NATO treaty was expressed in Article 5:

> The Parties agree that an armed attack against one or more of them in Europe or North America shall be considered an attack against them all and consequently they agree that, if such an armed attack occurs, each of them, in exercise of the right of individual or collective self-defense recognized by Article 51 of the Charter of the United Nations, will assist the Party or Parties so attacked by taking forthwith, individually and in concert with the other Parties, such action as it deems necessary, including the use of armed force, to restore and maintain the security of the North Atlantic area.[334]

NATO's Article 5 was what truly granted the authorization of the Western Alliance to use military force against any hostile aggressor with the intent of enforcing the Cold War containment fence to keep Soviet Russia at bay. The phrase "that an armed attack against one or more of them in Europe or North America shall be considered an attack against them all" utilizes the force of a global community. This phrase conveys the idea that a global society of nations can collectively be authorized to utilize military action whenever they deem it necessary. Also, Article

---

[333] Jim Garamone, *A Short History of NATO*, April 2, 2019, US Department of Defense. Source accessed November 16, 2023, from https://www.defense.gov.

[334] NATO/OTAN, *The North Atlantic Treaty*, Washington D.C., April 4, 1949. Source accessed November 16, 2023, from https://www.nato.int.

51, Chapter VII of the U.N. Charter is invoked to further enhance this international authority:

> Nothing in the present Charter shall impair the inherent right of individual or collective self-defense if an armed attack occurs against a Member of the United Nations, until the Security Council has taken measures necessary to maintain international peace and security. Measures taken by Members in the exercise of this right of self-defense shall be immediately reported to the Security Council and shall not in any way affect the authority and responsibility of the Security Council under the present Charter to take at any time such action as it deems necessary in order to maintain or restore international peace and security.[335]

Whereas NATO's Article 5 lays the framework for a global community to justify the use of military force against any perceived aggressor of member nations, U.N. Article 51 is the "glue" of the international order that cements the solidarity of a one-world military force. This article provides the authorization for the U.N. Security Council to make decisions calling for action against aggressors with the intent "to maintain or restore international peace and security." There are fifteen members of the U.N. Security Council who can cast one vote per member to ratify a decision that calls for military action. Currently the five permanent members are China, France, Russia, the UK, Northern Ireland, and the US. The ten temporary members are Albania, Brazil, Ecuador, Gabon, Ghana, Japan, Malta, Mozambique, Switzerland, and the United Arab Emirates. The U.N. and NATO, along with the CFR and the WEF would become the gatekeepers for the new world order.

---

[335] Charter of the United Nations and Statute of the International Court of Justice, (New York: UN Publications, 2015), 33-34.

George W. Bush's Global War on Terror

All the events of early 20th century, from the first major shifts away from the Monroe Doctrine through the Roosevelt Corollary and the foundations of progressive internationalism all come to a grand consummation leading to the New World Order. George Bush, Sr. was the first to use the term in his famous speech on September 11, 1990, just a mere eleven years to the day of the 9/11 attacks: "Out of these troubled times, our...objective – a new world order – can emerge...Today, that new world is struggling to be born, a world quite different from the one we have known."[336] The larger context of Bush, Sr.'s speech made reference to the founding of the U.N.: "Forty-five years ago, while the fires of an epic war still raged across two oceans and two continents, a small group of men and women began a search for hope amid the ruins. They gathered in San Francisco, stepping back from the haze and horror, to try to shape a new structure that might support an ancient dream." Here Bush refers to the founding U.N. conference in San Francisco as the backdrop of his phrase for a new world order. It is no surprise that Bush was a member on the CFR board of directors from 1977-1979.

The groundwork of the UN and NATO would provide Bush Senior's son George W. Bush with the catalyst for activating the new world order after 911. The Article 5 collective-defense clause would be invoked for the first time in fifty-two years after its initial signing in response to the 911 attacks in 2001. Several NATO mutual support agreements were activated in the international collective against terrorism: deployment of NATO naval forces to the Eastern Mediterranean, enhanced intelligence sharing, and military resources. According to the US State Department, NATO policy included the following with the Article 5 provisions: "Terrorism is now a standing item on the agendas of both the North Atlantic Council and the Euro-Atlantic Partnership Council.

---

[336] Bart R. Kessler, *Bush's New World Order: The Meaning Behind the Words*, Research Presented to Air Command & Staff College (Maxwell AFB, AL: Air Command Staff College, 1997). 1 – 5.

Regular consultations on terrorism among Allies and Partners and with other organizations promote common assessments and concerted action, thereby helping to ensure a unified international response in the fight against terrorism."[337] Just as the Second World War had granted broad powers to NATO and the U.N. so would the 911 terrorist attacks also bring about a resurgence of international authority for war. The U.N. Security Council passed Resolution 1441 on November 8, 2002, and warned of "serious consequences" if Iraq did not offer unrestricted access to weapon inspectors.[338] The invasion into Iraq authorized by George W. Bush never found any solid evidence for the existence of weapons of mass destruction (WMD's). The regime of Saddam Hussein was overthrown, and Bush declared six weeks later after the outset of the military operation that the "mission was accomplished." However, the goals to remove an ally of al-Qaeda and to establish a connection between Hussein and Osama Bin Laden proved to be as worthless as the U.N. directed search for WMD's.[339] NATO Article 5 along with the U.N. Article 51 would open Pandora's Box for the development of an international police state. The failures of the Iraq mission also empowered Iran, because a power vacuum was created with the overthrow of Hussein, and opened further access to the Middle East for Russia and China. The 2002 Authorization for Use of Military Force against Iraq was railroaded through Bush's War on Terror to have Congress to simply rubber-stamp the authorization. NATO's Article 5, along with the U.N. Article 51 helped to create a globalist war for Bush's new world order. Recall from the previous chapter that abuses occurred regarding the surveillance of American Citizens under the Patriot Act which was

---

[337] US Department of State Archive, *NATO Information Release 2001*. Source accessed November 16, 2023, from https://2001-2009.state.gov.

[338] National Archives, *The Iraq War; Global War on Terror*, Source accessed November 16, 2023, from https://www.georgewbushlibrary.gov.

[339] Tyler Koteskey, *Mission Accomplished Was a Massive Failure – But It Was Just the Beginning*, Responsible Statecraft, May 4, 2023. Source accessed November 16, 2023, from https://responsiblestatecraft.org.

created under the Bush administration. This global war on terror would open a Pandora's Box leading to the surveillance of ordinary American citizens later under the Obama administration as referenced in the previous chapter. The new world order ideology is promoted by both Republicans and Democrats. President Joe Biden, in an address to a group of leaders at a roundtable event at the White House, focused on the world economy and the war in Ukraine: "Now is the time when things are shifting. There's going to be a new world order out there. We've got to lead it, and we've got to unite the rest of the free world in doing it."[340] The Biden administration has fully embraced all the ideals of the liberal international order: "green" ecosystem practices, borderless societies, pandemic "science," abortion on demand, LGBTQ and transgender rights, along with identity politics. The liberal international order is driven toward globalism and the new world order.

The Rise of the International Order & Concepts of Globalism

Seventeenth-century English philosopher Jeremy Bentham is credited with creating the term "international" in his 1789 book titled *Introduction to the Principles of Morals and Legislation*.[341] Political scientists such as Lorenzo Cello at Marbella International University even further maintain that Bentham was also the first to conceptualize a "vision of an international order of liberal nations."[342] Although most progressives see an international liberal order in terms of noble humanity that unites together for the common good of society, the

---

[340] Heather Hamilton, *Biden Says There's Going to Be a New World Order and the US Must Take the Lead*, November 21, 2023, Washington Examiner. Source accessed November 21, 2023, from https://www.washingtonexaminer.com.

[341] Carolina Kenny, *Jeremy Bentham, Principles of International Law (1786-1789/1843)*, Classics of Strategy and Diplomacy. Source accessed November 21, 2023, from https://classicsofstrategy.com.

[342] Lorenzo Cello, *Jeremy Bentham's Vision of International Order*, Cambridge Review of International Affairs; Vol. 34, 2021 – Issue 1. Source accessed November 21, 2023, from https://www.tandfonline.com.

utopian dream falls short when it requires that individual liberty and freedom must be relinquished for achieving the collective order. Hoover Institution senior fellow Victor Davis Hanson (Stanford University) remarked about how Americans are deluded with this promise of international utopia: "The threat to citizenship comes not from foreign countries curtailing our liberties but from Americans themselves deliberately widening the idea of citizenship to include the peoples of the entire world, thereby rendering Americans mostly unexceptional. And never has this been truer than in the current era of globalization."[343] I will be referencing Hanson's work throughout the conclusion of this book and chapter because he offered an extensive analysis on the principles of globalism. Hanson's reference to "the threat to citizenship comes not from foreign countries…but from Americans themselves" is quite significant here. Most Americans are readily willing to relinquish their national sovereignty (citizenship) in the interest of the broadened collective of "the peoples of the [entire] world." Big government is bad enough when our own nation is under the tyranny of a runaway police state, but an even bigger global governance will require extensive military power for the control of nations. Whenever nations relinquish their national sovereignty for the sake of an international order, the result will be tyranny. Mattias Desmet stated that this tyranny of a collective state is a one-party system: "The first half of the twentieth century saw the emergence of Nazism and Stalinism, a completely new form of government commonly referred to as *totalitarianism*. It is immediately distinguishable from democracies by its on-party structure and its disregard for basic democratic principles, such as the right to free speech and self-determination."[344] The global utopian dream heralded by the Wilsonian principles of a League of Nations and the Bush manifesto for a new world order comes with an enormous price: our individual rights,

---

[343] Victor Davis Hanson, *The Dying Citizen: How Progressive Elites, Tribalism, & Globalization Are Destroying the Idea of America*, (New York: Basic Books, 2021), 269.

[344] Mattias Desmet, *The Psychology of Totalitarianism*, 90.

freedoms, and liberties when we relinquish our national sovereignty to global leadership entities such as the UN and WHO. I believe that the COVID pandemic was merely a dress rehearsal for a totalitarian one world government with its vaccine mandates and isolation and quarantine restrictions. The UN 2030 Sustainability Goals seeks to encompass much more in terms of world authority, and it is up those who love our great Constitutional republic to resist the global cabal.

When we compare the concepts of internationalism and globalism, each term has common ground as well as a distinctive meaning. At the most basic level the term international refers to "that which reaches beyond national boundaries in relation to an association of members of multiple nations." Globalism however, "treats the whole world as a sphere of political influence."[345] Globalism is not a new concept, the fourth century philosopher Diogenes stated: "I am a citizen of the world." Hanson further adds: "Globalism is not a new. It is recurrent, cyclical, and at best a morally neutral phenomenon, at worst a destroyer of local customs, traditions – and citizenship…Yet globalism's recent manifestation carries greater chances of dangerous consequences for American citizenship in our era of electronic interconnectedness."[346] In the history of civilizations, empires of tyrannical rulers and dictators (i.e., Babylon, Greece, Rome, etc.) progressed to sovereign nation states. And in our own American history when British tyranny threatened the individual freedoms of our Founders, the Revolutionary War cast off the shackles of tyranny and oppression giving birth to our beloved constitutional republic. However, in the twentieth century, with the move towards a progressive international order, the U.N. and NATO were at the forefront of a global collective society. That is the resurgence of globalism which also has a cultural impact Hanson referred to: "Globalization's real transnational cultural and political harmony encompasses a group of a few million elite architects of pan-worldism. They

---

[345] Merriam Webster Dictionary, Definitions of *International & Globalism*. Online edition.

[346] Hanson, *The Dying Citizen*, 269-273.

are heavily invested in ending nationalism and making Americanism incidental rather than essential to Americans as they synchronize their values, laws, and traditions with those abroad." Ernest Gellner who was the former director of the Center for the Study of Nationalism of the Central European University in Prague, (a Soros-funded institution) is an outspoken critic of nationalism. Gellner addressed Nazi fascism in the same light of "ethnic nationalism" which the Allied war alliance sought to terminate.[347] Gellner further adds to his critique of nationalism: "Nationalism is not what it seems, and above all it is not what it seems to itself. The cultures it claims to defend and revive are often its own inventions or are modified out of all recognition…In a nationalist age, societies worship themselves brazenly and openly, spurning the camouflage. At Nuremberg, Nazi Germany did not worship itself by pretending to worship God or even Wotan; it overtly worshipped itself." Gellner's attack on nationalism seems absurd because it postulates nationalists as being in lockstep with Hitler's fascist Third Reich.

This is not surprising given the prominence that such groups as Antifa and BLM have had during the lawless burning, looting, and rioting of 2020. Antifa, a group with European-German roots, has proudly worn the badge pf an anti-fascist, left-wing extremist organization. BLM is a communist-led organization with claims of being an anti-racist group calling for social justice. Both groups are equally opposed to nationalism because they burn American flags, condemning our country as fascist and white supremist. The so-called peaceful protests conducted by Antifa and BLM destroyed millions of dollars of property, and resulted in massive theft from businesses, outright attacks on law enforcement, and the murder of innocent citizens. Their rampage of anti-nationalist anarchy was applauded by progressives, the liberal international order and by global elites as a call for global revolution and the cause of a new world order. When Trump called for Antifa to be considered as a terrorist group, there was considerable criticism

---

[347] Ernest Gellner, *Nations & Nationalism*, second edition (New York: Cornell University Press, 2006), xvii & 55.

from the left and mainstream media saying that because the group is not a centralized organization, they could not qualify to be listed on the State Department watchlist: "Antifa is a domestic entity and as such not a candidate for inclusion on the State Department's list of foreign terror organizations."[348] The tragedy is that justice is preferential for dangerous militant radicals as millions of these violent protestors across the nation have not been called to account. The January 6th protests were largely peaceful except for a handful of instigators, yet nearly 1,000 have been charged and the FBI has placed over 350 suspects on their violent offender list. Many of these are still in prison waiting for a fair trial. Such is the travesty of an out-of-control police state where the rule of law is dictated by anti-nationalist and anti-conservative Deep State operatives. These are the markings of a liberal progressive international order. This is the spirit behind the Davos community's global elites that focuses on agendas promoting a world economic system with shared wealth distribution, borderless societies, green-eco system environmentalism, and the dictates of a global health system endorsed by the WHO. These global elites are not content with having only a small collective entity to comply with their agenda, but they demand worldwide conformity and sovereign nationalism only stands in the way to accomplishing their vision of a one-world governance. This conformity requires that freedom of speech one of our first cherished American amendments be subservient to media censorship. In a one-world global community there cannot be any voices that do not comply with the state narrative. In America we are seeing the tragic results of a one-party narrative where we have been censored on issues concerning vaccines, medical freedom, and traditional moral values. Hanson comments on the progressive marginalization of traditional religious values: "Much of the more traditional and religious world abroad may perhaps wish to opt out of what we now consider our norms – from gay marriage to racial quotas and identity politics, to abortion on demand – as we

---

[348] PBS News, *What is Antifa? A Look at the Movement Trump is Blaming for Violence at Protests*, June 1, 2020. Source accessed November 22, 2023, from pbs.org.

might their own religious intolerance, tribal violence, state atheism, or absence of constitutional freedoms."[349]

I have already addressed the role of the UN, CFR, NATO, and the EU in the progressive international order. There are many other think-tanks and foundations equally ambitious about influencing American foreign policy and a couple are worth mentioning here. The Global Policy Institute (GPI) in Washington, D.C. promotes research for "government officials, business professionals, journalists, academics... to increase the understanding of global events, domestic and international policies in the fields of Energy, Education, Economy, and Immigration."[350] In addition to confidently predicting that by 2050 the US will be completely weaned off fossil fuels, the GPI website chides Republican conservatives that if they threaten to cut military aid to Ukraine, then "GOP congressional districts will suffer economic fallout" because of cuts in demands for military contractors such as munitions plants to supply the Russo-Ukraine war effort. Although I seriously doubt that the conservative GOP will be impacted by refusing to fund the proxy war in Ukraine, at least GPI is transparent that they love billions of dollars being poured into military-industrial complex. Behind the GPI is what is known as the World Federalist Movement which they promote as follows: "A world federation would have authority on issues of global reach...Proponents maintain that a world federation offers a more effective and accountable global governance structure than the existing United Nations."[351] Did you catch that – a world federation offers more authority. A world federalist movement would come with the authority to enforce their mission: "To create more effective, transparent, and accountable global governance leading to a democratic world federation."

---

[349] Hanson, *The Dying Citizen*, 282-83.

[350] Global Policy Institute, globalpi.org.

[351] Ibid.

Concluding Thoughts

From the principles of the liberal international order and globalism, it is time to bring us again to full circle: the proxy war in Ukraine. The course of disastrous foreign policy in Ukraine was forged during the administrations of Carter, Clinton, Obama, and Biden. The foundations upon which this disastrous foreign policy course was established upon was what was laid in the nineteenth century with the demise of the Monroe Doctrine and the one world visions of Wilson, Willkie, FDR, and Truman. From here the institutions of the United Nations, Council on Foreign Relations, NATO, and the EU became the custodians of globalism and the Davos World Economic Forum served as the gatekeeper for global elites to usher in the new world order. Ukraine is merely a pawn on the geopolitical chessboard of the global elites. It is not about a cruel and autocratic Russian Federation or even an authoritarian Putin oppressing the weaker vassal state of Ukraine. It is rather about consolidating the power of a global regime behind the veil of a proxy war which has created an enormous sink hole into which billions of dollars around the world are poured at the bidding of global elites. For this reason, for decades governments in Ukraine have been overthrown and puppet rulers have been placed into power to be subservient to the international order.

Where do we go from here? First, we must demand that the billions of dollars of funding for the proxy war in Ukraine must stop now. This insane spending spree at the expense of taxpayers has further escalated our national debt into the trillions with no end in sight. Second, there needs to be a greater call for accountability from the corrupt Ukrainian government. We should be able to see audit trails tracking every dollar being spent on weapons and munitions. Thirdly, we must demand a return to an America first policy that seeks to protect our borders, enhance our national security and to strengthen our nation's military so they can defend us from enemies both foreign and domestic. An America first policy would mean that we return to the application of the Monroe Doctrine as intended by our Founding Fathers. This requires that we yield to the commonsense virtues avoiding foreign entanglement into international wars and conflicts which do not have an impact upon our national security interests. Unless there is a clear moral prerogative, we should not interfere in the affairs of foreign nations. I would use an example from the Second World War with the brutal holocaust of Jews in the hands of the Nazis. Here there was a direct violation of moral law, namely the Nazi death camps and the Hitler's ambitions of conquest through the Third Reich. I believe that the US could have assisted the war efforts in defeating Nazi Germany without the entanglement of NATO or the U.N. Because of FDR and Truman, America has been obligated through NATO's Article 5 and U.N. article 51 to be part of the "international police force." We must sever our ties to these organizations – both the U.N. and NATO. Although Trump was criticized for pulling back on support of these organizations, he bravely put America first and that philosophy is what we must return to for our nation. The America First Policy Institute (AFPI) is a great conservative organization that serves our country's national values. AFPI is a non-profit, non-partisan research institute with the following stated mission: "AFPI exists to advance policies that put the American people first. Our guiding principles are liberty, free enterprise, national greatness, American military superiority, foreign-policy engagement in the American interest, and the primacy of American workers, families, and communities in all we do."[352] The second conservative organization that is worthwhile supporting is the Center for Security Policy (CSP). CSP is also a non-profit organization that states its mission as follows: "Our mission is to secure America's founding principles and freedom through forthright national security analysis and policy solutions."[353] CSP has an impressive group of advisors from

---

[352] America First Policy Institute, source accessed November 22, 2023, from americafirstpolicy.com.

[353] Center for Security Policy. Source accessed November 22, 2023, from forsecuritypolicy.org.

a wide spectrum of security subject matter fields and was founded by Frank J. Gaffney, Jr. who served as the acting Assistant Secretary of Defense for International Security Affairs during the Reagan administration. Because our national intelligence has gone Deep State, and our foreign policy is driven by progressive globalists, both the CSP and the AFPI are hopeful prospects for restoring an America first policy in our nation. I alluded to the other action item worth supporting was alluded to in the previous chapter the work of Senators Ron Johnson (R-Wis.) and Chuck Grassley (R-Iowa) with their criminal probe on the Biden family titled *Hunter Biden, Burisma, and Corruption*. Members of the Biden administration must be held accountable for their corrupt ties to Ukraine. Members of the Obama administration along with Hillary Clinton must also be held accountable for their role in the Russian collusion narrative and the Deep State collaboration of Project Crossfire Hurricane which launched the assault not only upon Trump's team and staff but also countless other American Patriots who were victim of the Police State. The proxy war in Ukraine is the grand culmination point for this Deep State covert operation against the American people and will continue to lead us further down the path of a global new world order. This is the plan of the Global Elites.

www.ingramcontent.com/pod-product-compliance
Ingram Content Group UK Ltd.
Pitfield, Milton Keynes, MK11 3LW, UK
UKHW021313180426
11947UKWH00015B/1209